# REFORMING PASTORAL MINISTRY

*1 Tim 4:13-15*

# REFORMING PASTORAL MINISTRY

*Challenges for Ministry
in Postmodern Times*

# John H. Armstrong

GENERAL EDITOR

Crossway Books • Wheaton, Illinois
A Division of Good News Publishers

*Reforming Pastoral Ministry*

Published by Crossway Books
    A division of Good News Publishers
    1300 Crescent Street
    Wheaton, Illinois 60187

Cover design: Cindy Kiple

Cover illustration: © Theo Rudnak/SIS

First printing, 2001

Printed in the United States of America

**Library of Congress Cataloging-in-Publication Data**
Reforming pastoral ministry : challenges for ministry in postmodern
times / John H. Armstrong, general editor.
    p.    cm.
    Includes bibliographical references and index.
    ISBN 1-58134-179-2 (TPB : alk. paper)
    1. Church renewal.    2. Pastoral theology.    I. Armstrong, John H.
(John Harper), 1949-    .
BV600.2.R395    2001
253—dc21                                  2001000478
                                                    CIP

| 15 | 14 | 13 | 12 | 11 | 10 | 09 | 08 | 07 | 06 | 05 | 04 | 03 | 02 | 01 |
|----|----|----|----|----|----|----|----|----|----|----|----|----|----|----|
| 15 | 14 | 13 | 12 | 11 | 10 | 9 | 8 | 7 | 6 | 5 | 4 | 3 | 2 | 1 |

*For the reformation of the church
and the revival of biblical Christianity
in an increasingly dark time in history when
integrity in both life and doctrine is the
crying need of evangelical Christianity.*

*And for my first grandchild,
Graciela Noel Armstrong,
who brings delight to me every day.
I pray you will soon come to know Him in whom
there is true life, and that you will be cared for
all your life by a faithful minister and
ministry that is always reforming.*

# CONTENTS

# ACKNOWLEDGMENTS

The editor would like to again thank the board of Reformation & Revival Ministries, Inc., for their support and genuine friendship in the work that Christ has given to me as His servant. Each of these men has given in various ways to make this ministry possible—Bruce Bickel, Gerald Kamphuis, Bob Mulder, Bill Ladd, William Thrasher, Art Azurdia, Andy Froiland, Irv Queal, Mark Talbot, and Richard Johnson.

*John H. Armstrong*

# THE CONTRIBUTORS

GENERAL EDITOR

*John H. Armstrong* (B.A., M.A., Wheaton College; D.Min., Luther Rice Seminary) is founder and president of Reformation & Revival Ministries in Carol Stream, Illinois. He served as a Baptist pastor for twenty-one years before becoming a conference speaker, editor of *Reformation & Revival Journal*, a quarterly publication for church leadership, and *Viewpoint*, a bimonthly magazine for the church. He was the general editor of *Roman Catholicism: Evangelical Protestants Analyze What Unites & Divides Us*, *The Coming Evangelical Crisis: Current Challenges to the Authority of Scripture and the Gospel*, and *The Compromised Church: The Present Evangelical Crisis*. He is author of *The Stain That Stays: The Problem of Fallen Pastoral Leadership*, *The Catholic Mystery*, *True Revival: What Happens When God Moves*, and *Five Great Evangelists*. He serves as a theological consultant to several ministries and has contributed to numerous books and periodicals. He also directly assists congregations in biblical reformation and travels internationally in a conference-speaking ministry.

OTHER CONTRIBUTORS

*Arturo Azurdia III* (B.A., Cal State University; M.Div., American Baptist Seminary of the West; D.Min., Westminster Seminary in California) is senior pastor of Christ Community Church, Cordelia, California. He serves as an instructor in Bible exposition and theology at Grace School of Theology and Ministry, Pleasanton, California. He is the author of *Spirit Anointed Preaching*.

*Joel R. Beeke* (B.A., Thomas A. Edison College; M.Div., Netherlands Reformed Theological School; Ph.D., Westminster Theological Seminary) is president and professor of systematic theology and homiletics at Puritan Reformed Theological Seminary; pastor of the Heritage Netherlands Reformed Congregation in Grand Rapids, Michigan; editor of *Banner of Sovereign Grace Truth*; president of Reformation Heritage Books and Inheritance Publishers; and vice president of the Dutch Reformed Translation Society. He has written numerous books, most recently *Truth That Frees: A Workbook on Reformed Doctrine for Young Adults*, *The Quest for Full Assurance: The Legacy of Calvin and His Successors*, *A Reader's Guide to Reformed Literature*, *Puritan Evangelism: A Biblical Approach*, and *Gisbertus Voetius: Toward a Reformed Marriage of Knowledge and Piety*. He has also coauthored, edited, and introduced many volumes and has contributed hundreds of articles to Reformed books, journals, periodicals, and encyclopedias.

*Mark Coppenger* (B.A., Ouachita Baptist University; M.Div., Southwestern Baptist Theological Seminary; Ph.D., Vanderbilt University) is the pastor of Evanston Baptist Church, Evanston, Illinois. He previously taught at Wheaton College (1975-1981) and was president of Midwestern Baptist Theological Seminary (1995-1999). He has taught both philosophy and ethics and is the author of *A Christian View of Justice*. He has contributed to numerous published books and publications including *Leadership*, *Christian Scholar's Review*, and *Reformation & Revival Journal*. He has served the Southern Baptist Convention in a number of capacities including executive director (Indiana Baptist Convention) and vice-president of the SBC Executive Committee (1990-1995).

*Mark E. Dever* (B.A., Duke University; M.Div., Gordon-Conwell Theological Seminary; Th.M., Southern Baptist Theological Seminary; Ph.D., Cambridge University) is senior pastor of Capitol Hill Baptist Church, Washington, D.C. A frequent conference speaker, he serves as contributing editor to the *Cambridge Papers*. He has contributed to numerous periodicals and is visiting professor at both Beeson Divinity School and Southern Baptist Theological Seminary. He is the author of *Nine Marks of a Healthy Church*.

*Jim Elliff* (B.A., Ouachita Baptist University; M.Div., Southwestern Baptist Theological Seminary) is president of Christian Communicators Worldwide and a consultant for the Midwestern Center for Biblical Revival at Midwestern Baptist Theological

Seminary. He is the author of numerous booklets distributed through Christian Communicators Worldwide and regularly contributes to various publications. He is the author of *Led By the Spirit*.

*Wilbur C. Ellsworth* (B.S., Ithaca College; M.Div., Los Angeles Baptist Theological Seminary; D.Min., Trinity Evangelical Divinity School) has been a pastor for over thirty years and is senior pastor of Christ Church, Wheaton, Illinois. He is the author of *The Power of Speaking God's Word*.

*Joseph Flatt, Jr.* (Th.B., Baptist Bible Seminary; M.Div., Grace Theological Seminary; D.Min., Trinity Evangelical Divinity School) is senior pastor of First Baptist Church, Carmel, Indiana, where he has served for twenty-six years. He also actively serves as a chaplain (colonel) in the U.S. Army Reserve. He has contributed to several theological journals.

*David W. Hegg* (B.A., Los Angeles Baptist College; M.A., Western Conservative Baptist Seminary; D.Min., Westminster Seminary in California) is senior pastor of Corona Evangelical Free Church, Corona, California. He is the author of *Appointed to Preach* and has contributed to several publications, including *Reformation & Revival Journal* and *African National Pastoral Review*. He is an adjunct professor of theology at The Master's College.

*R. Kent Hughes* (B.A., Biola University; M.Div., Talbot Theological Seminary; D.Min., Trinity Evangelical Divinity School) is senior pastor of College Church, Wheaton, Illinois. He has written numerous books including *Disciplines of a Godly Man, Are Evangelicals Born Again?, The Gift, Liberating Ministry from the Success Syndrome*, and thriteen volumes in the highly regarded Preaching the Word commentary series.

*Jerry Marcellino* (B.A., University of Hawaii; M.Div., Capital Bible Seminary) is senior pastor of Audubon Drive Bible Church, Laurel, Mississippi. He is the author of *The Lost Treasure of Family Worship* and has contributed to several publications including *Tabletalk, Reformation Today*, and *Pulpit Helps*. He is the editorial director for Audubon Press and has ministered as a conference speaker across the United States.

*T. M. Moore* (B.A., University of Missouri; M.Div., Reformed

Theological Seminary; M.C.E., Reformed Theological Seminary; doctoral studies in theology, University of Pretoria) is a poet, writer, and theologian. He served in pastoral ministry for more than twenty years and also as a seminary president. He is the author of numerous books and book chapters, as well as dozens of essays and articles in a wide range of publications. He serves as theological advisor to Prison Fellowship Ministries and Charles Colson; North American editor for Scripture Union Publications; a distance learning specialist with Reformed Theological Seminary Virtual Campus and a visiting instructor with Reformed Theological Seminary, Charlotte; and a ministry associate with the Jonathan Edwards Institute. He is in frequent demand as a conference speaker and seminar leader. He lives in Philippi, West Virginia.

*Phil A. Newton* (B.A., Mobile College; M.Div., New Orleans Baptist Theological Seminary; D.Min, Fuller Theological Seminary) is senior pastor of South Woods Baptist Church, Memphis, Tennessee. He is an adjunct professor at Crichton College, Memphis, and the Institut Theologique de Nimes in France. He has contributed to several theological journals.

*Thomas N. Smith* is pastor of Randolph Street Baptist Church, Charleston, West Virginia. He has preached widely in both the United States and Great Britain He has served as associate editor of *Reformation & Revival Journal* since its inception in 1992 and is a feature columnist for *Viewpoint: A Look at Reformation & Revival in Our Time.*

# FOREWORD

by Erwin W. Lutzer

You can be grateful for the book you hold in your hands.

When I was given the manuscript, one glance at the writers and their topics assured me that this would be a good book. But not until I read it did I realize how excellent and necessary this book is for today's pastors. This volume has the potential for transforming the life and ministry of any pastor who reads it and takes it to heart. And no matter how many years we have been in ministry, there is something here for us all.

As pastors, we've all attended conferences to find the "key" to a successful ministry. We are interested in learning the latest data regarding church growth, the latest theories on church management, and the best way to organize our small groups. While it can be argued that all of these have their place, the reality is that many ministers are being drawn away from the biblical center, substituting the peripheral for that which is most important. What is lacking is a profound commitment to holy living, a passionate desire for the spiritual health and salvation of the congregation, and in short a radically biblical approach to the whole of church work.

Our greatest danger is that we might not even be aware of the secularization of the evangelical church. In his opening chapter, John Armstrong writes that "The culture has moved us increasingly to full-scale secularism, even in the lives and labors of our pastors. The pressures of this secularizing influence are quite real." Pastors do not openly deny the truth, Armstrong says, but they evade it. And evade it, they do.

Glance through these pages and you will notice the following. First, the writers cover a wide variety of topics, touching on all the important aspects of ministry—everything from preaching to pastoral care to worship. These and many other themes are discussed from a radically biblical perspective. They also draw on insights that have been left for us by a previous generation of ministers who have modeled godly leadership and pastoral concerns. As I read these chapters, I found both encouragement and correction for my own life and ministry.

Second, these topics are practical, helping us with the how-to of ministry. Every one of the writers has years of experience in facing both the joys and sorrows of pastoral ministry. You get the feeling that they are fellow travelers who know the pitfalls along the ministerial path. They know contemporary evangelicalism with its penchant for chasing the latest fads, but they also love the church passionately and believe that she is to be God's vibrant and visible witness to a weary world. And they believe that the pastor has a great and holy calling to lead God's people in proven biblical paths.

To put it briefly, this book is written to help us return to those truths that made the church great. Contemporary evangelicalism convinces us that Luther was right when he said that the church is in need of constant reformation. Not until we are willing to return to the biblical center will we see a reformation that God might choose to use to bring a revival to our continent.

If you are in the ministry, read this book, savoring its challenges and exhortations, and be willing to accept its corrections. If you are not in ministry as such, read it for your own growth and edification, and then pass it along to a friend in ministry. Pray that God will use it to challenge, encourage, and instruct him along the arduous journey to our permanent home.

This morning in my devotional time, I happened to read the comments the apostle Paul made about some believers who brought him news about the progress of the church. In my opinion, these words could also be said about the authors of this book. "For they refreshed my spirit and yours also. Such men deserve recognition" (1 Cor. 16:18).

Enough said. Now begin to read.

Dr. Erwin W. Lutzer
Pastor, Moody Church
Chicago, 2001

# EDITOR'S INTRODUCTION

John H. Armstrong

Books challenging and articulating models of pastoral practice are not common in our time. It seems the entire field has been taken hostage by the modern academic disciplines of social science and psychology. This was not always the case in evangelical churches. There was a time when the primary aim of much formal and informal thought about the ministry of the Gospel was directed toward the *pastoral* work of the minister.

Indeed, practical theology, which appears to have developed within the Scottish tradition, is an umbrella term concerned with relating theology to the actual practice of ministry. Derek J. Tidball has noted:

> Traditionally, its subject-matter was preaching, worship and liturgy, education and catechetics and pastoral care. Although Schleiermacher and others attempted to provide it with a disciplined and systematic theological foundation, in which the application was informed by theology, the field tended to become handy tips for ministers.[1]

The present volume arose out of a very specific context. After pastoring in a local church ministry for more than twenty years, I began to regularly preach across North America in 1992. As a result of this wider public ministry, or perhaps as the cause of it, I also began to work more particularly with hundreds of ministers in smaller groups and private fellowships. As I listened to the heart of faithful pastors and observed their labors more intensely, I saw clearly the great pressures modern ministers face every day. If pastors are to do the work they believe God has called them to do, it will cost them more than ever in this postmodern age. As clouds of opposition and persecution begin to gather over the church in North America, pastors must be more intentionally equipped to serve faithfully "in season and out of season" (2 Tim. 4:2).

In looking over the field of pastoral work and the many books published in the 1970s and 1980s, I began to reflect more deeply upon one of the greatest classics of pastoral ministry ever penned, *The Reformed Pastor* (1656). Written by the esteemed English minister Richard Baxter, it has been my companion for nearly thirty years now. Baxter, who served in the English village of Kidderminster in the mid-seventeenth century, clearly faced different challenges than modern pastors; in another way Baxter faced the same challenges modern ministers deal with every day. He ministered in a place where the Word of God was not understood and the name of God was barely known. Yet he went into this field of ministry with faith and hope. He sowed, and God gave the increase. Out of this inconsequential little village and from the life of this little-known pastor came a magnificent work, which was actually "a heartfelt appeal to other Puritan ministers for good pastoral practice, and is an extended discussion based on Acts 20:28, 'Guard yourselves and all the flock of which the Holy Spirit has made you overseers.'"[2]

So great has been the influence of Richard Baxter's thought and ministry upon my own that I felt a modern book about reforming pastoral ministry (which is primarily what Baxter meant by his use of the term *Reformed* in the title) was needed. This book does not try to reproduce Baxter. Such an attempt would be, considering the sheer brilliance and depth of Richard Baxter's celebrated work, unadulterated folly. But it is a work that seeks to understand the age in which we presently live, the challenges modern ministers actually face, and the need for congregations and lay leadership to better understand what pastoral life and work is really about. I sought for contributors from various churches both large and small. These contributors are ministers who come from different parts of the kingdom and who have had some very different experiences of ministry. They are all practitioners (like Baxter), not theorists (like so many of our modern role models)! These are contributors whose preaching is powerful in the best and truest sense. And these are ministers who have had experience in dealing with the souls of real people under their own care. They are ministers who have shown love for the church over many years of faithful service and who believe in preaching "all the counsel of God" (Acts 20:27, KJV) to the entire church. They are ministers who take their work seriously and view their calling as their highest privilege.

James I. Packer summarizes the overall life and ministry of the best Puritan ministers when he observes: "The great Puritans were as humble-minded and warm-hearted as they were clear-headed, as fully oriented to people as they were to Scripture, and as passionate for peace as they were for truth."[3] My prayer is that the chapters of this book, coming profoundly out of the lives of those who write them, will model the same. Each of us has attempted to be as "humble-minded and warm-hearted" as possible, both in what we write and how we write it. We have also labored to be "clear-headed" in a time of profound confusion. All of us love people and want to be "as passionate for peace as [we are] for truth." I humbly pray readers will sense this as they meditate upon these collected essays.

## NOTES

1  Derek J. Tidball, "Practical Theology," in *New Dictionary of Theology*, eds. Sinclair B. Ferguson, David F. Wright, and J. I. Packer (Downers Grove, IL: InterVarsity Press, 1988), p. 525.

2  Wallace Benn, *The Baxter Model: Guidelines for Pastoring Today* (Hartford, Northwich, Cheshire, England: Fellowship of Word and Spirit, 1993), p. 1.

3  James I. Packer, *A Quest for Godliness* (Wheaton, IL: Crossway, 1990), p. 32.

# 1

## SEMPER REFORMANDA:

### The Pastoral Role in Modern Reformation

■

John H. Armstrong

There is a profound sense in which everything said about the work of reforming pastoral ministry can be summarized in a slogan of the Protestant tradition: *semper reformanda* ("always reforming"). This  Latin phrase (often debated both in terms of its origin and modern misuse) contains the essence of what will be argued throughout *Reforming Pastoral Ministry*. When properly rendered, this helpful phrase underscores the idea that the church genuinely reformed by the Holy Scripture must always be a church that is "continually being reformed."[1]

Evangelical Christianity is necessarily rooted in the historic Protestant Reformation of the sixteenth century. The church before the time of the sixteenth century had "groaned under the papacy" (as one lesser-known catechism put it) for several centuries. Through the passionate concern of the Reformers for the Word of God, the Lord renewed the church, giving back to His people many of the major doctrines and practices of Holy Scripture. Along with this great recovery of doctrine came a re-forming of ideas about pastoral ministry. The role of ministers changed from that of priests, who primarily performed actions *for* the church, to that of shepherds who proclaimed the truth of God *to* the church. In short, the exposition of Scripture was powerfully recovered. And through this recovery the pastoral ministry could now be radically and continually reforming through generations to follow.

But the goal of confessing evangelical churches, since the sixteenth century, has never been to create a fixed system of theology and ministry, thereby ending all meaningful theological interactions with the questions and issues of each present age. Though the Reformation era produced numerous confessions of faith as well as several distinct theological traditions (Lutheran, Reformed, Anabaptist, etc.), evangelical Protestantism has generally agreed that no single system of theology should be seen as *the* truth about God, Jesus, human life, sin, and the world. Theology, of all historic genres and types, is at its best an inadequate and fallible human effort to understand the truth and to confess Jesus as "the way and the truth and the life" (John 14:6) more faithfully.

Because the church militant is never pure, its tendency has always been toward decline. There are two apparent reasons for this reality. One is that those who truly believe upon Christ are still sinners, though the life of obedience has definitely begun in them and their faith is living (cf. Rom. 1:5; 16:25-26). The other is that the very best church is still, at best, a mixed congregation. Carnal and worldly elements will always be present, even in healthy churches. (This seems to be implicitly denied by the modern self-confident demeanor of many mega-church leaders!)

Because of these realities the task of each generation is to think biblically and theologically in light of the particular challenges of its own time. Indeed, it is the responsibility of the church to question every single statement of faith as the *only* confession of faith for that era. At the same time this continual need for reformation does not mean that all Christians are free to believe whatever they will or say whatever they like. With biblical freedom of conscience comes a profound personal and corporate responsibility. We are free to confess Christ faithfully, but we are never free to stand against the catholic, apostolic Gospel of Jesus Christ.

To me it seems self-evident that the evangelical church lost its grasp upon confessional integrity over the last half of the previous century. We lost our bearings in terms of the very truths the Reformation set forth with such power and clarity—e.g., a massively God-centered perspective that plainly asserts the primacy of grace in the salvation of humanity through Jesus Christ alone with the glory of God's divine sovereignty at the center of the entire theological framework. Because of this tragic loss the very idea of reforming the church now takes on new meaning. This work is not optional—it is urgent! While sociologists of religion remind us that the church in America is precipitously declining in both its impact and the number of faithful members, we would do well to rethink several important questions: What is really happening to us as evangelicals? How did we get to this point, and how can we possibly change our situation? And more to the point of this present book, what kind of pastoral ministry is called for in terms of the magnitude of the problems we now face?

This question is especially pertinent when it comes to both the calling and labor of the parish minister, the local church pastor. When we speak of reforming the church, we dare not approach this vital subject without considering pastoral ministry more carefully and theologically. John Calvin insightfully noted in his commentary on Isaiah that "To pastors and ministers the Lord commits his Church as his beloved wife."[2] Because the Lord loves the church, He is profoundly jealous over the life and ministry of the ministers that He gives to serve the church.

Consideration of pastoral ministry, then, is clearly vital to the health of the entire church. It calls to mind both a history and a present reality. It calls to mind the reality of historical pastoral images that served the church well in the past. One can recall, as an example of this historical tradition, the massive corpus of work that came from the pen of the esteemed Richard Baxter, whose pastoral labors served a generation (1641-1661) powerfully in his ministry at little Kidderminster. Here the world saw the effect of one pastor upon a very small field of service (a town of some 2,000 adults). Yet it was here that a careful and God-directed pastoral effort plainly had a disproportionate effect for good far beyond the flock he served in a seventeenth-century small village. This consideration also calls to mind the Pastoral Epistles, rich with their practical insights into both human nature and pastoral care. Here we see the beloved apostle Paul pouring out his heart for the churches by opening a window to his own pastoral soul so that Timothy, and all of us since, would "preach the Word" and "be prepared in season and out of season" in order to "correct, rebuke and encourage—with great patience and careful instruction" the church of Christ (2 Tim. 4:2).

Actually, the evangelical tradition is resplendent with models of careful pastoral ministry. Indeed, it was within this tradition that the subject of pastoral theology finally became a separate discipline of theological study. A gifted teacher of pastoral theology notes:

> The increasing need to provide an adequately trained ministry led to the emergence of pastoral theology as a separate discipline in a more modern sense in the late 18th century. During the following century numerous works were published which drew on contemporary science and philosophy in an attempt to provide a systematic and comprehensive understanding of ministry. At the turn of the century, however, a decline had set in and works on pastoral theology had become practitioners' handbooks rather than works of theological depth.[3]

To say the least, this later development has not been altogether salutary. Even within some of our most esteemed evangelical seminaries and colleges, the "psychological captivity" of the Christian ministry seems to have dominated the field of pastoral ministry for several decades now. And recent reactions against this psychotherapeutic tendency have not always replaced seriously flawed tendencies with more mature and careful biblical ones. It seems far easier to tell the church what is wrong, especially in the field of pastoral theology, than it is to set forth a definitive Christ-centered pastoral theology that is both academically sound and biblically nuanced.

## THE LOST WORD

It is not too dramatic to say that the contemporary ministry lost its grip on the Word of God; or better put, the Word of God no longer held a serious grip upon the life and practice of modern ministers over the last fifty years or so. David Wells has stated this concern plainly: "The problem is not, of course, that the Bible itself has disappeared. There are, in fact, enough Bibles in America to put one in every home. No, the problem is that we are not hearing the Word of God. It does not rest consequentially upon us."[4]

Referring to the 1970s and 1980s, Wells observes that while evangelicals were struggling for the truth of biblical inerrancy, their practice was actually being radically altered. I submit that the place where this was happening most profoundly was in the pastoral ministry. The consequences of biblical authority were "not worked out for our preaching, our techniques for growing the Church, [and] our techniques for healing our own fractured selves. These all happened largely without the [obvious and intentional] use of Scripture. It is as if we think that while the Bible is inspired, it is nevertheless inadequate to the tasks of sustaining and nourishing the twentieth-century Church!"[5]

The way evangelical ministers presently deal with scriptural authority leaves them in a profoundly vulnerable position. While affirming the Bible's authority, large numbers of pastors now use it ever so lightly (inconsequentially) in preaching popular sermons aimed at restoring the emotional and spiritual health of their flocks. They counsel with profound dependence upon the newest fads and popular psychological books while they lead with the sharpest managerial techniques of the most successful corporations of our age.

What most distinctly marked the great recovery of the sixteenth century was that ministers began to preach and counsel in a way that was radically distinct from the methods of their time, those of the medieval Schoolmen. As Nehemiah recorded of an ancient reformation in his own day: "They read from the Book of the Law of God, making it clear and giving the meaning so that the people could understand what was being read" (Neh. 8:8). The sixteenth-century Reformers did the same, opening up the Word of God and giving the plain sense of the text's meaning, both in public and in private. And they pointed their hearers to Christ through faithful expositions, which in some cases literally happened every day!

These Reformers understood that the great impact of Pentecost was not the mighty rushing wind or the divided tongues of fire but the preaching of the Word. It was the sheer authority of the Word that pierced the hearts of the hearers straight through (Acts 2). This same pattern can be seen throughout the book of Acts (cf. 6:1-6; 8:4; 19:20; etc.).

This was preaching that was supremely focused upon the person and work of Christ. The problem in our age is not so much that evangelicals have entirely stopped reading their Bibles and explaining certain texts to congregations. (There is, however, a growing awareness as I travel from place to place across the continent that Bible reading in public worship is getting shorter and shorter, if not totally absent! With the constant focus upon the visual arts we clearly are in danger of losing the reverent public reading of the Holy Scriptures, especially in the more non-liturgical traditions; see 1 Tim. 4:13.) The problem is actually more subtle: How do we use the texts of the Bible we read and speak week by week?

The late A. W. Tozer lamented this tendency long before it became popular in our circles. In 1963, just two days after his death, an article appeared from his pen that prophetically underscored the very problem I am speaking about. Tozer asserted:

> Jesus Christ today has almost no authority at all among the groups that call themselves by His name. Now, I'm not referring to Roman Catholics, those who are liberal in their theology, or members of the various quasi-Christian cults. I do mean Protestant churches generally, especially those who protest the loudest that they are in spiritual descent from our Lord and his apostles: the evangelicals.
>
> It is a basic doctrine of the New Testament that after his resurrection, Jesus was declared by God to be both Lord and Christ (Acts 2:36). The Father invested him with absolute lordship over the church, which is his body. All authority is his in heaven and on earth (Matt. 28:18). In his own proper time he will exert it fully, but during this period in history he allows his authority to be challenged or ignored. And right now it is being challenged by the world and ignored by the church.[6]

This problem must be clearly understood or evangelical ministers will never correct it. What I am saying is quite simple: The Bible is still preached, after a certain fashion. But it is preached as a handbook for daily living, an inspiring resource for solving practical problems in life and home, a how-to book for busy modern living. We teach Bible stories to our children, but the stories we teach have become moral lessons in how to be better children. As more than one critic has noted, we still teach the Bible story of David and Goliath. The problem is, we teach the story as a means for inspiring adults and children to slay the giants that arise in their daily lives. We do not teach this biblical story, in other words, with a proper Christocentric focus.

But what is the actual purpose or intent of the Word of God? What does God desire for His flock to get from the text that faithful ministers preach week after week? Jesus answered this question when He responded to the manner in which the Pharisees handled the text: "You diligently study the Scriptures because you think that by them you possess eternal life. These are the Scriptures that testify about me, yet you refuse to come to me to have life" (John 5:39-40). This reveals the dangers of any group, including the most conservative, in turning the Scriptures into a "practical" word for life today. We must get beyond this "practical" use of the Bible or we will never see true reforming of the church's life and ministry.

If we do not get this focus right, it is not too dramatic to say that we will get nothing else right. The focus of the Bible is not upon plans for successful living. It is not upon the family. It is not on growing large and successful churches. It is not about dealing with codependency or self-esteem. And it is certainly not about political concerns the church must address prior to every national election. From Genesis to Revelation the Bible is about Christ. Christ alone is the heart and soul of the entire canon. Older evangelicals understood this when they confessed their confidence in *solus Christus*, Christ alone. Modern evangelicals may use the same Bible, even the same familiar texts, but they no longer use it in the same way.

Ministers must especially understand afresh that God always deals with His people by granting them revelation. But this personal revelation comes out of the explicit claims of the Holy Scripture, not simply out of our experience; i.e., not "The Lord told me . . ." This personal revelation must come by a right dealing with the text of Holy Scripture. If evangelical ministers do not determine again to "know nothing . . . except Jesus Christ and him crucified" (1 Cor. 2:2), there is no hope for reforming local churches in our present North American context. We may continue to build hugely successful large churches, but there is no realistic way we can build faithful congregations that love and obey God as their first priority.

## THE LOST PERSPECTIVE

As a result of losing the Word of God, modern ministers have also lost a vital perspective on the role and place of the ministry. Our present perspective on pastoral ministry is more directly shaped by George Barna's statistical insights (which are helpful if used for what they really are—i.e., religious data) and the church growth experts than by Holy Scripture. Let me explain.

This volume is about reformation in pastoral ministry. It would be helpful here to make a distinction between revival and reformation. Revival, understood in the corporate sense, is an extraordinary outpouring and empowering of the Holy Spirit that brings fresh life to the experience of large numbers of people in the Christian church at the same time. Such seasons of unusual Christian experience come like "showers of blessing" from God Himself. There can be little doubt that pastors and congregations all across North America need revival showers in our time. But revival showers as we have known them in more recent decades will only create more mud and greater confusion if we do not see a significant change in the direction of pastoral life and ministry. Therefore, we also need reformation. But what exactly is the difference between revival and reformation?

We will again let A. W. Tozer guide us. He noted on several different occasions that "A revival of the kind of Christianity which we have had in America the last 50 years would be the greatest tragedy of this century, a tragedy which would take the church a hundred years to get over."[7] After spending much time preaching on the subject of revival and praying for such a divine awakening, with pastoral and lay leaders alike, I strongly concur with Tozer's insight.

The revival of *Christian experience* (if it really is Christian at all) without the recovery of *Christian truth* would be an unmitigated disaster. What is needed, now more than ever, is a Word-driven, reformational revival. We already have staggering numbers of people who profess faith in Christ but show little or no evidence of savingly knowing Him. Because we have lost the centrality of the Word of God in our ministries, as previously noted above, we seem to long all the more for techniques and programs that will help us pastor our churches. The only lasting solution is to regain a pastoral perspective deeply rooted in God and His holiness.

Consider, as noted briefly above, that in the decade of the 1970s we had a major battle over the Bible. Evangelicals debated the issue of inerrancy with great vigor. Major papers and statements of faith were issued, and numerous books were published. Large conferences were held, and evangelicals made their presence widely known throughout American Christendom. Every statistical survey I have seen since the late 1970s indicates that to some measure we won major victories through this effort. At the same time the belief, life, and practice of Christians and churches has seriously declined. I am personally afraid that many who fought for the inerrancy of the Bible have practically denied its authority! Let me explain what I mean.

If the Bible has no real authority in the realms of personal belief and the actual practice of individual Christians and local congregations, what difference does it make that we have argued over its trustworthiness? If the Bible does not make ministers more holy and churches more humble, have we really won the debate? I wish I had a dollar for every time I have heard pastors tell me why they could not (or would not) seek to reform the practices of their own church by the obvious teaching of Holy Scripture. I would be a rich man. The guilt of most of us does not lie in our outright denials of the Scripture. We still preach biblical sermons. (Or at least we call them biblical sermons!) The problem is not in outright denial; it is in sheer neglect! We have, whether intentionally or not, neglected the tough issues of pastoral ministry. But why?

I suspect there are at least two reasons. One is pragmatism. We know too many stories about ministers who have been faithful, only to see their membership rolls decline. This is a hard trial for the average pastor. Unless one's life is deeply rooted in God and His holiness, there is little hope that most ministers can, or will, pay this extremely high price. The other reason for this neglect is fear. Pastors, like other mortals, have human fears. There are legitimate fears about their family, their job security, and their entire future. They know, by instinct and example, that when a pastor takes a stand for reforming the church, the price will always be steep! The simple fact is that in many cases it will not be long until the faithful minister is looking for another place to serve. Only those who have lost members and who have night after night agonized over the flock of God and have been accused of relational insensitivity can adequately understand this very real pressure. (These attacks are rarely waged over real doctrinal subjects since most church members know very little real doctrine in the first place! They are usually aimed at the pastor's inability to keep the entire flock happy and positive toward his overall ministry.)

What I am arguing here is that we have actually lost, in the last several decades, a perspective or outlook that once shaped the pastors who serve the churches of North America. The culture has moved us increasingly toward full-scale secularism, even in the lives and labors of our pastors. The pressures of this secularizing influence are quite real. The church is increasingly accepting the modern perspective on life in the world in place of the ancient perspective of a consciously and intentionally God-directed vision.

We may still confess the same creeds and statements of faith, but we do not confess them in a way that makes a real difference. The famous theologian J. Gresham Machen noted this problem in 1925 when he wrote about Modernist ministers:

> It makes very little difference how much or how little of the creeds of the Church the Modernist preacher affirms, or how much or how little of the biblical teaching from which the creeds are derived. He might affirm every jot and tittle of the Westminster Confession, for example, and yet be separated by a great gulf from the Reformed faith. It is not that part is denied and the rest

affirmed; but all is denied, because all is affirmed merely as useful or symbolic and not as true.[8]

In such an environment it is not that pastors deny the truth openly so much as they learn, whether consciously or not, to be imprecise and evasive. They usually learn this by observing how "successful" pastors have done it. Modernism in theology seventy-five years ago did not so much deny confessed revealed truth as it evaded precise and clear statements of what truth was and what difference it actually made. The older Modernism of the 1920s desired to reduce the consensus of what was truth to the lowest possible common denominator so that the widest possible arena for unity could be constructed. Evangelical ministers of that era successfully resisted this temptation precisely because they knew what they believed and why they believed it. They had a mind-set that was strongly informed by categories of right and wrong, truth and error. But a whole new temper of mind has arisen in modern evangelicalism because we have lost our shared perspective upon the work of faithful ministry. Listen to J. Gresham Machen again:

> This temper of mind is hostile to precise definitions. Indeed nothing makes a man more unpopular in the controversies of the present day than an insistence upon definitions of terms. . . . Men discourse very eloquently today upon such subjects as God, religion, Christianity, atonement, redemption, faith; but they are greatly incensed when they are asked to tell in simple language what they mean by these terms.[9]

The great difference between our day and Machen's is that people still discourse on religion, spirituality, and God, but there is no longer a distinct Christian framework in the culture. The question I am asking comes down to this: Is there still a distinct Christian framework in the church? The temper of mind inside the church is surely more hostile to precise definitions than it was in Machen's day. In his time a debate was actually waged and evangelicals had the courage to stand up against both great ecclesiastical machinery and major cultural obstacles. Today it is hard to find anyone who wants to seriously debate anything of substance. The only thing that seems to matter is, "Does the perspective being touted produce a growing and success-ful church?"[10]

The reason ministers have lost their way is not hard to find. There is no vivid sense of otherworldliness among us. God as absolutely holy no longer matters. We live for the now! We actually think the Gospel is a message that is primarily about putting lives back together. We have no sense of the eternal. As a result we have a Mr. Fix-it mental-ity about the Christian ministry. The church wants a pastor who can fix the problems of the congregation—social, emotional, marital, financial, and spiritual. (And when the pastor no longer does this suc-cessfully, he is calmly told to relocate!) If the church and its message are about meeting people's needs, then the pastor has become a highly trained "need fixer." In previous generations the minister was under-stood to be the "man of God." He handled the Word and cared for the souls of his people. Today if he is truly successful, he is more likely to be the manager of a local corporation. (Indeed, many of our largest churches no longer seek theologically trained staff members but rather successful businessmen to develop and lead their programs. Some are even bold enough to openly say so!) Let's face it, in the minds of many evangelical parishioners the minister is there to make God enjoyable and the church as user-friendly as possible.

The pressure this puts upon pastors, in the present context, is immense. Only the spiritually courageous will survive.[11] The simple fact is this: Market-driven churches and pastors who buy into this approach engage in complete capitulation to the debilitating and destabilizing effects of worldliness. David Wells is surely prophetic when he writes:

> The stream of historic orthodoxy that once watered the evangel-ical soul is now damned by a worldliness that many fail to rec-ognize as worldliness because of the cultural innocence with which it presents itself. . . . The older orthodoxy was driven by a passion for truth, and that was why it could express itself only in theological terms. The newer evangelicalism is not driven by the

same passion for truth, and that is why it is often empty of theological interest. . . . We now have less biblical fidelity, less interest in truth, less seriousness, less depth, and less capacity to speak the Word of God to our own generation in a way that offers an alternative to what it already thinks.[12]

The first way for pastors to lead the church toward meaningful biblical reformation is to get a true sense of how great the need really is. The second is to be gripped by the immensity of God's holiness personally. When this has happened, the reforming pastor is then ready to consider the need for the kind of divine power that is necessary for ministry in our time.

## THE LOST POWER

As a result of these first two losses, evangelical ministers have generally stopped asking for the power of the Holy Spirit upon their own lives and ministries. They either assume they already have this power due to some experience in the past, or they believe it is not proper to ask for power because of a theological position wrongly or inadequately developed. Many think that all they will ever need was given to them at their conversion, or perhaps in their ordination. Some even assume the divine equipment needed is part of their graduation from Bible college or seminary.

Pastors are weak human instruments who must be filled with divine authority. There is no other way to accomplish the true work of pastoral ministry. True authority never comes from within our human persona or from the office (or gifting) itself, but from a divinely given mandate and from a scripturally based message. God save us from evangelical mini-popes who rule the church as if it were their own flock. Many of us grew up observing the carnage of this style of ministerial authority in an earlier generation. We who minister the Word of Christ to this present generation have no right to impose our human opinions and traditions upon those whom Christ has made free by the Gospel. We do, however, have a responsibility to bind the consciences of our hearers with the Word of God. The proper way to destroy false traditions and practices is always by showing the church the right way to think and act through the proper use of Holy Scripture.

Pastors, pressured to become managers and therapists, now seem to turn more and more to specialized insights and unique training (often offered by how-to seminars and endless denominational workshops on growing healthy churches). David Wells observes:

> As the nostrums of the therapeutic age supplant confession, and as preaching is psychologized, the meaning of Christian faith becomes privatized. At a single stroke, confession is eviscerated and reflection reduced mainly to thought about one's self. . . . Thus it is that the pastor seeks to embody what modernity admires and to redefine what pastoral ministry now means in light of this culture's two most admired types, the manager and the psychologist.[13]

We must begin this reformation of pastoral ministry by earnestly seeking for the power of God again. We need what the apostle spoke of so plainly when he said that his preaching of the Gospel was "not simply with words, but also with power, with the Holy Spirit and with deep conviction" (1 Thess. 1:5). Until we have this true power we shall never move modern men and women, immersed in a culture that stands in such utter hostility to God's holiness and all divinely delegated authority. We must, if we are biblical, reforming ministers, be fully persuaded that the Gospel "is the power of God for the salvation of everyone who believes" (Rom. 1:16).

But where are we to begin? I offer Luke 11:13 as the starting point for ministers who are seeking to recover the power of God to conduct their ministry with integrity, passion, and profound conviction. In this passage Jesus tells us to "ask," "seek," and "knock" that we might get from God the gift of the Holy Spirit. Our Lord says: "If you then, though you are evil, know how to give good gifts to children, how much more will your Father in heaven give the Holy Spirit to those who ask him!"

It will not do to argue that since I already have the Holy Spirit living within me, I do not need to ask for His power and presence. This text will not bear such a conclusion by any means of serious exegesis. Just as we accepted another person in our marriage and still ask them for deeper knowledge and a greater felt presence of their personality in our lives, so we must hunger and thirst for more of God's Spirit working in and through us by the power of Christ's resurrection. A ministry that "asks not" will be a ministry that "has not" (cf. Jas. 4:2).

## THE WAY HOME

The only road that leads the ministry home again is to believe, teach, and practice nothing more and nothing less than what the Holy Scripture requires of us. This might sound rather simplistic. The fact is, if this counsel were followed by thousands of pastors throughout North America, a new reformation might well break out over the next few years. This reformation might well result in a holy outpouring of real revival that would change our generation much as the church was changed by the events of the sixteenth century.

It has often been with ministers that God has first begun the work of reforming and renewing the life of the church. Consider the effect of one man, Martin Luther, in Germany. Or consider the labors of Jonathan Edwards in early America. Consider what has happened when godly ministers have joined with one another in holy concert to seek the Lord's favor upon their labors.

The mandate for the reforming pastor will always be quite simple, whether in good times or bad, whether in eras of judgment or eras of true revival. It is and will always be: "Trust God to produce in the hearers his chosen purposes—irrespective of whether the results are readily visible."[14]

## CONCLUSION

I write as an evangelical minister, as one who has been engaged in pastoral ministry for three decades. I also write as one who has observed the church in almost every imaginable setting and style across North

America. If the faithful minister of the Gospel is to labor for the reformation of the church in a real congregational setting, great courage
and clear vision must become the order of the day.

We must have shepherds who are "continually being reformed"
by the Spirit and the Word. Even in the early days of the Reformation
in sixteenth-century Europe, the human instruments God used to
purge the medieval church realized their deep personal shortcomings.
John Calvin, the most biblical of all the early reformers, recognized
that reformation was not so much an event as it was the beginning of
a process. He understood that true reform was brought about, ultimately, by God alone. Reforming the church was ultimately not the
work of the minister, but the work of God, through Jesus Christ, by
the Spirit of Christ, in the hearts of those who were the called of God.
This conviction is borne out by the famous *Heidelberg Catechism*
when it says:

> Q. What do you believe concerning the *holy catholic Church*?
> A. That the Son of God, out of the whole human race, from
> the beginning to the end of the world, *gathers, defends, and pre-*
> *serves for Himself, by His Spirit and Word, in the unity of the true*
> *faith, a Church chosen to everlasting life*; and that I am, and for-
> ever shall remain, a living member thereof.[15] (emphasis mine)

The work of reforming the church is ultimately Christ's work. He
alone "gathers, defends and preserves for Himself, by His Spirit and
Word, in the unity of the true faith, a Church chosen to everlasting
life." Only when the faithful pastor understands this theological reality will he undertake earnest pastoral labor for reforming the church
with holy confidence balanced with proper dependence upon the
Spirit of God.

> Indeed, Luther and Calvin were in very close agreement about the
> actual nature of the church. They understood that the true
> church, known to God alone, is a company of justified sinners.
> But the visible church will by necessity always be a mixed com-
> pany. Only when the visible church ensures the right preaching
> of the Gospel and the right administration of the sacraments will

it be a true church. Calvin, unlike Luther, believed that in view of this it was necessary for the church to submit itself to continual self-examination. Its members must accept a system of pastoral discipline that would purify it, just as its ministers must be diligent to test all their doctrine and ministerial practice by the Word of God. This is extremely important for the reader of this present volume to understand. It is the belief of each contributor that the reformation of the church is not a single act but an ongoing process. The truly reformed church must always be a reforming church, not a church that emulates Rome's boast of *semper idem*, always the same.[16]

This continual need for the church to always be reforming itself must always be by *sola Scriptura*, by Scripture alone. The church requires, by its very nature, an ongoing purging and renewing of its life by the power of the Spirit. It is not an institution, like a modern corporation with a profit-driven purpose, but rather a living body, an expression of Christ in visible human form. As a living body, the church needs much more than evangelical correctness and managerial attention. Far too many of us have settled for comfortable new waves of technological wizardry without the power of God. It is time that we thought more intentionally about reforming pastoral ministry by the Word of God alone.

## NOTES

1 The phrase is sometimes translated by the English "continually reforming," but the Latin is a passive gerundive, which means it could be better translated, "continually being reformed." It would appear that the essence of this cry was not heard in the church, at least in these precise words, until post-Reformation times between the seventeenth and eighteenth centuries. Further historical work on this term clearly needs to be undertaken. The fact that the idea arose and was frequently appealed to is beyond dispute. The precise origin of the expression is properly in dispute.

2 Graham Miller, *Calvin's Wisdom: An Anthology Arranged Alphabetically* (Carlisle, PA: Banner of Truth, 1992), p. 209.

3 Derek J. Tidball, "Pastoral Theology," in *New Dictionary of Theology*, eds. Sinclair B. Ferguson, David F. Wright, and J. I. Packer (Downers Grove, IL: InterVarsity Press, 1988), pp. 493-494.

4 David F. Wells, *The Bleeding of the Evangelical Church* (Carlisle, PA: Banner of Truth, 1995), p. 10.

5   A. W. Tozer, "All Authority Was Given to Me," reprinted in *Masterpiece* (November/December 1990), p. 20. Excerpted from *God Tells the Man Who Cares*.

6   Ibid.

7   Quoted by Jim Elliff in "Reformation or Revival?" in *Heartcry: A Journal on Revival and Spiritual Awakening*, No. 3, Fall 1997, p. 20.

8   J. Gresham Machen, *What Is Faith?* (Carlisle, PA: Banner of Truth, 1991 reprint), p. 34.

9   Ibid., pp. 13-14.

10  Consider the recent debates among evangelicals regarding "The Openness of God" proposal. In the past this kind of thinking would have been called "heresy" without much further discussion. (*Heresy* seems to be the one word no one wants to use in the modern context.) A generation ago evangelical ministers would have run away from such an idea as fast as possible. Today leading evangelical publishers and magazines entertain this "new" perspective while insisting that though the view might not be orthodox, we must allow it within the big tent of evangelicalism since it is taught by some of our most respected pastors and theologians. In one such debate we are told repeatedly that the proponent of this view of God is the pastor of a successful, growing, evangelistic church. What more could a person need for general acceptance and approval than this? In fact, look at the descriptions of popular authors on the jackets of many modern titles and you will see the same used as the criteria for why this particular author should be read by an evangelical audience.

11  In reality it is the "weak" who survive; cf. 2 Corinthians 3:1—4:18. Also see 2 Corinthians 12:10. What is really needed is "weak" ministers who properly delight in their sufferings for the sake of the church of Christ.

12  David Wells, *No Place for Truth, Or: Whatever Happened to Evangelical Theology?* (Grand Rapids, MI: Eerdmans, 1993), pp. 11-12.

13  Ibid., p. 101.

14  This quotation comes from a longer statement called *The Preacher's Mandate* and is used by permission of The Cornerstone Trust, Box 1906, Cave Creek, Arizona 85327. The full statement, which can be secured as a bookmark by writing to The Cornerstone Trust, reads as follows:

*The Preacher's Mandate*

Pray as though nothing of eternal value is going to happen unless God does it.

Prepare as giving "my utmost for his highest."

Seek not to "get a message" from the scripture, but seek "the message" of the scripture.

Be satisfied not with producing good content, but with producing good people.

Attend carefully to a private and public walk with God, knowing the congregation never rises to a standard higher than that being lived by the preacher.

Be "persuaded that the gospel is the power of God unto salvation."

"Preach the word"—not *about* the word, not *from* the word, not *with* the word—affirming it is only proclamations of God's word that carry God's authority and his promise to bless.

Exalt Christ preeminently, trusting he will then draw people to himself.

Balance declarations of "salvation by faith alone" with declarations describing the life Christ produces when he sees *saving faith*; transformed heart, desire to serve the Lord not self, growing affection for his word, increasing obedience, fruit of the Spirit, saltiness in society, maturing Christlikeness.

Depend solely upon God for translation of spiritual truth into life.

Preach Christ's word in Christ-like demeanor.

Agree it is impossible at one and the same time to impress people with Christ and with oneself.

Allow the preaching to exude the fruit of the Spirit, lest the preaching fail to produce Christ-like lives.

Preach with humble gratitude, as one privileged to be an oracle of God.

Trust God to produce in the hearers his chosen purposes—irrespective of whether the results are readily visible.

15  *The Heidelberg Catechism*, Lord's Day 21, Question 54.

16  R. T. Jones, "Reformation Theology," in *New Dictionary of Theology*, p. 567.

# 2

## DELIVER US FROM PROFESSIONALIZATION:

### Recovering Pastoral Ministry

■

### Mark Coppenger

How to Become Bishop

In his 1965 book *How to Become a Bishop Without Being Religious*,[1] Methodist Minister Charles Merrill Smith pronounced "In the Garden" "the greatest hymn ever written"[2] and urged young ministers to make a two-door, dark compact their first car purchase.[3] His test for hymns was simple: "If it emphasizes the attributes of God—his majesty, power, mercy, goodness, love, etc.—or recounts in some manner the story of Jesus, it is an objective hymn and thus, with possible rare exceptions, unsuitable for a public worship service. If, on the other hand, the hymn is preoccupied with the feelings, reactions, desires, hopes and longings of the individual worshiper it is subjective and guaranteed to have a religious kick in it."[4] By Smith's account, the people would much rather sing about themselves ("And He walks with *me*, and He talks with *me*, and He tells *me* I am His own") than to work through the sort of material you get in "A Mighty Fortress."

As for the car, you might finish your ministry with a metallic green Oldsmobile, but you must not begin there. It would be unseemly.

The book is full of such tongue-in-cheek counsel, with chapter titles on the order of "The Techniques of Being Unmistakably

Clerical," "Selecting the Clerical Wife," and "Getting Into the Major Leagues."

## HUMOR ASIDE

Of course, Smith's book is overstated humor, but with a strong element of truth. I was surprised to read the following words in a Doctor of Ministry seminar paper: "To this day I can't understand why a larger church has not considered me seriously for their pastor. . . . If the Lord is saving the best for last in my ministry, then he or I need to do some serious maneuvering before it's too late. I know he called me to prepare. I just can't figure out what for. I was pastoring the same size church with a college education; it seems like such a waste." That minister's Master's and doctoral studies hadn't given him the leverage he thought they would for career advancement, and he was bitter.

On reflection I realized that my surprise came not so much from his thinking as from his candor in this context. For through the years I'd heard a number of men express their career longings, their desire to "step up" in one way or another.

From my days as a youth director, I'd been given professional counsel, things to embrace and things to avoid. Some of it was godly, stewardly wisdom; much of it was eyewash.

I remember the moments before I entered the sanctuary on the Sunday I came "in view of a call" as youth director. My role that morning was to be introduced on the platform, lead in prayer, and then go down into the congregation to sit with friends from the church. I handed my Bible to the college acquaintance I'd be joining in the pew and turned toward the entrance door. An overweight, chain-smoking usher asked, "Don't you think you ought to carry your Bible up there? It looks better." And I did.

Multiply that advice by the hundreds, and you have the makings of comprehensive career counseling, tips for success and advancement. From seminary I gained "Don't get too far out in front of your troops, or they'll mistake you for the enemy and start shooting at you." And "Never ride alone with a woman who's not family." A seasoned minister once suggested, "Never schedule more than three counseling sessions with an individual. If it takes more than that, they need a professional." Another gave his staff copies of *Dress for Success*, with its "power ties" and such. Yet another told me, "If you don't marry these folks, you'll never be able to minister to them." And so it went, for better or worse.

## THE VALUE OF PROFESSIONAL CODES

I don't mean at all to gainsay our being circumspect and professional in our behavior. We might well look to ministerial codes of conduct. From the time of Hippocrates, doctors have had such codes. Attorneys and psychiatrists have used them extensively. But ministers have been slow to embrace them. Some see them as an insult, monitoring God's monitors. Others worry about enforcement. Nevertheless, they have appeared in this century, and they offer some good things to us.

In the 1930s several denominations largely replicated each other's wording as they laid out standards. For instance, the minister was to "reserve sufficient time for serious study," "meet his bills promptly," and "tell the truth as he sees it and present it tactfully and constructively."[5] He "will not plagiarize" and "will not be party to funeral or marriage rackets."[6]

One interesting exercise is to picture the minister who would be the opposite of these codes. He has no devotional life, is physically unfit, ignores his family, lives outside his income, fails to study, shows racial bias, seeks special gratuities, plays favorites in the congregation, violates confidences, and gossips.[7] Perhaps we have seen ministers who fill this bill, and it's not a pretty sight. If professional codes can help here, more power to them.

Furthermore, the language of these codes can be inspirational, for they offer ideals as well as rules: "I am a minister of the Lord Jesus Christ, called of God to proclaim the unsearchable riches of his love. Therefore, I voluntarily adopt the following principles in order that through dedication and self-discipline I may set a more worthy example for those whom I seek to lead and serve. . . . I will cultivate my devotional life, continuing steadfastly in reading the Bible, meditation and prayer."[8] We also read, "Faith, hope, and love in all relationships shall be shared,"[9] and "We are dedicated to upholding the dignity and worth of every person who seeks or is reached by our care and proclamation."[10] These are good expressions, worthy of reflection.

## THE PERIL OF PROFESSIONAL CODES

There are, however, troubling features in these codes. On first reading they may not seem to be problematic, for they follow the canons of gentlemanly behavior. But some parts don't wear well in light of the early church. First, they are conspicuous for what they omit. For example, few if any mention church discipline, one of the most difficult and neglected tasks of the pastor. Second, they can be self-serving, in that members of the profession typically write them for themselves. One critic says they "are shot through with collusive self-interest."[11] As valid as the following rule may be, it still sounds a bit odd for ministers to put it into their code of conduct as a moral obligation: "A weekly holiday and an annual vacation should be taken and used for rest and improvement."[12]

Let's take a closer look at several other examples:

*"It is unethical for a minister to take sides with factions in his parish."*[13] If by this you mean that the minister should not have a party spirit, that he should not let his preferences skew or diminish his devotion to pastoral duty, then you do well enough. You could say there is only one right side, and that is the Lord's side. But what is the application? What would Paul make of this in the Galatian church? The Judaizers say that all new converts should be circumcised. Another group, made up largely of Gentile converts, objects. Paul turns to the ministerial code and decides that he should not take sides, and thus we have no letter to the Galatians.

You might pay grudging respect to this approach of not taking sides in that it's a formula for long life in the ministry of a particular church. Yes, people will be irritated with you if you don't stand with them, but they'll get over it. Stay out of their way, and they'll excuse you. They will less likely forgive you if you stand against them. But where is leadership in this? And for that matter, where is truth?

Perhaps this rule simply applies to petty squabbles, things upon which a minister should not squander his good will. Perhaps "taking sides" is nefarious by definition, implying low motives and murky means. But if the rule demands ministerial neutrality on all live issues in the church, then it is not a biblical rule.

*"It is unethical for a minister to speak ill of the character or work of another minister . . . ,"*[14] and *"I will consider all ministers my co-laborers in the work of Christ, and even though I may differ from them, I shall respect their Christian earnestness and sincerity."*[15] This is a nice enough *prima facie* rule, for it is good to give one another the benefit of the doubt and to refrain from nit-picking each other to death. On a practical level, what goes around comes around, and you may very well find yourself on the receiving end of withering criticism should you violate this standard. But one's mind runs to a number of passages, including Ezekiel 34. Here God commanded his man to prophesy against "the shepherds of Israel."

In the New Testament Jude attacked "shepherds who feed only themselves." And, of course, we remember the repeated words of Jesus in Matthew 23: "Woe to you, teachers of the law and Pharisees, you hypocrites!"

It seems that the Christ of the professional codes is tamer than the Christ of the New Testament. Consider the references to our Savior's character and manner in these codes.

*"I will seek to be Christlike in my personal attitudes and conduct toward all people regardless of race, class or creed."*[16] And again, *"I will seek to be Christlike in attitude and action toward all persons regardless of race, social class, religious beliefs, or position of influence within the church and community."*[17] In common parlance, this means that the minister will be gentle, gracious, courteous, and nonjudgmental, unwavering in his own principles, but not so fixed upon them as to dismiss others.

Yes, Jesus said we should not judge lest we be judged (Matt. 7:1), but five verses later He said we should not cast our pearls before swine. To obey this latter commandment, you must judge some to be swine.

Yes, over protests Jesus gathered children unto Himself, ate with sinners, and went meekly to the cross. He gave us the parable of the Good Samaritan, rebuking racists. But this was also the Jesus who called people "whitewashed tombs" to their faces and even called a disciple "Satan." This is the Jesus who hated the practice of the Nicolaitans and who wanted to spit the Laodiceans out of His mouth. Was His attitude in these latter cases Christlike? Yes, by definition. But is this what the code writers had in mind? Probably not.

The issue of Christlikeness has been raised in the popular question, "What Would Jesus Do?" As many have observed, the more proper question is, "What would Jesus have me do?" For we have no business cursing fig trees, and we may well run for political office and marry, though Jesus would have considered neither. But not to quibble; the problem with the admonition to Christlikeness is its linkage with a hyper-tolerant image of Christ. As Allan Bloom has demonstrated in *The Closing of the American Mind*,[18] this kind of tolerance is the national ideal, and a minister who exhibits it may well go far. But he may fail in his prophetic office.

"*I will strive with evangelistic zeal to build up the church I serve, but will not proselyte the members of other religious groups.*"[19] Also, "*In my evangelistic responsibilities, I will seek to lead persons to salvation and to church membership without manipulating converts, proselytizing members of other churches, or demeaning other religious faiths.*"[20] Yes, we are to be careful in our witness, relying upon the power of the Gospel and not our cleverness. No, we are not to be "stealing sheep" to boost our membership and financial numbers. No, we are not to take cheap shots at other faith groups. But these code statements go beyond that. They make it sound as if one church is the Rotary, another the Lions, a third the Kiwanis.

This was not the view of the apostles. They understood that union with mistaken faith groups was toxic and that it was the preacher's responsibility to say so and beckon others to the true church. In 2 Corinthians 6:14-18 Paul disparaged yoking with error and urged people to come out and be separate. In Colossians 2:8 he warned of captivity to "hollow and deceptive philosophy," and in 2:18 of angel worship. And there is no mystery over what he might say to the homosexually-oriented Metropolitan Community Churches in light of Romans 1.

In sum, the minister of the professional codes is scarcely a prophet.

And insofar as the minister has a role as prophet, he must resist the domestication of the profession. Yes, he must exercise all due courtesy, be as impartial as possible, and show measure in his pronouncements. He must guard against churlishness. But he must not be muzzled in the name of cordiality, for this is to ignore Paul's mandate in 2 Timothy 4:2: "Preach the word; be prepared in season and out of season; correct, rebuke and encourage—with great patience and careful instruction." If he is too concerned with offending the ministers and members of The Church of the Itching Ears, he may well be a pillar of his community, but he will not be God's man.

*"Ministers and staff limit their practice to those positions and responsibilities for which they are qualified."*[21] On the face of it, this standard is quite reasonable, but it is not so uncomplicated as it may seem. It touches the matter of Christian counseling, where the debate rages over the competence of pastors with Scripture alone to do the heavy lifting. Should the pastor quickly refer the troubled soul to a psychologist or psychiatrist lest he misdiagnose things and do damage through untutored methods? The therapeutic society cries, "Yes." But many believers are saying, "Not so fast."

One of the basic criticisms of professional thinking and professional codes is their self-protective nature, their fascination with turf. One cynic speaks of "a code of Professional Manners oriented toward a Professional Image for the protection of Professional Compensation."[22] Criticism of the American Medical Association along these lines is commonplace. Many have argued that there is an economic interest in doctors' setting standards that artificially limit the number of competitors through unreasonably tight medical school admission practices, standards that essentially demean their counterparts in acupuncture, midwifery, osteopathy, homeopathy, and chiropractic, and that eliminate advertising that could drive down fees. Of course, there is a strong point to be made for upholding the quality and dignity of the profession, but it is fair to ask if that is all that is in play here.

Most seminaries now offer Master of Divinity degrees with a non-language track, and preachers who want a simpler walk through seminary often take it. Some even take the two-year Master of Christian Education, even though they are headed for the pastorate. When view-

ing these strategies, one appreciates the code's insistence upon qualification. You want to ask the hiring church how they can hope to hear
consistently pointed biblical preaching if they will settle for such slim
study in the language and preaching fields. But no one can deny that
there are those without these courses who have done creditable work
as lifelong, self-taught, thoughtful students of the Word, and we
would border on professional arrogance to gainsay their ministry.

Furthermore, this standard could squelch some perfectly reasonable development in ministry, such as the discovery that a music minister filling in for a departed senior citizens' minister was just the ticket.
Must he take courses in gerontology before he proceeds? What sort of
qualification grants him admission to this ministry? And who is to say?

## THE PROFESSIONS

The term *profession* comes from the Latin for public statement or vow.
Originally it was connected with religious orders. But through the
years it took on a more general meaning. Some see four distinctives in
the professions.[23] First, their members possess "specialized skills and
knowledge not possessed by the population at large." This knowledge
is theoretical at base and is "acquired by extended formal education."
There is legal theory and there is musical theory in a way that there is
no theory of bricklaying or pipefitting.[24] Second, members "enjoy professional autonomy, which encompasses both self-governance, or reg-
ulation, and liberty of professional action." Third, they concern the
achievement of some lofty goal, such as physical health, spiritual
health, justice, or knowledge. Fourth, their members exhibit "an atyp-
ical moral commitment to the interests and well-being of the client,"
a level of commitment we do not normally expect in business or the
trades. These latter enterprises have customers rather than clients. To
the non-professional, "the customer is always right." For the professional, the client is often wrong and needs to be told so.[25] Some add a
fifth item, "the professional culture."[26] This culture includes informal
groups, social protocols, emblems, distinctive dress, jargon, heroes,
and villains.

Of course, the second criterion does not jibe so well with the typical minister's situation. He does not take "clergy boards" as doctors take their "medical boards." He cannot be disbarred by other ministers the way a lawyer may be disbarred from his practice. But one could argue that ministers have their counterparts in ordination councils and denominational placement offices, run by ministers and capable of either advancing or retarding other minister careers. And insofar as churches insist upon theological studies and these schools of theology are sanctioned by accrediting agencies made up largely of clergy, there is a measure of ministerial self-governance.

Though the term *professional* has a nice ring to it, the professions have their detractors. Some say the members are too paternalistic and too tightly aligned with one another. One writer observed, regarding the medical profession, "There are two kinds of information that doctors routinely withhold from patients: one kind has to do with facts about the patient's illness; the other kind has to do with evaluations of the competence of performance of the other doctors involved in the case, or the wisdom of the treatment that other doctors have recommended."[27]

The medical profession is not the only one where the members cover for each other. Ministers do it as well. When I was a college professor, my pastor was in over his head. Without a background of serious study, he had little heart or aptitude for the preaching ministry, at least in the context of an evangelical witness to a white-collar, largely Catholic suburb of Chicago. He enjoyed soliciting free materials from local merchants for vacation Bible school use and comparison-shopping for light bulbs, but hours in the study were not his cup of tea. He was largely indifferent to evangelism, content to build a "you all club" of transplanted Southern Baptists. One thing led to another, and the pastor left. The feelings of all involved were raw.

We invited a denominational worker to speak, hoping he would give us some encouragement and wisdom on how to proceed. Instead he essentially scolded us for a deficiency in love. And it was then I began to see that ministers had a tendency to hang together, instinctively taking each other's sides in disputes, circling the wagons against the laymen and their machinations.

Of course the ministry, done right, is harder than laymen suppose. Of course there are dangerous "longhorn deacons" (as my Texas friends put it), busybodies, and a menagerie of curiosities in the congregation. But those in the ministry are too quick to count other ministers in trouble as "wounded heroes." Some are. Many aren't—heroes, that is.

In our focus on professional solidarity, we can forget the point to it all—the glory of God. As Richard Baxter put it, "The ultimate end of our pastoral oversight is that which is the ultimate end of our whole lives; even the pleasing and glorifying of God. . . ."[28] Baxter provides us this template: "It is the first and great work of the ministers of Christ to acquaint men with the God that made them, and is their happiness; to open to them the treasures of his goodness, and tell them of the glory that is in his presence, which all his chosen people shall enjoy; that so by shewing men the certainty and the excellency of the promised felicity, and the perfect blessedness in the life to come, compared with the vanities of this present life, we may turn the stream of their cogitations and affections, and bring them to a due contempt of this world, and set them on seeking the durable treasure; and this is the work that we should lie at with them night and day."[29]

One might say that this is an eloquent statement of the professional standard, one that matches what is said in the codes we've examined. But it is the nature of professions to take on a life of their own, and, as was the case with the visiting denominational worker, the profession can prompt men to downplay those very standards, shifting focus to the plight of their fellow professional. When you take your eyes off the high calling and the pleasure of God and turn it to the professional affairs of men, however nobly expressed, you run the danger of substituting earthly agendas for heavenly things.

When you set your heart on pleasing God, good professional things will follow. You will want to avoid, in Baxter's words, "an undervaluing of unity and peace," "want of serious, industrious, unreserved laying out of ourselves in the work of God: discovered by negligent studies, by dull, drowsy preaching, by not helping them that want abroad, by neglect of acknowledged duties, e.g., church discipline," and "giving in to the power of worldly, carnal interests, manifested by temporising, worldly business, and barrenness in works of charity."[30] Of course, it does not follow that by doing hard work, framing interesting sermons, and stirring ourselves to acts of charity, we will either please God or insulate ourselves from self-regarding professional pride. But first things first, and professionalism is not first.

## CAREERISM

Closely aligned with the notion of profession is that of career. In the 1980s, the Association of Theological Schools conducted a study published under the title, *Clergy Assessment and Career Development.*[31] Four thousand clergy and laity from denominations associated with ATS were surveyed. This would seem to be a reasonable thing to do, in that career development and career tracks are besetting cultural concerns, and the insights of practitioners are critical. But we should also ask what the Bible says about career development.

We might begin by scanning a concordance for references to *career*. We soon find that the concordance will be no help, for *career* does not appear. And upon reflection we see that the very notion of career planning for Paul and Timothy is an odd one.

The word *career* comes from the French word *carriere*, meaning the road we take or the course a horse runs. In fact, we sometimes read the expression, "He careered around the track." (The Greek equivalent would be *dromos*, as in *hippodrome*.) Of course, Christians do follow a course throughout their lives. In 2 Timothy 4:7 Paul said he had finished his race. But the problem lies in sketching that course in advance. That's a commonplace practice in the world, but this is no sure commendation of its fitness for the ministry.

A quick visit to a management school library shows an interest in careers. The card catalogue is full of books with such titles as *Building a Great Resumé; Targeting the Job You Want; Dynamite Networking for Dynamite Jobs: 101 Interpersonal, Telephone, and Electronic Techniques for Getting Job Leads, Interviews and Offers; Personal Best: 1001 Great Ideas for Achieving Success in Your Career; Creating You & Co.: Learn to Think Like the CEO of Your Own Career; Strategic Job Jumping: Fifty Very Smart Tactics for Building Your Career; The New Rules: Eight Business Breakthroughs to Career*

*Success in the 21st Century; The $100,000 Club: How to Make a Six-Figure Income; Career Barriers: How People Experience, Overcome, and Avoid Failure.* The sad thing is that anyone who has been around the ministry for any time will recognize these sentiments at play in that arena as well.

In this vein, we read the words of Michael Korda. He speaks of the "geography of power," the need to insure that you have a corner office and to seize the "power corners" at the office party.[32] He goes on to say that you can unnerve somebody by putting your hat or briefcase on his desk.[33] Better yet, carry no briefcase at all, just a manila envelope. This shows you're not accustomed to lugging things around like the proletariat do.[34] We may laugh at these and other manipulative techniques, but who can deny that similar if not identical moves have made their way into the ministry.

To be fair, we should note that techniques are not just for the carnally acquisitive, but also for the relatively innocent, those who find themselves in perilous waters in the parish. As Lyle Schaller puts it, "The institutional skill the churches have developed to the highest level of competence is the ability to keep secrets. Or it can be stated in the form of a cynical question. Why should you as a pastor cut your own throat, or undercut your own ministry, when there are so many volunteers willing to do this for you?"[35] But we need to remember that with each gain in self-preservational cleverness, even for the best of causes, we sacrifice transparency and the sort of vulnerability that makes ministry genuine. One can very quickly overdo guile.

The very idea of career planning means that you anticipate a long, "upward" progression through assignments. This may clash with the call to die. Yes, you may write your plans in pencil, standing ready to erase them at God's leading. But pencil has a way of setting up on the paper, and what was once easily erasable becomes more resistant as the years pass.

In my military studies I was disappointed to see that the Army manual on leadership (*Field Manual 22-100*) changed in the 1970s to incorporate the perspectives of Abraham Maslow, with his pyramid of motivational cues. At the base were such human needs as food and shelter. At the peak was human fulfillment. The military leader was counseled to lead his men by attending not only to their desire for survival and comfort, but also to their desire to maximize their well-being through meaningful projects—"Be all that you can be!" The problem comes when they are called upon to die in place, to hold a hill at all dreadful costs in order that the enemy might be delayed in his attack on the main body. Where is the career enhancement in that? Similarly, where is the career enhancement in the act of standing for the truth at the expense of your church job? How will that look on your resumé? In Army terms, we blink when we substitute career planning for "duty, honor, country." The analogue in ministry should be clear.

It is perhaps not too much of a strain to imagine a modern Paul hearing the Macedonian call and responding with the question, "Have you got dental?" But beyond the problems of self-attention to comfort, security, and advancement, there are epistemological problems. How in the world do we know what the Lord will have us do ten years down the road? How can we anticipate with any meaningful confidence where our walk with the Lord will take us? Yes, we have careers, but I submit we discover rather than chart them. We see them looking backward, not forward. And God is much better at engineering careers than we are.

Certainly we take steps in particular directions; we prepare for specific tasks by going to seminary or taking our shots for a trip to the mission field. But if we are to be book-of-Acts Christians, we stand ready to bypass Bithynia in a moment and head for Troas and Macedonia, whatever the cost. And as the decades pass, should we have decades, we can just begin to make out the careers that God has given us. At the same time, we can feel for those who designed their own careers in the flesh.

We should note that one may just as surely damage his career by being Barnabas as by being Peter or Paul. We tend to focus on the fiery prophet who alienates his backslidden congregation with his demands for holiness and sacrifice. As he goes from forced termination to forced termination, we say he paid the price for faithfulness to the biblical task. Some have; some haven't. Some are simply needlessly offensive people; some are the genuine item. But it is important to note that gentleness and restraint can cost you just as well. For if denominational reform is afoot and you are disinclined to join in the fray on the cause of right, you may well be judged a slacker. Some are; some aren't. Some are feckless. Others are called to a positive role of steadying the ship while the king's men and the pirates struggle on deck. When the struggle is over, they may be nobodies, but better to be God's nobodies than careerish somebodies.

In God's economy, we need Peter to be Peter, Paul to be Paul, and Barnabas to be Barnabas. If career tracking lures us from our God-given roles, we have cheated the kingdom and injured ourselves.

## MODELS

We are drawn to what we admire, and I fear that we increasingly admire the smooth CEO of a pastor, and not the die-in-place, content-with-humble-station minister, more esteemed in my youth. Our focus then was upon the Jim Elliot of *Through Gates of Splendor* and the Lottie Moon of the Southern Baptist memorial mission offering. Beset by murderous Ecuadorian Aucas, missionary Elliot fired his pistol into the air. He knew that he was surely bound for heaven, and just as surely that his murderers were bound for hell; so he chose his death over theirs.[36] Similarly, Lottie Moon resolved to eat no more, an act of sympathy with the starving Christians of her region. Her letters were marked with accounts of "the strange appearance of the drought-stricken sky, roads strewn with corpses, and mothers hanging themselves in country villages."[37] In her last moments on shipboard home, she conversed with "Chinese friends long since gone on before her." These were our heroes.

Those more familiar with rental car upgrades and Big Bertha drivers than the smell of burning garbage and diesel exhaust in a mission field slum, the weary late-afternoon trek through hospital visits, and the fifteenth hour of preparation for a single sermon may, sadly, be our models today.

Some argue that Judas would fare well in today's environment. Here is a short version of a widely circulated piece of humor (source unknown) on pastoral search committee judgments:

Moses: He stutters, and his former congregation says he loses his temper over trivial things.

Abraham: He took off to Egypt during hard times. We heard that he got into trouble with the authorities and then tried to lie his way out.

David: He is an unacceptable moral character. He might have been considered for minister of music had he not "fallen."

Elijah: He proved to be inconsistent and is known to fold under pressure.

Amos: He comes from a farming background and is better off picking figs.

Peter: He has a bad temper and was heard to have even denied Christ publicly.

Paul: We found him to lack tact. He is too harsh, his appearance is contemptible, and he preaches far too long.

Timothy: He has potential but is much too young for the position.

Jesus: He tends to offend church members with His preaching, especially Bible scholars. He is also too controversial. He even offended the search committee with His pointed questions.

And our choice is:

Judas: He seemed to be very practical, cooperative, good with money, cares for the poor, and dresses well. We all agreed that he is just the man we are looking for to fill the vacancy as our Senior Pastor.

Are we saying that the standards for pastor given in 1 Timothy 3 are to be ignored? Are marriage history, reputation, and maturity irrelevant? Of course not. And yes, there is a difference between the role of Old Testament itinerant prophet and New Testament pastor. The point is simply that God is pleased to work outside the bounds of what the world counts as professional circumspection and decorum, and we would do well to be slow to speak in gainsaying one's credentials. Clark Kerr has explained a lack of university leadership by the trusty practice of looking for people in "no trouble." Instead, they need to look for people in "good trouble."[38] There is wisdom there for the church, but it is not clear that there is ample room for the expression "good trouble" in a culture of professionalization.

## CONCLUSION

In John 10:11 Jesus said that "the good shepherd lays down his life for the sheep." Insofar as we are willing to lay down our life, our career, our professional standing, for our sheep, we are pastors in His image.

It is the shepherd's duty to love, feed, rescue, attend, comfort, guide, watch, and guard the sheep.[39] It is not the shepherd's duty to impress other shepherds and gain their acclaim. Neither is it his duty to seek or hold the flock that enhances his fortunes. Nor is it his duty to cover for shepherds who neglect to feed, rescue, attend, comfort, guide, watch, and guard their sheep.

Should the task of shepherding become professionalized, these confusions of duty might well threaten.

## NOTES

1  Charles Merrill Smith, *How to Become a Bishop Without Being Religious* (Garden City, NY: Doubleday, 1965).

2  Ibid., p. 82.

3  Ibid., p. 12.

4  Ibid., p. 79.

5  "The Congregational Code," adopted by the New Haven, Connecticut, Association for Congregational Ministers and published in *Church Administration* by Cokesbury Press in 1931. Reprinted in Joe Trull and James Carter, *Ministerial Ethics* (Nashville: Broadman & Holman, 1993), pp. 220-221.

6  Ibid.

7  Ibid.

8  "The Disciples Code," entitled "My Ministerial Code of Ethics" (Indianapolis: Department of Homeland Ministries—Christian Church [Disciples of Christ], 1990). Reprinted in Trull and Carter, *Ministerial Ethics*, pp. 226-227.

9  "Eastern Oklahoma Presbyterian Code," entitled "Report from the Task Force on Ministerial Ethics," Eastern Oklahoma Presbytery, adopted by *Presbytery*, February 13, 1990. Reprinted in Trull and Carter, *Ministerial Ethics*, p. 229.

10  "Code of Ethics for Ordained and Licensed Ministers and Lay Speakers in the Church of the Brethren," *Ethics in Ministry Relations—1992*, approved by 1992 Annual Conference of the Church of the Brethren, Elgin, Illinois, September 1992. Reprinted in Trull and Carter, *Ministerial Ethics*, p. 240.

11  Gaylord Noyce, *Pastor Ethics* (Nashville: Abingdon, 1988), p. 198. Cited in Trull and Carter, *Ministerial Ethics*, p. 240.

12  "The Congregational Code," p. 220.

13  Ibid.

14  Ibid.

15  "The Disciples Code," p. 227.

16  Ibid.

17  "Sample Codes of Ethics: Pastor or Senior Minister Code," in Trull and Carter, *Ministerial Ethics*, p. 253.

18  Allen Bloom, *The Closing of the American Mind* (New York: Touchstone Books, 1988).

19  "The Pastor's Code of Ethics (UCC)," provided by the First Congregational Church, Chesterfield, Virginia, affiliated with the United Church of Christ. Reprinted in Trull and Carter, *Ministerial Ethics*, p. 237.

20  "Sample Codes," p. 254.

21  "Eastern Oklahoma Presbyterian Code," p. 228.

22  Lisa Newton, "A Professional Ethic: A Proposal in Context," in John E. Thomas, ed. *Matters of Life and Death* (Toronto: Samuel Stevens, 1978), p. 264. Cited in Trull and Carter, *Ministerial Ethics*, p. 190.

23  James Wind, J. Russell Burch, Paul Camenisch, and Dennis P. McCann, eds., *Clergy Ethics in a Changing Society: Mapping the Terrain* (Louisville: Westminster/John Knox Press, 1991), p. 121.

24  Ernest Greenwood, "Attributes of a Profession," in *Moral Responsibility and the Professions*, Bernard Baumrin and Benjamin Freedman, eds. (New York: Haven Publications, 1983), p. 22.

25  Ibid., p. 23.

26  Ibid., pp. 28-29.

27  Marcia Millman, *The Unkindest Cut* (New York: William Morrow, 1978), p. 137, quoted in John Kultgen, *Ethics and Professionalism* (Philadelphia: University of Pennsylvania Press, 1988), p. 291.

28  Richard Baxter, *The Reformed Pastor* (London: James Nisbet and Co., 1860), p. 107.

29  Ibid., p. 109.

30  Ibid., chapter IV, pp. 183-282.

31  Richard A. Hunt, John E. Hinkle, Jr., and H. Newton Maloney, eds., *Clergy Assessment and Career Development* (Nashville: Abingdon, 1990).

32  Michael Korda, *Power: How to Get It, How to Use It* (New York: Random House, 1975), pp. 64-65, 85.

33  Ibid., p. 177.

34  Ibid., p. 192.

35  Lyle Schaller, *Survival Tactics in the Parish* (Nashville: Abingdon, 1977), p. 11.

36  Frank Drown, February 9, 1999, chapel address, Midwestern Baptist Theological Seminary, Kansas City, Missouri.

37  Irwin T. Hyatt, Jr., *Our Ordered Lives Confess: Three Nineteenth-Century*

*American Missionaries in East Shantung* (Cambridge, MA: Harvard University Press, 1976), p. 123.

38  Cited by David Adamany, March 24, 1996, in a keynote address to the annual meeting of the North Central Association of Colleges and Schools, Chicago, Illinois.

39  Charles Jefferson, *The Minister as Shepherd* (Hong Kong: Living Books, 1973 reprint), pp. 39-66, cited by Richard Mayhue, "Watching and Warning," in John MacArthur, *Rediscovering Pastoral Ministry* (Dallas: Word, 1995), p. 338.

# 3

## THE UTTER NECESSITY OF A GODLY LIFE:

### *The Foundation of Pastoral Ministry*

■

Joel R. Beeke

"God saves all kinds of people, even ministers," wrote John Kershaw, a nineteenth-century Baptist pastor. Kershaw went on to explain that though the ministry is a great vocation for removing a pastor from the attractions of a cursing, sinning world, one of a minister's greatest dangers is that he handles the sacred so frequently that it becomes banal to him.[1] As ministers, we can handle the Word of God as if it were no more than the words of men. We can take that which is holy for granted even as we live unholy lives. We can exhort others to holiness but, like the Pharisees, not move an inch in that direction ourselves. Charles Spurgeon called this fatal error "ministerialism."

Regarding such ministerialism, this article addresses questions we need to raise as pastors. Why is a godly life an utter necessity for us? What means or spiritual disciplines can we use to cultivate the sanctification of our own hearts toward God? How should we exercise those disciplines? What ought to motivate us, in dependence on the Spirit, to maintain holy living in the midst of busy and challenging pastorates?

### PURSUE GODLINESS

To be godly means to live and be like God (Eph. 5:1-2). Without holiness or godliness, no man—ministers included—will see God,

Hebrews 12:14 says. Perhaps no definition of godliness (or sanctification) matches that of the *Westminster Shorter Catechism*: "Sanctification is the work of God's free grace, whereby we are renewed in the whole man after the image of God, and are enabled more and more to die unto sin, and live unto righteousness" (Q. 35).

It is impossible to separate vibrant, godly living from a vibrant spiritual life and a God-owned ministry. The sanctification of our own heart is not an ivory-tower topic or experience. It is an absolute necessity—both personally and in relation to our calling as ministers of the Gospel—if we are to live to the glory of God.

Scripture says there should be no disjunction between the heart, character, and life of a man who is called to proclaim God's Word and the content of the message he proclaims. "Watch your life and doctrine closely. Persevere in them, because if you do, you will save both yourself and your hearers" (1 Tim. 4:16).

Jesus condemned the Pharisees and scribes for not being and doing what they proclaimed. They were condemned for carrying on a professional ministry in which a great disparity existed between lip and life, between the doctrine professionally proclaimed and the doctrine assimilated and manifested in daily living.

Professional clerics, more than anyone else, should seriously consider the scathing words of Christ: "The teachers of the law and the Pharisees sit in Moses' seat. So you must obey them and do everything they tell you. But do not do what they do, for they do not practice what they preach" (Matt. 23:2-3). We ministers are called to be as holy in our private relationship with God, in our role as husbands and fathers in our families, and in our ministry as shepherds among our people, as we appear to be in the pulpit. There must be no disjunction between our calling and living, nor between our confession and practice.

Scripture posits a cause-and-effect relationship between the character of a man's life as a Christian and his fruitfulness as a Christian minister (Matt. 7:17-20). The fruitfulness of a minister's work is proportional to the sanctification of his heart toward God. We as ministers must therefore seek grace to build the house of God with the hand of sound preaching and doctrine as well as with the hand of a sanctified life. Our doctrine must shape our life, and our life must adorn our doctrine. "He doth preach most who doth live best," wrote John Boys. We must be what we preach and teach, not only applying ourselves to our texts but applying our texts to ourselves. Our hearts must be transcripts of our sermons.[2] Otherwise, as John Owen warned, "If a man teach uprightly and walk crookedly, more will fall down in the night of his life than he built in the day of his doctrine."

## ACQUAINT YOURSELF WITH GOD

The heartbeat of a godly life is personal acquaintance with God. "Acquaint now thyself with him, and be at peace: thereby good shall come unto thee," Eliphaz says in Job 22:21 (KJV). Though this verse may not mean everything Eliphaz envisioned, it is true that acquaintance with God will not only affect our entire ministry—it will also influence our redeemed humanity spiritually, intellectually, emotionally, and physically. This chapter focuses on the spiritual dimension of a pastor's life: A healthy spiritual life with God will promote godliness in every area of one's life.

According to James Stalker, a preacher must possess three aspects of spiritual communion with God: "a large, a varied, and an original life with God."[3] Each aspect is essential to produce freshness, spiritual power, and unction in our preaching and pastoral work from week to week, year after year.

*A large acquaintance with God.* Peter admonishes us to "grow in the grace and knowledge of our Lord and Savior Jesus Christ" (2 Pet. 3:18). Paul describes being changed by the Holy Spirit from one stage of glory to another (2 Cor. 3:18).

The implication is clear: Spiritual life begins in the heart and, as a dynamic reality, is fueled by grace and knowledge. When our hearts as preachers are increasingly sanctified toward God, new hues and subtle nuances will be added to our preaching that will reflect our inner growth. We will be expressing the same eternal truths, but they will be enriched by various dimensions of our growing relationship with God. Though we speak of the same Father, the same Christ, the same Spirit, and the same covenant of grace, with all its attendant Trinitarian blessings, that we spoke of years ago when we were first

*change of heart*

ordained into the ministry, those great themes will become richer and deeper as they are punctuated with the freshness of a growing relationship with God.

In a good marriage love is expansive; the partners remain the same, but the relationship is never static. The relationship remains alive and dynamic as husband and wife grow in knowing, loving, and serving each other. If this is true between two finite personalities, how much more of a pastor's relationship with God, in which he explores the depths of God's being and the glory of His salvation.

Preaching is the mirror of a pastor's expanding relationship with God. Woe to the congregation that is lulled to sleep by wooden messages from a pastor who is not growing in acquaintance with his Master.

*freshness*
*annointing*

As ministers, we stand at the edge of the ocean of God's vast being and inscripturated truth. Spurgeon felt that way. He said after years of preaching that his problem was finding too many texts to preach on rather than not enough. The awareness that we are just beginning to know God in Christ and His gracious truths ought to stimulate us to grow. There is so much more to explore and experience. Like Paul, we must press on: "But one thing I do: Forgetting what is behind and straining toward what is ahead, I press on toward the goal to win the prize for which God has called me heavenward in Christ Jesus" (Phil. 3:13-14).

*A varied acquaintance with God.* The Psalms eloquently testify that knowing God and walking with Him on earth is a varied experience. Some people view the Christian life as nothing but joy and victory. But such a view would eliminate nearly half of the Psalms, which describe pain, sorrow, frustration, and loneliness as authentic parts of a theology of Christian experience. We ought, therefore, to look to the Psalms for a more complete understanding of what we will encounter in our walk with God. As Luther says, "If you can't find your life in the Psalms, you have never become a child of God."

Walking with God is a varied experience. A godly person may experience days of ecstatic joy and unspeakable peace followed by days of staggering struggle and groaning heaviness. There are times when pastors sing with David, praising God "with singing lips" (Ps.

63:5). But there are also times when we must cry out with Asaph, "Will the LORD reject forever? Will he never show his favor again? Has his unfailing love vanished forever? Has his promise failed for all time? Has God forgotten to be merciful? Has he in anger withheld his compassion?" (Ps. 77:7-9).

Preaching that does not incorporate large segments of the Word of God because the soul of the preacher is estranged from this varied experience of walking with God is truncated and narrow. Such preaching will not satisfy deeply exercised children of God as Paul's preaching did. Because Paul knew what anxiety was, he could teach believers how not to be anxious. Because he had personally battled fear and sin and mortification, he could preach to the fears and groanings of other believers (2 Cor. 1:3-7).

This varied walk with God permeates Paul's pastoral letters. He uses the gentleness of a mother to describe pastoral work in 1 Thessalonians 2:7 ("But we were gentle among you, like a mother caring for her little children"), then switches to a more fatherly image of discipline four verses later, saying, "For you know that we dealt with each of you as a father deals with his own children" (v. 11). Paul's shepherding of the Thessalonians reflects his varied acquaintance with God.

Someone who spends a day working with lilies in a greenhouse will come out smelling like a lily. A man who has been alone with God will preach words that are permeated with that communion. Thus Stalker says to preachers:

> There are arts of study by which the contents of the Bible can be made available for the edification of others; but this is the best rule: Study God's Word diligently for your own edification; and then, when it has become more to you than your necessary food and sweeter than honey or the honey-comb, it will be impossible for you to speak of it to others without a glow passing into your words which will betray the delight with which it has inspired yourself.[4]

*An original acquaintance with God.* God's Word is filled with concepts of solidarity and community. The book of Numbers speaks dozens of times about God working among families. True believers are like leaves that belong to the same tree of life, Scripture teaches.

Yet believers are also individuals; no two leaves on a tree are precisely identical. The purest, noblest form of individualism is manifest in Scripture. For example, Jesus says, "The very hairs of your head are all numbered" (Matt. 10:30). That's astonishing individualism. He also says that He knows all of His sheep by name (cf. John 10:3, 14). What is more individual than a person's name?

If our acquaintance with God is genuine, it will be original. We will not parrot the language or experience of another person, but we will confess with John "what we have seen and heard, so that you also may have fellowship with us" (1 John 1:3).

A. W. Tozer once compared walking with God to crossing an ocean in a ship. One ship does not carve out a path for another to follow. There is a sense in which each one of us must walk alone with God with a sense of pure, holy originality. We must trust God to sanctify us in every experience we are led through in order to make us "competent as ministers of a new covenant" (2 Cor. 3:6). He leads us through these experiences to sanctify us in a way that perfectly fits us as individuals. He tailor-makes all our afflictions, joys, and experiences to perfectly fit His will for us.

If we are to be effective preachers and pastors, we must resolve, by God's grace, to be godly or we must leave the ministry. We must have a growing, varied, and original life with God.

## USE ORDINARY SPIRITUAL DISCIPLINES

How are we as pastors to cultivate godly living? Discouragements and obstacles abound. In our ministries many of us confront much that is disheartening and rubs against our efforts to walk the King's highway of holiness. We often feel frustrated, disappointed, near despair, and often quite unholy. So much of what we are makes us unprofitable and so much of what we do appears to be fruitless. As John Stott says, "Discouragement is an occupational hazard of the Christian ministry."

Still, the way to cultivate godly living is surprisingly simple: We are to walk with God in the way of His appointment, diligently using the means of grace and the spiritual disciplines, waiting upon the Holy Spirit for blessing. Note that godly living involves both discipline and the continued grace of the Holy Spirit. This dual emphasis upon duty and grace is fundamental to Puritan thinking on godly living.[5] As John Flavel wrote, "The duty is ours, though the power be God's. A natural man has no power, a gracious man hath some, though not sufficient; and that power he hath, depends upon the assisting strength of Christ."[6]

To this John Owen adds, "It is the Holy Ghost who is the immediate peculiar sanctifier of all believers, and the author of all holiness in them." The Spirit supplies what we lack so that we may "press toward the mark." The Spirit enables us as believers to "yield obedience to God . . . by virtue of the life and death of Jesus Christ."[7]

The believer then is empowered with "a diligent and constant use and improvement of all holy means and duties, to preserve the soul from sin, and maintain its sweet and free communion with God," Flavel said.[8] Taking encouragement from Owen's wise advice ("If thou meanest to enlarge thy religion do it rather by enlarging thy ordinary devotions than thy extraordinary"), let us examine in more detail what spiritual disciplines or means of grace the preacher may use to enlarge his walk with God.

## Read Scripture

Pastors will cultivate godly living through the discipline of diligent, systematic, prayerful, and meditative reading of the Holy Scriptures (1 Tim. 4:13; 2 Tim. 2:15). In this they must do the following:

| *Be diligent.* Physical health is profoundly affected by one's daily diet. Unusual times of feasting or fasting are a factor, of course, but not nearly as important as a daily regimen of eating. In the same way, our spiritual health is affected by our habitual spiritual intake. There are times of great crisis in ministry when we are driven to extraordinary times of prayer, and there are times when we are too hard-pressed to pray. But these are not the normal times. Similarly, if we are to have an expanding, varied, and original acquaintance with God, we must cultivate the discipline of setting aside a regular time in which we immerse ourselves in the Scriptures. Richard Greenham said that we

ought to read our Bibles with more diligence than men dig for hidden treasure. Diligence makes rough places plain, the difficult easy, and the unsavory tasty.[9]

*Be systematic.* We must study the whole range of God's revealed mind from Genesis to Revelation, keeping in mind who God is, who we are, what His relationship is to us as our Creator and Redeemer, and what our relationship is to Him and His world. We must immerse ourselves in the Word of God, not the word of man concerning what God has revealed. Too many ministers are more influenced by what others have told them about the Scriptures than by the Scriptures themselves.

Paul warns us about such a practice in 2 Timothy 3:16-17: "All Scripture is God-breathed and is useful for teaching, rebuking, correcting and training in righteousness, so that the man of God may be thoroughly equipped for every good work." In effect he was saying, "Timothy, those Scriptures that your God-fearing mother and grandmother taught to you are adequate in all their richness and fullness to furnish you completely and to produce a godly life."

If all Scripture is given to equip men for the work of ministry, we cannot help but be crippled by neglecting any part of the revealed Word of God. How often must Christ warn us as pastors, "Ye do err, not knowing the scriptures" (see Matt. 22:29)? The Word of God is the lifeline of our souls, the very heartbeat of our sanctification. We must be able to say with Jeremiah, "When your words came, I ate them; they were my joy and my heart's delight" (Jer. 15:16).

Proper preparation for reading the Bible is critical, however. Without it, our reading will seldom be blessed. Such preparation, according to Richard Greenham, consists of three things:

> 1) We must approach Scripture with a reverential fear of God and his majesty, being "quick to listen, slow to speak" (James 1:19), and determined like Mary to lay up God's Word in our hearts.
>
> 2) We must approach Scripture with faith in Christ, looking on him as the "lion out of the tribe of Judah to whom it is given to open the book of God."
>
> 3) We must approach Scripture with a sincere desire to learn

about God. We often do not profit from Bible-reading because we come without a heart for divine teaching.[10]

For how many of us has the Bible ceased to be a living testimony of personal, devotional relationship to Christ? Yes, we read it, and we prepare sermons from it, but for whom? Only for other people? Is it surprising, then, that our ministries are marked by coldness and doctrinal imbalance when we no longer personally search, love, and live the Scriptures?

*Be prayerful and meditative.* Ask for the Spirit's light. Stop presuming that knowing the original languages of Scripture and using exegetical tools are sufficient to unlock the mysteries of Holy Scripture. None of us knows Hebrew and Greek like the scribes and Pharisees; yet they searched the Scriptures daily and missed their true meaning. Didn't Jesus say to them, "You diligently study the Scriptures because you think that by them you possess eternal life. These are the Scriptures that testify about me, yet you refuse to come to me to have life" (John 5:39-40)?

We must pray with David, "Open my eyes that I may see wonderful things in your law" (Ps. 119:18). Only then will the message and spirit of the Scriptures penetrate our minds and conquer our hearts.

We must also ask God for light from the Scriptures to scrutinize our hearts and lives. Ezra 7:10 says, "For Ezra had devoted himself to the study and observance of the Law of the Lord, and to teaching its decrees and laws in Israel." Ezra's meditative preparation involved a three-step process: studying, doing, and teaching. That kind of meditative reading of the Scriptures requires us to reflect on what the Scriptures speak to us, that we might more fully worship God in spirit and in truth, both in private and in public.

After reading Scripture, meditation is critical. Reading may give knowledge, but meditation and study will add depth to that knowledge. The difference between reading and meditation is like the difference between drifting in a boat and rowing toward a destination.

The Puritans spoke often of such meditation. Thomas Hooker defined the art of meditation as "a serious intention of the mind, whereby we come to search out the truth and settle it effectually upon the heart."[11] He and other Puritans suggested the following ways of meditating on Scripture:

1) Pray for the power to harness the mind, to focus the eyes of faith on this task.

2) Read the Scriptures, then select a verse or two or a doctrine upon which to meditate.[12]

3) Memorize the selected verse(s) to stimulate meditation, to strengthen faith, to witness to and counsel others, and to serve as a means of divine guidance.

4) Sing Psalms that relate to your selection. Singing the Word can be immensely helpful to help us look Godward. As Luther said to Melanchthon, "Come Philip, let us sing the Word and let the devil do what he will."[13]

5) Meditate on what you know about your verse(s) or subject. As you meditate, think of applications to your own life. "Take every word as spoken to yourselves," said Thomas Watson.[14] Take every truth as directed to you.

6) Pray and sing again and again. Pray through the verse(s) or doctrine.[15]

Spurgeon relates how one Puritan, a county magistrate named John Row, occupied himself in meditation. "Sometimes in a morning, before he rose, he would be meditating an hour or two together," Spurgeon writes. "When he was riding or walking abroad, he would still be in meditation. When he went about his worldly affairs he would contrive them beforehand, and spend what spare time he had in heavenly contemplation. He seldom prayed in secret without preparing himself for it by meditation, saying he preferred a short prayer after long meditation above a long prayer without meditation."[16]

We have lost the art of meditation. We have forgotten that disciplined meditation on the Scriptures helps us focus on God. Meditation helps us view worship as a discipline to be cultivated. It involves our mind and understanding as well as our heart and affections. It transfuses Scripture through the texture of the soul. David says, "Oh, how I love your law! I meditate on it all day long. Your commands make me wiser than my enemies, for they are ever with me. I have more insight than all my teachers, for I meditate on your statutes" (Ps. 119:97-99; cf. Josh. 1:8; Ps. 1:2; 104:34; 119:48).

Meditation on Scripture is absolutely crucial for a pastor (1 Tim. 4:13-15). Meditation helps prevent vain and sinful thoughts (Matt. 12:35) and provides inner resources on which to draw (Ps. 77:10-12), including direction for daily life (Prov. 6:21-22). Meditation is a weapon against temptation (Ps. 119:11, 15), provides relief in afflictions (Isa. 49:15-17), benefits others (Ps. 49:3), and glorifies God (Ps. 145:7).

Meditation also enriches public prayer. "Out of the overflow of the heart the mouth speaks," says Matthew 12:34. The minister who interacts with God during the week through prayerful, meditative study of the Scriptures—who has tasted new dimensions of the grandeur and majesty of God that week, and new depths of his own indwelling sin and the riches of Christ to atone for him—will not have a cold, dry prayer on Sunday morning but will radiate the presence of the Almighty.

## Pray Unceasingly     *prayer, then ministry*

Men "should always pray and not give up," Jesus says in Luke 18:1. "Should" means that the obligation of prayer rests upon us at all times regardless of our present frame of mind. Christ knew that "giving up" was one of the greatest hindrances to the habit of prayer; hence His warning not only to pray but also not to give up doing it.

Why is it that we as ministers, unlike other workers, are not required to punch a clock or work a certain number of hours a week, yet are able to receive our livelihood from the Gospel? It is because a precedent was established by the apostles in Acts 6 when they refused to take time away from their calling to do other things, even legitimate acts of mercy to widows. Since to "neglect the ministry of the word of God in order to wait on tables" was not pleasing to Christ who had commissioned them to preach, they determined to give their attention "to prayer and the ministry of the word" (vv. 2, 4).

Note the order here: first prayer, then ministry. As Charles Bridges once wrote, "Prayer is one half of our ministry; and it gives to the other half all its power and success."[17] Likewise, Jean Massillon (1663-1742), a famous French preacher, said to a group of ministers:

A pastor who does not pray, who does not love prayer, does not belong to that Church, which "prays without ceasing." He is a dry and barren tree, which cumbers the Lord's ground. He is the enemy, and not the father of his people. He is a stranger, who has usurped the pastor's place, and to whom the salvation of the flock is indifferent. Wherefore, my brethren, be faithful in prayer, and your functions will be more useful, your people more holy; your labors will prove much sweeter, and the Church's evils will diminish.

Later he added:

That man ceases, if I may use the expression, to be a public Minister from the time he ceases to pray.[18]

Our consciences may condemn us here more than in any other part of our ministry. You may admit this, saying, "I have never been careless in the preparation of my sermons, neither in the hard work of exegesis nor in the sweating work of sermonic application. But I am plagued with guilt when I ask, 'Have I given *myself*—not just time, but myself—to prayer?'"

Part of our problem is that we view prayer as an appendix to our work rather than as our work. Notwithstanding all our failures, we must sustain the habit of secret prayer if we are to live godly lives. The only way to learn the art of sacred wrestling and the art of holy argument with God is to pray. Praying is the only way to turn the promises of God into the horns of His altar by which we lay hold of God Himself. Our preaching about prayer and all the treatises we read on prayer will be of no help unless we pray with Jacob, "I will not let you go unless you bless me" (Gen. 32:26).

Lack of prayer is the downfall of many ministries. If Thomas Brooks could say, "A family without prayer is like a house without a roof, open and exposed to all the storms of heaven," should not we add, "And a pastor without prayer is like a church without a roof, open and exposed to all the storms of heaven, earth, and hell"?

If the giants of church history dwarf us today, perhaps it is not because they were more educated, more devout, or more faithful as much as because they were men of prayer, possessed with the Spirit of grace and supplication. They were Daniels in the temple of God. As Owen wrote, "A minister may fill his pews, his communion roll, and the mouths of the public, but what that minister is on his knees in secret before God Almighty, that he is and no more."

Let us seek grace to be men of prayer, like the great Reformers were. Luther prayed three hours daily. "Meditation, temptation, and prayer make a minister," he wrote. To Melanchthon, Luther once said, "I must rise an hour early tomorrow, for, given all that I need to do, I must spend more time in prayer."

John Welsh, the son-in-law of John Knox, prayed seven hours a day. "I often wonder how a Christian could lie in his bed all night, and not rise to pray," he said. Welsh kept his robe at his bedside each night so he wouldn't catch cold when he rose to supplicate with his God. Once his wife found him weeping on the hard floor after midnight and asked him why he was crying. "Oh, my dear wife," he said, "I have 3,000 souls to answer for, and I know not how it is with many of them!" On another occasion she heard him pleading in broken sentences, "Lord, wilt Thou not grant me Scotland?"

It would not be wise for us to suddenly attempt to pray three hours a day, much less seven, but let's refuse to relinquish the inner prayer chamber, for here true reformation will either be established or broken. Let's refuse to be content with the shell and husk of religion without the inner core of prayer. When we grow drowsy or sloppy in prayer, let us pray aloud, or write down our prayers, or find a quiet place outside to walk and pray. Just don't stop praying.

Don't abandon stated times of prayer, but also pray in response to the least impulse to do so. Conversing with God through Christ is our most effective antidote to warding off spiritual backsliding and discouragement. Prayerless discouragement is like an open sore ripe for infection, whereas prayerful discouragement is like an open sore that's ripe for the balm of Gilead.

Keep prayer a priority in your personal and official life. As John Bunyan said, "You can do more than pray after you have prayed, but you cannot do more than pray until you have prayed. . . . Pray often, for prayer is a shield to the soul, a sacrifice to God, and a scourge to Satan."[19] Pray before and after every church duty you perform, be it preaching, family visitation, teaching catechism class, or counseling a troubled couple.

Failure to pray unceasingly (1 Thess. 5:17) is the primary reason why there is so little unction in most preaching today. This problem is two-sided to be sure. It is our fault as ministers because we relinquish prayer time too easily, and it is the fault of our people when they make too many demands of us. Too many churches indirectly pressure ministers to abandon prayer time by filling their days with administrative duties, committee meetings, and counseling sessions. Today many pastors are busy studying the problems of the church and providing a smorgasbord of solutions, but where are the Daniels, Luthers, and Welshes who are giving themselves to prayer?

Often we lack genuine communion with our people in preaching because we lack genuine communion with God in our inner closets. How can we preach on heaven and hell without feeling the truths of eternity in our soul throughout the week? M'Cheyne once asked Andrew Bonar what he had preached on the previous day. Bonar answered, "On hell." M'Cheyne replied, "I trust you did it with tears."

Margin notes in some editions of the *King James Version* of James 5:17 say that Elijah "prayed in his prayer." We as ministers ought to be doing that as well. As Spurgeon wrote: "To you as the ambassadors of God, the mercy-seat has a virtue beyond all estimate. The more familiar you are with the court of heaven, the better shall you discharge your heavenly trust. . . . All our libraries and studies are mere emptiness compared with our closets. We grow, we are mighty, we prevail in private prayer."[20]

## Read and Listen to Sermons

Sound books that promote godly living are a powerful help to pastors. Read the spiritual classics, letting great writers be your spiritual mentors and friends.

The Puritans excelled in this. "There must scarcely be a sermon, a treatise, a pamphlet, a diary, a history or a biography from a Puritan pen which was not in one way or another aimed at fostering the spiritual life," said Maurice Roberts.[21]

Read on a diversity of subjects for a diversity of needs. If you would foster godly living by remaining sensitized to sin, read Ralph Venning's *The Plague of Plagues*, Jeremiah Burroughs's *The Evil of Evils*, Thomas Watson's *The Mischief of Sin*, or Thomas Boston's *Human Nature in Its Fourfold State*.

If you long to be drawn closer to Christ, read Thomas Goodwin's *Christ Our Mediator*, Alexander Gross's *Happiness of Enjoying and Making a Speedy Use of Christ*, Isaac Ambrose's *Looking Unto Jesus*, John Brown's *Christ: The Way, the Truth, and the Life*, or Friedrich Krummacher's *The Suffering Savior*.

If you are sorely afflicted, read Samuel Rutherford's *Letters*, J. W. Alexander's *Consolation to the Suffering People of God*, James Buchanan's *Comfort in Affliction*, or Murdoch Campbell's *In All Their Affliction*. If you are buffeted with temptation, read John Owen's *Temptation and Sin*. If you want to grow in holiness, read John Flavel's *Keeping the Heart* or Octavius Winslow's *Personal Declension and Revival of Religion in the Soul*. Or read J. C. Ryle and Jerry Bridges on holiness.

Since I was fourteen years old, such literature has enriched me. Good books have drawn me closer to God, enlightened me in His Word, and prompted meditation, conviction, and allurement.

Organize your private time so you can read at least thirty minutes each day for your own godliness. When you read, don't be in a hurry. Look up cited texts. Be content to read some books more slowly than others. Some books may be tasted, while others should be chewed on before being digested.

Read as an act of worship. Read with the goal of being elevated into the great truths of God, so that you may worship the Trinity in spirit and in truth. Read and meditate and apply. Pray before, during, and after you read; then put into practice what you have read, insofar as it is biblical.

Be selective about what you read. Subject all your reading to the touchstone of Scripture. So much of today's Christian literature is shallow froth, riddled with Arminian theology or secular thinking. Time is too precious to waste on unprofitable reading. Read more for eternity than time, more for spiritual growth than professional advancement. Remember John Trapp's admonition: "As water tastes of the soil it runs through, so does the soul taste of the authors that a man reads."

Ask of each book: Would Christ approve of this book? Does this book increase my love for the Word of God, help me to kill sin, impart abiding wisdom, and prepare me for the life to come? Could I better spend my time by reading another book?

Speak to others about the best of what you read. Godly conversation upon godly reading promotes godly living. And in all your reading, aim for the psalmist's petition: "Teach me your way, O LORD, and I will walk in your truth; give me an undivided heart, that I may fear your name" (Ps. 86:11).

Some people prefer listening to reading. Do both to live a godly life. Listen to great preachers, either in person or on tape, who will enrich your spiritual welfare. Select those preachers who encourage your sanctification. Today there are a wealth of excellent sermon and conference tapes available.

Listen to sermon tapes in the car—on your way to pastoral calls, for example. What a boon such preaching can be for one's ministry! Here are some suggestions on how to listen to such tapes:

1) Prepare your soul with prayer.

2) Listen with a holy appetite and a tender, teachable heart. Avoid a critical spirit.

3) Be attentive to what is preached, receiving with meekness the engrafted Word (Jas. 1:21), mingling it with faith (Heb. 4:2).

4) Retain and pray over what you hear. As Joseph Alleine advised, "Come from your knees to the sermon, and come from the sermon to your knees."

5) Live out the sermons you hear, remembering that doers of the Word are the best hearers (Jas. 1:22-25). Speak to your closest friends about what you hear.[22]

## Celebrate the Sacraments

God's sacraments complement His Word. They point us away from ourselves. Each sign—water, bread, and wine—directs us to believe in

Christ and His sacrifice on the cross as the source for godly living. The sacraments are visible means through which Christ invisibly communes with us and we with Him. They spur us to Christlikeness and therefore to holiness.

Grace received through the sacraments is not different from that received through the Word. Both convey the same Christ. But as Robert Bruce put it, "While we do not get a better Christ in the sacraments than in the Word, sometimes we get Christ better."[23]

### Fellowship Regularly with Believers

"As the communion of saints is in our creed, so it should be in our company," wrote Thomas Watson. That's good advice. Pastors who would be godly should seek fellowship in the church and associate with mentors in godly living (1 Cor. 11:1; Eph. 4:12-13), especially fellow pastors in various denominations who will keep confidences.

The church ought to be a fellowship of caring and a community of prayer (Acts 2:42; 1 Cor. 12:7). So converse and pray with fellow believers whose godly walk you admire (Col. 3:16). Association promotes assimilation. A Christian who tries to live in isolation from other believers will be defective; likewise, a pastor who does not commune with others usually will remain spiritually immature.[24]

### Keep a Journal

The ministry can be a lonely occupation. Recently *U.S. News and World Report* did a study of 100 occupations in relation to loneliness. Pastoral ministry ranked No. 2 on the list, right after night watchman.

As a minister you should take care not to divulge too many of your feelings to office-bearers or church members. Such words could be used against you. Some people in the congregation may even become jealous if you become a close friend with others. You must use caution concerning in whom to confide. Journaling or diary-keeping can help take the edge off your loneliness by helping you express thoughts to God and to yourself that otherwise remain buried. Journaling can serve numerous benefits that promote godliness, including assisting you in meditating and praying, in remembering the Lord's works and faithfulness, in understanding and evaluating yourself, in monitoring your goals and priorities, and in maintaining other spiritual disciplines.[25]

### Cultivate Other Disciplines

Cultivate godly living through other disciplines, ascertaining over time which profit you the most. Add your own disciplines to this list.

*Sabbath-keeping, or sanctifying the Lord's Day.* This can greatly improve personal spirituality. Pastors need a weekly, extended private time with God, either on Sunday or another designated day. Though we must be careful not to bind ourselves with legalistic observances for our pastoral Sabbath, secular matters should not be allowed to infringe upon this time. We ought to view this time as a joyful privilege, not a tedious burden, in which our private worship of God and use of spiritual disciplines can be sustained without interruption. As J. I. Packer says, "We are to rest from the business of our earthly calling in order to prosecute the business of our heavenly calling."[26]

*Stewardship of time and money.* Time is short and must be used wisely, for the days are evil (Eph. 5:15-16). The godly pastor uses time to prepare himself, his family, and his congregation for eternity (2 Cor. 6:2).

The disciplined use of money is rooted in the principle that God owns everything we have (1 Cor. 10:26). Giving reflects faith in God's provision (Mark 12:41-44) and is an act of worship (Phil. 4:18). Giving should be sacrificial and generous (2 Cor. 8:1-5) and motivated by love, thankfulness, and cheerfulness (2 Cor. 9:7). Giving reaps bountiful blessing (Luke 6:38). The godly man experiences the words of the Lord Jesus that "it is more blessed to give than to receive" (Acts 20:35).

*Evangelizing and serving others.* Christ expects us to evangelize and serve others (Matt. 28:19-20; Heb. 9:14). We are to be motivated in this discipline by obedience (Deut. 13:4), gratitude (1 Sam. 12:24), gladness (Ps. 100:2), humility (John 13:15-16), and love (Gal. 5:13). Serving is often hard work, but we are called to use every spiritual gift God has granted us (see Rom. 12:4-8; 1 Cor. 12:6-11; Eph. 4:7-13).[27] As pastors, one of our greatest rewards is serving people. To see people drawn closer to Christ through the Spirit's blessing upon God's

Word and the use of our gifts is a profoundly humbling experience. It also draws us closer to God.

Finally, *the ministry of the Word* is itself a spiritual discipline that promotes godliness. Often the best times of communion with God occur when one is preaching or writing on a spiritual subject. One of the ministry's profoundest joys are those rare occasions when we sense from the beginning to the end of our sermon that we are God's mouthpiece. During such times God rushes before us, and we have all we can do to keep up with Him. Inevitably we realize that we are preaching to ourselves as well as to the people. Afterwards we yearn to be alone with God to savor the sacredness of renewed communion with Him.

For some ministers, writing is an obligation rather than a pleasure. Some find writing difficult but rewarding and pregnant with blessing. When one is granted the Spirit's freedom in writing, the heart is drawn inexpressibly close to God and His Word. Sacred truth then enlarges the soul, and the fingers cannot fly over the keys fast enough.

Writing is also a blessing because it is so lasting; what is written now may be blessed by the Spirit to someone next week or fifty or 100 years from now. Even a short article may be used to save or profit a soul. As M'Cheyne said, "The smallest tract may be the stone in David's sling. In the hands of Christ it may bring down a giant's soul." Writing promotes scriptural truth and wages war on the forces of evil. "We must throw the printer's inkpot at the devil," Luther said.

Studying, learning, and teaching on various levels can also promote godliness. As ministers, we profit most when we work on three levels. It is good for our spiritual life when we teach something that compels us to move beyond our present level of knowledge, something that stretches us both intellectually and spiritually. That is often true of seminary teaching or lecturing at ministers' conferences. But it is also good to teach gospel truths at an elementary level, such as catechizing or evangelizing neighborhood children. Such simplicity can enhance appreciation for the Gospel. Then, too, teaching near or slightly below our level, as in preaching, reinforces truth that is most edifying for our souls.

CONCLUSION

Ministers must live godly lives. Reading, singing, memorizing, and meditating upon Scripture; engaging in secret prayer; reading orthodox literature; listening to the preached Word; using the sacraments; pursuing spiritual fellowship; journaling; sanctifying the Lord's Day; exercising stewardship; serving others for Christ's sake; preaching, teaching, and writing—these are the spiritual disciplines that, if diligently pursued in dependence upon God's gracious Spirit, will greatly sanctify our hearts toward God. That in turn will work two great benefits:

1) *It will promote godly living in every area of our life.* The call to holiness and godly living is a comprehensive call. By cultivating the spiritual disciplines in private with God, we will cultivate godly living in our homes as fathers and family worship leaders; in our preaching and teaching as well as relating to ministerial peers, office-bearers, staff, and church members; in the pleasures of social friendship; and in relationships with our unevangelized neighbors and the world's hungry and unemployed. As Horatius Bonar wrote: "Holiness . . . extends to every part of our life, influences everything we are, or do, or think, or speak, or plan, small or great, outward or inward, negative or positive, our loving, our hating, our sorrowing, our rejoicing, our recreations, our business, our friendships, our relationships, our silence, our speech, our reading, our writing, our going out and our coming in—our whole man in every movement of spirit, soul, and body."[28]

Godly living is a daily task. It is the core of religious faith and practice. Our entire lives, Calvin said, "must be an exercise in piety."[29] In short, the call to godly living is a lifetime commitment of faith to live "through Christ before God" (2 Cor. 3:4), to be set apart to the saviorhood and lordship of Jesus Christ.

Holiness begins in our minds with a present-tense, total commitment to God and works outward in our actions through all of life (Phil. 2:12-13).[30] As Thomas Boston said, "Holiness is a constellation of graces." Through the Spirit's blessing upon the spiritual disciplines and as we experience gratitude to God, we are called to cultivate the fruits of holiness, such as love, joy, peace, patience, kindness, goodness, faithfulness, gentleness, and self-control (Galatians 5:22-23).[31]

2) *A life of godliness will promote and sustain an effective ministry.* The people we serve will have a model to emulate and, by God's grace, will do so.

The level of godliness in our personal lives does more to influence people than all of our busyness. M'Cheyne scarcely exaggerated when he said, "My people's greatest need is for my own holiness." Our lives are our visible rhetoric.

When hearing or reading sermons from ministers used greatly by God, such as Whitefield, Boston, M'Cheyne, and Spurgeon, some ask, "Why were they so blessed?" The sermons of these writers are excellent, but their content is not unlike that of many others who were not so signally used. Is this difference only because of God's sovereignty? The answer is that these men lived exemplary lives of piety. Spurgeon even dared to say that he would be willing to write his entire life in an open sky for all to read.

Richard Cecil, a close friend of John Newton, once wrote: "Example is more forceful than precept. People look at me six days a week to see what I mean on the seventh day." William Burkitt put it more quaintly: "The minister's life is the people's looking-glass by which they usually dress themselves."

Many evangelicals have forgotten the central truth that piety is the pastor's greatest weapon for reformation. As M'Cheyne said, "A minister's life is the life of his ministry. . . . In great measure, according to the purity and perfections of the instrument, will be the success. It is not great talents that God blesses so much as likeness to Jesus. A holy minister is an awful weapon in the hand of God."

Let us remember that a ministerial calling will not save an unholy man. Let us remember that Satan strives after us more than after others, knowing that there are many who will see every act of unkindness or ungodliness that we do. Let us be moved by the glory of God, the honor of our calling as His heralds and ambassadors, love for our people, and the brevity of life to seek the Spirit's grace to live godly in the midst of God's church and in this present evil world. As 1 Thessalonians 5:22-23 says, "Avoid every kind of evil. May God himself, the God of peace, sanctify you through and through. May your whole spirit, soul and body be kept blameless at the coming of our Lord Jesus Christ."

Finally, let us remember that as we fight the good fight of faith and wrestle for greater sanctification of heart, we have Jesus Christ, the best of generals, to help us. We have the Holy Spirit, the best of advocates, to console us. We have the best of assurances to comfort us—the promises of the Father. And we have the best guarantee for eternal results: "And we know that in all things God works for the good of those who love him, who have been called according to his purpose" (Rom. 8:28).

However hard the task is to strive for godliness, let us not forget that godliness is ultimately God's work, blessing the exercise of spiritual disciplines as He has promised to do. The *Shorter Catechism* is right: "Sanctification is God's work of grace in us." God preserves his servants in holiness, saving us *from*, not *in*, our sins. He promises eternal salvation by the only path that will get us to heaven—the King's highway of holiness.[32] What a blessing that the outcome of the task of godliness doesn't depend on us! It rests with the King of kings who sanctified himself so that He might sanctify His people (Heb. 2:9-11). And He that sanctifies and they that are sanctified are one. This provides unspeakable peace and freedom to fulfill in some measure the chief goal of our lives: "To glorify God and enjoy Him forever."

NOTES

1 *John Kershaw: The Autobiography of an Eminent Lancashire Preacher* (Sheffield, England: Gospel Tidings Publications, reprint 1968), p. 112ff.

2 Gardiner Spring, *The Power of the Pulpit* (Edinburgh: Banner of Truth Trust, reprint 1986), p. 154.

3 *The Preacher and His Models* (New York: A.C. Armstrong and Son, 1891), lecture 2.

4 Ibid., pp. 53-54.

5 Daniel Webber, "Sanctifying the Inner Life," in *Aspects of Sanctification*, 1981 Westminster Conference Papers (Hertfordshire, England: Evangelical Press, 1982), pp. 44-45.

6 *The Works of John Flavel*, Vol. 5 (London: Banner of Truth Trust, reprint 1968), p. 424.

7  *The Works of John Owen,* Vol. 3 (Edinburgh: Banner of Truth Trust, reprint 1976), pp. 385-386.

8  *Works of John Flavel,* Vol. 5, p. 423.

9  *The Works of the Reverend and Faithfull Servant of Jesus Christ, M. Richard Greenham,* ed. H[enry] H[olland] (London: Felix Kingston for Robert Dexter, 1599), p. 390.

10  Ibid., pp. 392-393.

11  *The Application of Redemption by the Effectual Work of the Word and Spirit of Christ, for the Bringing Home of Lost Sinners to God,* Vol. 2 (London: Peter Cole, 1659), p. 210.

12  For a list of profitable subjects for meditation, see *The Works of Stephen Charnock,* Vol. 3 (Edinburgh: James Nichol, 1865), p. 307.

13  Cf. Joel R. Beeke and Ray B. Lanning, "The Transforming Power of Scripture," in Don Kistler, ed., *Sola Scriptura!: The Protestant Position on the Bible* (Morgan, PA: Soli Deo Gloria, 1995), pp. 258-260.

14  Thomas Watson, "How We May Read the Scriptures with Most Spiritual Profit," in *Heaven Taken by Storm,* ed. Joel R. Beeke (Pittsburgh: Soli Deo Gloria, 1992), pp. 113-129.

15  See Nathanael Ranew, *Solitude Improved by Divine Meditation, or A Treatise Proving the Duty, and Demonstrating the Necessity, Excellency, Usefulness, Natures, Kinds, and Requisites of Divine Meditation* (Morgan, PA: Soli Deo Gloria, reprint 1995).

16  Charles Spurgeon, "How a Puritan Lived," *Banner of Truth* (U.K.), No. 92, May 1971, p. 24.

17  *The Christian Ministry* (London: Banner of Truth Trust, reprint 1967), p. 148.

18  Quoted in ibid., pp. 147-148.

19  John Bunyan, *Prayer* (Edinburgh: Banner of Truth Trust, reprint 1999), p. 23ff.

20  Charles H. Spurgeon, *Lectures to My Students* (London: Passmore and Alabaster, 1881), p. 41.

21  "Visible Saints: The Puritans as a Godly People," in *Aspects of Sanctification,* 1981 Westminster Conference Papers (Hertfordshire, England: Evangelical Press, 1982), pp. 1-2.

22  Watson, *Heaven Taken by Storm,* pp. 16-18, and *A Body of Divinity* (London: Banner of Truth Trust), pp. 377-379. Cf. Joel R. Beeke and Ray B. Lanning, "Reading and Hearing the Word in a Puritan Way," *Reformation & Revival* 5:2 (1996), pp. 67-76.

23  Read frequently *Westminster Larger Catechism,* Questions 161-175, for how to use the sacraments properly.

24  Joel R. Beeke, *Assurance of Faith: Calvin, English Puritanism, and the Dutch Second Reformation* (New York: Peter Lang, 1991), pp. 407-408.

25  Donald S. Whitney, *Spiritual Disciplines for the Christian Life* (Colorado Springs: NavPress, 1991), pp. 196-210.

26  J. I. Packer, *A Quest for Godliness: The Puritan Vision of the Christian Life* (Wheaton, IL: Crossway Books, 1990), p. 239; Errol Hulse, "Sanctifying the Lord's Day: Reformed and Puritan Attitudes," in *Aspects of Sanctification,*

1981 Westminster Conference Papers (Hertfordshire, England: Evangelical Press, 1982), pp. 78-102.

27  Whitney, *Spiritual Disciplines,* p. 93ff.

28  Horatius Bonar, *God's Way of Holiness* (Pensacola, FL: Mount Zion Publications, reprint 1994), p. 16.

29  Quoted in Donald G. Bloesch, *Essentials of Evangelical Theology,* Vol. 2 (New York: Harper & Row, 1979), p. 31.

30  Joel R. Beeke, *Holiness: God's Call to Sanctification* (Edinburgh: Banner of Truth Trust, 1994), p. 21.

31  Joel R. Beeke, "Cultivating Holiness," *Reformation & Revival* 4:2 (1995), pp. 83-84.

32  *Works of Owen,* Vol. 11, p. 254ff.; Joel R. Beeke, *The Quest for Full Assurance: The Legacy of Calvin and His Successors* (Edinburgh: Banner of Truth Trust, 1999), pp. 170-171.

# 4

---

# RESTORING BIBLICAL EXPOSITION TO ITS RIGHTFUL PLACE:

## *Ministerial Ethos and Pathos*

■

### R. Kent Hughes

I have had the unique privilege of teaching biblical exposition over the past two decades. My teaching grows naturally out of my regular, weekly handling of the text of the Bible. The natural and right place to begin such instruction on preaching is with the subject of *Logos*, the Word of God. Though the how-to's of expository preaching are important, I do not generally go into these with a great deal of detail at first. I much prefer to begin with the beliefs and understandings that are *indispensable* to the task, and in fact demand it—the *prolegomenon* to biblical exposition.

When this approach is adopted, the foundation point will always be a wholehearted belief in the authority of God's Word. Full confidence in its *inerrancy*, *sufficiency*, and *potency* is indispensable to a commitment to biblical exposition. To my knowledge no one does regular expository preaching who does not hold to this high view of Scripture—that it is God's inerrant Word.

But this alone is not enough. Exposition will not happen if one does not also view the Scriptures as *adequate and sufficient* for all of life, appropriating Moses' view that the Bible is "not just idle words for you—they are your life" (Deut. 32:47). The preacher must accept

the Lord's injunction that God's Word is his very food—"every word
that comes from the mouth of God" (Matt. 4:4).

But even this is not enough. No one will give his life to biblical
exposition who does not believe in Scripture's *potency*—that it can cut
through the hard, white bone and running marrow of any soul and
work salvation and that "the Word of God is living and active.
Sharper than any two edged sword . . ." The unsheathed Word can do
anything! But we must truly believe it—not believe that we believe it—
but believe it!

Second, the expositor must understand and hold to the insepara-
bility of the Spirit and the Word, that they are like breath and speech
to each other. This means that you must hold the conviction that when
the Word is authentically ministered, the Spirit ministers. The Word
and Spirit do not have separate ministries but are one.

Third, the expositor understands and rests his ministry on the fact
that apostolic preaching was expositional. Paul's instructions to
Timothy ("Devote yourself to the public reading of Scripture, to
preaching and to teaching," 1 Tim. 4:13) was lived out in the early
church's public readings from the Old Testament and the apostolic
writings followed by exposition—*paraklesis* and *didaskalia*. "It was
taken for granted at the beginning that Christian preaching was exposition, that is, that all Christian instruction and exhortation be drawn
out of the passage that had been read."[1] Therefore, any kind of
preaching in the church, other than exposition, is an aberration.

Fourth, the expositor understands and glories in the knowledge
that the preaching that brought about the Reformation and the
Protestant tradition was biblical exposition. Both Luther and Calvin
bear monumental evidence of this. Calvin saw parallels between the
sea of blood that launched the Old Covenant, when Aaron doused the
Word of the Old Covenant with the blood of sacrifices, and Jesus proclaiming the New Covenant in His blood. Calvin said that one ought
to regard the New Covenant Scriptures as if written in Christ's blood.
Indeed, this is the way Calvin treated the Scriptures of both Covenants,
as witnessed by his incredible sequential exposition of one book after
another.

*★ Heb 4:12 power, competance*
*God calls it to pass; exposes the heart*
*The Word that is alive in you*
*God will make it work*

So, in light of the four foundational reasons above, and in light of the grand pluses of exposition:

1) You will preach texts that you would never preach, and even avoid if possible.

2) You never have to fret about what to preach on Sunday.

3) Systematic biblical exposition aids your growth as a theologian.

4) Expository preaching keeps you subject to the text.

5) Expository preaching gives you the confidence to preach with "Thus saith the Lord" conviction.

6) Expository preaching gives you confidence that when the Word is opened, the Spirit speaks.

Because of all this I am compelled to believe that the week-after-week fare of the church must *not* be topical or doctrinal or even textual, but expositional. Further, the popular a-textual forms of "disexposition" are also clearly wrong.

For the purpose of this chapter I will assume that everything that could be discussed under *logos* is in order in the reader's thought process; i.e., that scriptural prolegomena are part of the preacher's heart and that he has prepared his exposition. He has prayerfully interpreted his text in its context, using the established canons of hermeneutics. He understands the text's application in its historical setting and in the whole of Scripture. He has discerned wherein it is a revelation of Jesus Christ and has made the appropriate intercanonical connections. He has made the trip "from Jerusalem to Chicago" and understands its present relevance. He has articulated the theme of the text, its "melodic line." He has outlined his exposition using the literary structure of the text as a guide to his sermon's symmetry. He has enlisted stories and illustrations that really do illuminate the text. And finally, he has written or outlined his sermon using language (metaphors and concrete words) that actually does communicate in today's culture.

What is left for the truly reforming minister now is the actual event of the preaching of the Word, which invites our consideration of the *ethos* and *pathos* that are essential to biblical exposition.

## ETHOS

*integrity*

Ethos, as I am defining it, is simply what you are—your character, you
as a person, and therefore you as a preacher handling God's Word
before the flock of Christ. Ethos has to do with the condition of your
inner life and with the work of the Holy Spirit within you, especially
as it relates to the text that you are preaching. Biblical exposition is
enhanced when the preacher invites the Holy Spirit to apply the text
to his own soul and ethical conduct so that the preacher is sympathetic
to and humbly pursues the application of the text to his own life.

Phillips Brooks, the famous Episcopal bishop of Boston and
author of "O Little Town of Bethlehem," touched on this when he
gave his famous definition of preaching in the 1877 *Yale Lectures on
Preaching*: "Preaching is the bringing of truth through personality."[2]
He then elaborated:

> Truth through Personality is our description of real preaching. The
> truth must come really through the person, not merely over his
> lips, not merely into his understanding and out through his pen.
> It must come through his character, his affections, his whole intel-
> lectual and moral being. It must come genuinely through him.[3]

In the early 1900s Methodist Bishop William Quail carried the
idea further by asking and answering a rhetorical question:
"'Preaching is the art of making a sermon and delivering it?' he asked.
'Why no, that is not preaching. Preaching is the art of making a
preacher and delivering that!'"[4]

These were helpful, groundbreaking observations when qualified
and not taken too far, at least not to the extent Bishop Quail did when
he concluded: "Therefore the elemental business in preaching is not
with the preaching, but with the preacher. It is no trouble to preach,
but a vast trouble to construct a preacher. What then, in the light of
this, is the task of a preacher? Mainly this, the amassing of a great soul
so as to have something worthwhile to give—the sermon is the
preacher up-to-date."[5]

The bishop seems to have forgotten in his enthusiasm Paul's declaration, "For we do not preach ourselves" (2 Cor. 4:5). Indeed, many modern preachers do preach themselves with their endless personal anecdotes and inner therapeutic explanations and confessions. Nevertheless Brooks is right. The truth of God's Word "must come through [the preacher's] character, his affections, his whole intellectual and moral being. It must come genuinely through him."

And here is the great professional danger, because it is possible for us preachers to imagine that we have spiritually been to places we have never visited. Phillips Brooks observed that in the repeated loud proclamation of the grand truths of the faith we can become like railroad conductors who imagine by saying, "All aboard for Albany" or "All aboard for Chicago" that they have actually been there. We can beg men to repent and yet grow so familiar with the whole doctrine of repentance that we are dulled to the fact that we have never ourselves repented[6] *get plank out of your own eye*

C. S. Lewis saw the same thing: "Those, like myself, whose imagination far exceeds their obedience are subject to a just penalty; we easily imagine conditions far higher than we have actually reached. If we describe what we have imagined we may make others, and make ourselves believe that we have really been there—and so fool both them and ourselves."[7] Richard Baxter warned, "Lest they offer the bread of life to others which they themselves have not eaten."[8]

In the light of these realities, Lewis once advised a friend who was considering theological studies to forgo them, observing: "Someone has said, 'None are so unholy as those whose hands are cauterized with holy things'; sacred things may become profane by becoming matters of the job. . . . I've always been glad myself that Theology is not the thing I earn my living by. On the whole, I'd advise you to get on with your tent-making."[9]

So let us all be warned as we preachers live our days amidst the wonders of God's Word and the immensities of its great truths that what we preach must come through our souls. As the godly John Owen said: "If the word do not dwell with power *in* us, it will not pass with power *from us*"[10]—Balaam's donkey notwithstanding! However, nothing is more powerful than God's Word preached by one whose heart has been harrowed and sanctified by the Word he is preaching.

The Puritan William Ames has it exactly right:

> Next to the evidence of truth, and the will of God drawn out of
> the Scriptures, nothing makes a sermon more to pierce, than
> when it comes out of the inward affection of the heart without
> any affection. To this purpose it is very profitable, if besides the
> daily practice of piety we use serious meditation and fervent
> prayer to work those things upon our own hearts, which we
> would persuade others of.[11]

Every appropriation of the truth preached will strengthen the
preacher for preaching. Every repentance occasioned in his soul by
the Word preached will give conviction to his voice. Then it will be
said of him: "His sermon was like thunder, because his life was like
lightning."[12]

Theologically, Jonathan Edwards in his *Treatise Concerning the
Religious Affections* has given us the best explanation of what must
take place within us. Edwards didn't use the word "affections" as
we do to describe a moderate feeling or emotion or a tender attach-
ment. By affections Edwards meant one's *heart*, one's *inclinations*,
and one's *will*.[13] Edwards said, "For who will deny that true religion
consists in a great measure in vigorous and lively actings and the
inclination and will of the soul, or the fervent exercises of the
heart?"[14] Edwards then goes on to demonstrate from a cascade of
Scriptures that real Christianity so impacts the affections that it
shapes one's fears, one's hopes, one's loves, one's hatreds, one's
desires, one's joys, one's sorrows, one's gratitude, one's compassing
or understanding, and one's zeal.[15]

This is what I believe needs to routinely happen to the preacher as
he prepares God's Word, so that the message comes through his whole
intellectual and moral being. When this happens, he is truly ready to
preach.

I have said it many times: Sermon preparation is twenty hours of
prayer. It is humble, holy critical thinking. It is repeatedly asking the
Holy Spirit for insight. It is the harrowing of your soul. It is ongoing
repentance. It is utter dependence. It is a singing heart.

*Spend time c̄ God*

## PATHOS

When we actually come to the preaching event, these moments must be an exercise in Spirit-directed *pathos* or God-centered passion, as I am using this word.

*Bogus passion.* Here it must be said that there is a lot of bogus passion in today's pulpits. I have known of a preacher who would run in place, swing his arms, and jump up and down in the vestry in order to affect a spiritual passion when he stepped into the pulpit. I heard of another who stood on his head before walking out to the chancel. Hollywood has a word for this: "method acting." But a false passion may have much subtler roots, as D. Martyn Lloyd-Jones observed:

> A man prepares a message and, having prepared it, he may be pleased and satisfied with the arrangement and order of the thoughts and certain forms of expression. If he is of an energetic, fervent nature, he may well be excited and moved by that and especially when he preaches the sermon. But it may be entirely of the flesh and have nothing at all to do with spiritual matters. Every preacher knows exactly what this means. . . . You can be carried away by your own eloquence and by the very thing you yourself are doing and not by the truth at all.[16]

So, sinners that we preachers are, we must be wary of ourselves and the source of our homiletic passion. No marginal annotations: "Weak point here. Raise voice, pound pulpit!"

*Scriptural passion.* Despite abuses, the Scriptures know of and enjoin a godly passion for preachers of the Word. Paul told the Thessalonians, "Our gospel came to you not simply with words, but also with power, with the Holy Spirit and with deep conviction" (1 Thess. 1:5). Paul wasn't referring to conviction among his hearers, but rather *his own* conviction ("full conviction," RSV, NASB; "strong conviction," NEB)—i.e., earnestness and passion. That is the way Paul preached. For Paul, preaching and weeping went hand in hand: "For three years I never stopped warning each of you night and day with tears" (Acts 20:31). This was also Jesus' way on occasion. Do you think that Jesus dispassionately intoned, "O Jerusalem, Jerusalem, you who kill the prophets and stone those sent to you, how often I have longed to gather your children together, as a hen gathers her chicks under her wings, but you were not willing" (Matt. 23:37)? Not a chance. It was a loud, passionate lament.

Scriptural preaching demands a passion that flows from the conviction that what you are preaching is true. When George Whitefield was getting the people of Edinburgh out of their beds at five o'clock in the morning to hear his preaching, a man on his way to the Tabernacle met David Hume, the Scottish philosopher and skeptic. Surprised at seeing Hume on his way to hear Whitefield, the man said, "I thought you did not believe in the gospel?" Hume replied, "I don't, but he does."[17] Precisely! Whitefield's famous passion bore substantial and convincing testimony to the authentic burden of the Gospel he preached. And so it always will be. Where there is no passion, there is no preaching.

At the same time we must realize that the display of passion must be requisite with your personality. There are some people, like the nineteenth-century Scottish elder, who are (by nature) so subdued that if they raise their left eyebrow and one corner of their mouth twitches, they are rolling in the aisles. Passion can be demonstrated when the preacher raises his voice and flails his arms so that it appears he is about to fly away. But it can be equally present when a preacher talks quietly and slowly—"This is about your soul. It is a matter of life and death."

It is a matter of historical fact that Jonathan Edwards, the author of *Sinners in the Hands of an Angry God*, read his sermons, holding his notes in front of his face so he could read them in a normal voice. According to John Piper, Serano Dwight asked a man who had heard Edwards preach if he was an eloquent preacher. The reply was:

> He had no studied varieties of the voice, and no strong emphasis. He scarcely gestured, or even moved; and he made no attempt by the elegance of his style, or the beauty of his pictures, to gratify the taste, and fascinate the imagination. But, if you mean by eloquence, the power of presenting an important truth before an audience, with overwhelming weight of argument, and

with such intenseness of feeling, that the whole soul of the speaker is thrown into every part of the conception and delivery; so that the solemn attention of the whole audience is riveted, from the beginning to the close, and impressions are left that cannot be effaced; Mr. Edwards was the most eloquent man I ever heard speak.[18]

Edwards was an immensely passionate man, and it oozed through his personality. Piper concludes, "By precept and example Edwards calls us to [quoting Edwards] 'an exceeding affectionate way of preaching about the great things of religion' and to flee from a 'moderate, dull indifferent way of speaking.'"[19]

Thomas Chalmers, the celebrated Scottish preacher, was described by James Stewart as preaching "with a disconcertingly provincial accent, with an almost total lack of dramatic gesture, tied rigidly to his manuscript, with his finger following the written lines as he read."[20] His secret? His "blood earnestness."[21] A universe of homiletical wisdom is contained in that phrase. However we preach, we must have a "blood earnestness."

Spurgeon asked, "'What in a Christian minister is the most essential quality for securing success in winning souls for Christ?' I should reply, 'Earnestness'; and if I were asked a second or a third time, I would not vary the answer, for personal observation drives me to the conclusion that, as a rule, real success is proportionate to the preacher's earnestness.[22]

> Be earnest, earnest, earnest—
> Mad if thou wilt;
> Do what thou dost as if the
> stake were Heaven,
> And that thy last deed before
> the Judgment Day.
> CHARLES KINGSLEY[23]

I have a framed picture of Charles Simeon that was printed in 1836, the year of his death. Simeon was the man who almost singlehandedly brought the evangelical resurgence to the Church of

England. Fellow of King's College Cambridge, he had secured the pulpit of Holy Trinity, Cambridge, where he preached for over fifty years. For the first ten years of his ministry, his unhappy parishioners chained their pews closed, so that all listeners had to sit in the aisles. But Simeon persevered. His twenty-one volumes of sermons, *Horae Homilaticae (Hours of Homilies)*, set the standard for preaching in the following generations. His Friday night tea was used to disciple a generation of preachers and missionaries, men like Henry Martyn. He not only prevailed but three times gave the university lectures. When you visit Cambridge, you can view his artifacts at his church: the black Wedgewood teapot from which he served students at his Friday night study group, his umbrella (the very first in Cambridge), and his twenty-one volumes of sermons.

Today if you visit the National Gallery in London, you can see a famous set of silhouettes depicting Simeon in various homiletical postures as he implored his people from the pulpit of Holy Trinity. A contemporary wrote:

> I have been at Trinity church thrice today. In the morning a very good sermon by Simeon, a decent one by Thomason, and in the evening to a crowded congregation, a superlative discourse by Simeon (on Acts 4:12), vital, evangelical, powerful and impressive in his animated manner. John Stoughton has a similar recollection. He felt that Simeon's sermons far from having the slow penetrating force of the dew came down like "hailstones and coals of fire." I was struck with the preacher's force, even vehemence. He spoke as one who had a burden from the Lord to deliver—as one who, like Paul, felt "Woe unto me if I preach not the gospel."[24]

Another of his curates, Charles Carus, wrote, "The intense fervour of his feelings he cared not to restrain; his whole soul was in his subject and he spoke and acted exactly as he felt."[25] One of his obituaries carried this remembrance of calling his hearers to faith:

> And after having urged all his hearers to accept the proffered mercy, he reminded them that there were those present to whom

he had preached Christ for more than thirty years, but they continued indifferent to the Saviour's love; and pursuing this train of expostulation for some time, he at length became quite overpowered by his feeling, and he sank down in the pulpit and burst into a flood of tears.[26]

> *I preached as never to preach again*
> *As a dying man to dying men.*

Richard Baxter's poem is not sentiment, but the heart of a preacher alive with God's Word!

## CONCLUSION

In *logos*, *ethos*, and *pathos* we have a simple outline of the anatomy of true biblical exposition. Here we have a simple way of restoring biblical exposition to its rightful place in the modern church. Here we can do the true work of biblical reformation in our preaching.

*Logos* means, simply, that what you believe about the Word is everything. As a preacher, if you believe that Scripture is wholly *inerrant*, totally *sufficient*, and massively *potent*, you will give yourself to the hard work of biblical exposition.

*Ethos* means that belief and hard work are not enough. You must let the Word of God course through your soul, inviting the Holy Spirit to winnow your soul, making you sympathetic to the truth you are preaching, and as much as is possible conforming your life to the truth you preach, so that God's Word "comes out of the inward affection of the heart without any affectation."

*Pathos*, therefore, means that you must stand to preach drenched in an authentic passion that causes you to speak with the utmost blood earnestness. You are preaching the Word. The wind of the Holy Spirit is in your sails. God's name is lifted high.

Glory alone to God!

## NOTES

1 John R. W. Stott, *Guard the Truth* (Downers Grove, IL: InterVarsity, 1996), p. 122, explains:

It was taken for granted from the beginning that Christian preaching would be expository preaching, that is, that all Christian instruction and exhortation would be drawn out of the passage which had been read.

We note, however, that the public reading of Scripture came first, identifying the authority. What followed was exposition and application, whether in the form of doctrinal instruction or of moral appeal, or both. Timothy's own authority was thus seen to be secondary, both to the Scripture and to the apostle. All Christian teachers occupy the same subordinate position as Timothy did. They will be wise, therefore, especially if they are young, to demonstrate conscientious integrity in expounding it, so that their teaching is seen to be not theirs but the word of God.

2 Phillips Brooks, *Lectures on Preaching* (Manchester, VT: James Robinson, 1899), p. 5.

3 Ibid., p. 9.

4 Paul Sangster, *Doctor Sangster* (London: Epworth Press, 1962), p. 271.

5 Ibid.

Preaching is the art of making a sermon and delivering it. Why no, that is not preaching. Preaching is the art of making a preacher and delivering that. Preaching is the outrush of soul in speech. Therefore the elemental business in preaching is not with the preaching, but with the preacher. It is no trouble to preach, but a vast trouble to construct a preacher. What then, in the light of this, is the task of a preacher? Mainly this, the amassing of a great soul so as to have something worthwhile to give—the sermon is the preacher up-to-date.

6 Brooks, *Lectures on Preaching*, p. 25.

7 C. S. Lewis, *The Four Loves* (New York: Harcourt, Brace, Jovanovich, 1960), p. 326.

8 This quotation is attributed to the great Baxter, though I have not been able to locate the source of the original words. The closest I have come upon is *The Reformed Pastor* (Edinburgh: Banner of Truth, 1994), pp. 54-55.

9 Sheldon Vanauken, *A Severe Mercy* (New York: Harper & Row, 1977), pp. 104-105.

10 William H. Goold, ed., *The Works of John Owen*, Vol. 16 (London: Banner of Truth, 1968), p. 76 reads:

But a man preacheth that sermon only well unto others which preacheth itself in his own soul. And he that doth not feed on and thrive in the digestion of the food which he provides for others will scarce make it savoury unto them; yea, he knows not but the food he hath provided may be poison, unless he have really tasted of it himself. If the word do not dwell with power *in* us, it will not pass with power *from* us.

11 Art Lindsley, "Profiles in Faith, William Ames: Practical Theologian," *Tabletalk*, [MONTH?] 1983, p. 14.

12 Harvey K. McArthur, *Understanding the Sermon on the Mount* (New York: Harper, 1960), p. 161 who quotes Cornelius A. Lapide, *Commentary on Matthew's Gospel* (on 7:28), who records this quotation that I have adapted: "A sermon of Basil's was like thunder, because his life was like lightning."

13 Jonathan Edwards, *The Religious Affections* (Edinburgh: Banner of Truth, 1994), p. 24, where he explains,

This faculty is called by various names; it is sometimes called the inclination: and, as it has respect to the actions that are determined and governed by it, is called the will: and the mind, with regard to the exercises of this faculty, is often called the heart.

Cf. pp. 24-27.

14  Ibid., p. 27.

15  Ibid., p. 31; cf. pp. 31-35.

16  D. Martyn Lloyd-Jones, *The Sermon on the Mount*, Vol. 2 (Grand Rapids, MI: Eerdmans, 1960), p. 266.

17  Clarence Edward Macartney, *Preaching Without Notes* (Grand Rapids, MI: Baker, 1976), p. 183.

18  John Piper, *The Supremacy of God in Preaching* (Grand Rapids, MI: Baker, 1990), pp. 49-50.

19  Ibid., p. 104.

20  Ibid., p. 50.

21  Ibid., p. 51.

22  C. H. Spurgeon, *Lectures to My Students* (Grand Rapids, MI: Zondervan, 1954), p. 305.

23  Elisabeth Elliot, *A Chance to Die, The Life and Legacy of Amy Carmichael* (Old Tappan, NJ: Revell, 1987), p. 13.

24  Hugh Evan Hopkins, *Charles Simeon* (Grand Rapids, MI: Eerdmans, 1977), p. 64.

25  Ibid., p. 65.

26  Ibid., p. 66.

# 5

# KEEPING THE MAIN THING
# THE MAIN THING:

## *Preaching Christ as the Focus of All Reformation*

■

## Thomas N. Smith

At age fifteen I was what was known among Baptists as a "preacher boy." "Preacher boy" meant, that while I was not ordained or permitted to hold pastoral office, I was allowed to preach. And preach I did (though admittedly it was very poor preaching), all over southern Oklahoma. I know now that the sheer novelty of a fifteen-year-old boy preaching was enough to get people to come at least once. These small congregations in places like Thackerville, Leon, Gene Autry, and Burneyville were kind, patient, and generous to boy-wonder preachers. While I doubt they learned much from me, I most certainly learned a great deal from them. Indeed, I keep learning from the lessons they taught me thirty-odd years ago.

One of these lessons came in the form of the offertory prayer. Almost infallibly when called upon to pray before "taking up" the offering, some wizened older man with sunburned face turning suddenly white at the juncture of his head where his cowboy hat was worn 365 days out of the year would implore the Lord to "bless this young man You have sent to us today. Give him Your message, and be pleased to hide him behind the cross."

I think often about those last words. They are striking, almost shocking. In no other public gathering that I can think of would the wish be expressed that a guest speaker be hidden. We want to see our speakers and entertainers; we want them, in seventies language, to "let it all hang out." "Hide him behind the cross" is a radically Christian prayer, expressing a radically Christian wish. This wish is to see not the preacher, but to see Christ, to see Christ crucified. Further, the striking manner in which this wish is expressed indicates a jealousy over the glory of Christ that eschews anything, even a boy wonder, that would intrude upon the supremacy of the Gospel. It was also, by the way, a gentle way to remind the preacher boy what his central responsibility was in the act of preaching: He was to show people Jesus Christ, Jesus Christ crucified for sinners. I wish I could personally thank each of those old deacons who prayed for me in that way. Someday I will.

## THE LONGING OF THE PEOPLE OF GOD

This, in a very real way, is the heart of the subject "Preaching Christ." It is personal, relational, and practical. In this sense the personal must come before the ideological, the relational must precede the theoretical, the practical must take precedence over the theological.[1]

We believe that Christians are a unique people. They are indwelt by the Holy Spirit of Christ. They are led by the Spirit of God. They have an anointing from the Holy One. Christians, by definition, believe that God's final revelation of Himself is found in the life, death, and resurrection of Jesus of Nazareth. They have come to know God in this revelation of this person.

One result of this is a desire in the heart of Christians to know Christ in an ever deepening way. Therefore they long to see Him preached and taught.

There is within every Christian's heart the longing expressed in a hymn attributed to Bernard of Clairvaux:

> We taste Thee, O Thou living Bread,
> And long to feast upon Thee still;
> We drink of Thee, the Fountainhead,
> And thirst our souls from Thee to fill.

*Our restless spirits yearn for Thee,*
*Where'er our changeful lot is cast;*
*Glad when Thy gracious smile we see,*
*Blest when our faith can hold Thee fast.*

The same sentiment is expressed in another hymn attributed to the same writer:

*Jesus, the very thought of Thee*
*With sweetness fills my breast;*
*But sweeter far Thy face to see*
*And in Thy presence rest.*

*Nor voice can sing, nor heart can frame,*
*Nor can the memory find*
*A sweeter sound than Thy blest name,*
*O Savior of mankind.*

*O hope of every contrite heart,*
*O joy of all the meek,*
*To those who fall how kind Thou art!*
*How good to those who seek!*

*But what to those who find? Ah, this*
*Nor tongue nor pen can show—*
*The love of Jesus, what it is,*
*None but His loved ones know.*

This gets to the heart of the issue because this gets to the heart. It is just here that so much contemporary preaching fails. It fails because it overloads the minds of Christians with expository and lexical detail, or, in the opposite direction, it "dumbs down" to the listener with no real Christian content at all. In other cases it views preaching as a matter of presenting theological propositions that never reach the affections, or as a subtle (or not so subtle!) manipulation of the emotions that bypasses the mind altogether. It fails by stressing the practical or moral lesson without anchoring the point in the fact and accomplishment of Jesus, or it presents a Jesus with no real connection to the ethical demands and struggles of everyday, contemporary life.

And while these things take place week by week, the Christians in the pews feel themselves without a real and clear *Christian* word of encouragement, confirmation, and direction. In the words of an anonymous writer, "The hungry sheep look up and are not fed." This is because the hearts of the people are not nourished in the truth as it is in Jesus. Again, a hymn expresses this well:

> *I love to tell the story,*
> *For those who know it best*
> *Seem hungering and thirsting*
> *To hear it like the rest.*

And at the root of this longing is the reality mentioned in an earlier stanza of the same song:

> *I love to tell the story,*
> *More wonderful it seems*
> *Than all the golden fancies*
> *Of all our golden dreams.*
> *I love to tell the story,*
> *It did so much for me;*
> *And that is just the reason*
> *I tell it now to thee.*

The preaching of Christ lies at the heart of all authentic Christian experience. This experience is initiated in such preaching and is advanced by such preaching. If it is objected, "But this is itself an argument from experience," we answer with Pascal, "The heart has reasons that reason knows nothing of."

## "I LOVE TO TELL THE STORY"

The mention of "the story" just now is not accidental. It is perhaps to the Gospel as story that failure or success in the preaching of Christ is really to be discovered.

| The Gospel is *the* story. For the Christian, the Gospel of Jesus Christ is *the* Story. This is because the Gospel of Jesus is the continuation of the story of God's mighty acts in the history of Israel as recorded in the Bible. The writers of the Gospels are at pains to connect the story of Jesus with these earlier, Israelite stories (see Matt. 1:1-17; Luke 1—2; John 1:1-18). The recorded preaching of the earliest Christian preachers comes in story form. The epistles themselves, even the most theologically structured of them—Romans and Hebrews—are really highly developed stories.[2] This fact is so obvious that it is easily missed.

And what is this Story? It is the story of the God who created all things including mankind, whom He created in His own image. It is the story of a good and beautiful creation made for mankind's benefit and pleasure. It is the story of man's ungrateful rebellion against his good Lord and of his subsequent plunge into depravity and misery. It is the story of the grace and action of the same God to rescue His human family from this plight, first in the history of Israel and finally in the history of Jesus Christ and His earliest followers. It is a story with a promised future when mankind in revolt will become mankind at rest in the fully restored glory of God. It is this uniquely Christian understanding of history that gave rise to the quip, "History is *His story*." Preaching, if it is to be Christian, must recover this understanding of history, of the Gospel as story.

The fact that this needs to be said at all shows just how much the evangelical churches have embraced the worldview of the Enlightenment of the eighteenth century. In response to the Modernist agenda, we have departed from the shape that the Bible itself gives its message and have opted instead to reshape it into a different, more impressive form. There is not a little arrogance in this project! So we have come to believe that unless we restate the stories of the Bible in propositional form, we cannot get to the heart of the matter. The fact is, when we reshape the Story into a non-story form, we lose the distinctive contours of the original form and lose vital aspects of its meaning. Those holding a high view of the inspiration and authority of the Scriptures need to do some serious thinking about the implications of this approach. Is it not at least possible that in adopting the Modernist method we have exchanged the weakness and foolishness of God for the wisdom and power of man (see 1 Cor. 1:18—2:16)? A return to preaching Christ, then, will mean a return to the form that the Bible itself, indeed God Himself, has given to the message.

## A STORY WITH A CLIMAX

In addition to constructing their books in a way that shows continuity with the Old Testament, the New Testament writers were concerned to emphasize something else in the strongest possible terms. Each one highlights in his own unique manner the fact that *Jesus of Nazareth is the culminating climax of Israel's story.* Matthew does this in presenting Jesus as the seed of Abraham who will be the blessing of God to all nations (cf. Matt. 1:1-17 with 28:18-20). Mark does the same in presenting the ministry of Jesus as a new beginning, a new Genesis (Mark 1:1). John does the same thing, only (if possible) more explicitly (John 1:1-3). Luke also presents the coming of Jesus in terms of a new Genesis, but also as the fulfillment of the expectations of the prophets (cf. Mal. 3:1 and 4:5-6). Each of the Synoptics puts this message of fulfillment into the mouth of Jesus Himself with the words, "the kingdom of God is near." All of the recorded sermons of Acts that have Jews as their audience present in the strongest possible terms this same idea of final, climactic fulfillment in Jesus of Nazareth (see, e.g., Acts 2:14-36 and 13:16-41). It is the same in the epistles. "Christ died . . . was buried . . . was raised . . . according to the Scriptures" (1 Cor. 15:3-4). ". . . the gospel of God he promised beforehand through his prophets in the Holy Scriptures" (Rom. 1:1-2).

Furthermore, this concept of climactic fulfillment is presented in eschatalogical "time language," language that at times seems coined for the occasion. Paul's use of the word "now" carries this eschatological connotation (see Rom. 3:21; 8:1). So does his "when the time had fully come" (Gal. 4:4) and "new creation" (Gal. 6:15; 2 Cor. 5:17), as well as the phrase "on whom the fulfillment of the ages has come" (1 Cor. 10:11). The same is true of John's "this is the last hour" (1 John 2:18) and the phrase "at the end of the ages" (Hebrews 9:26).

The apostles and prophets of the New Testament viewed the Old

Testament as the bearer of a valid story, but they viewed that story as incomplete in itself. They would have agreed with Karl Barth that "The Old Testament is going somewhere." And Barth, like themselves, was not at all uncertain where the Old Testament was going: It was going to the manger, to the cross, to the empty tomb of Jesus of Nazareth! The promises of the former era had met with their fulfillment in the Messiah, Jesus. Paul speaks for the whole body of New Testament writers when he summarizes this view in the words, "For no matter how many promises God has made, they are 'Yes' in Christ" (2 Cor. 1:20).

## AN OLD CANON AND A NEW HERMENEUTIC

What we have in the Old Testament, then, is an old canon, the same body of sacred writings accepted by Israel in the second Temple period (cf. 2 Tim. 3:14-17 with Luke 24:27, 44). The preachers and writers in the New Testament period are united in their loyalty to and dependence upon this canon.

But a radical shift has taken place in their thinking concerning the hermeneutical lens through which this canon is viewed and interpreted. This new perspective distinguishes them from every other grouping within Palestine in their day, whether the Sadducees, the Pharisees, or the Qumran sect. And this new, radical viewpoint is traced back to Jesus Himself.

In language that is breathtaking in its daring, Jesus regularly refers to the events of His life and ministry as the fulfillment of the expectations and promises of the Old Testament. Luke records Jesus' saying to the disciples, "Blessed are the eyes that see what you see. For I tell you that many prophets and kings wanted to see what you see but did not see it, and to hear what you hear but did not hear it" (10:23-24). In the same vein, He declares Himself to be greater than Solomon and Jonah the prophet (Luke 11:29-32). He claims to be greater than the Temple (Matt. 12:6—a daring utterance!). He declares that "Your father Abraham rejoiced at the thought of seeing my day," then goes even further, asserting, "Before Abraham was born, I am!" (John 8:56-

59). He announces that He Himself is the fulfillment of the prophetic promises of the gift of the Holy Spirit in the last days (John 7:37-39).

But perhaps the most authoritatively influential declarations made by Jesus concerning the Old Testament and Himself are to be found in Luke 24. In the story of the disciples on the road to Emmaus, Jesus chides their unbelief by declaring that all that has taken place in Jerusalem is in keeping with the Scriptures, and "beginning with Moses and all the Prophets, he explained to them *what was said in all the Scriptures concerning himself*" (vv. 25-27, emphasis added). Again, in His post-resurrection appearance to the disciples in Jerusalem, Luke records Jesus' saying, "This is what I told you while I was still with you: Everything must be fulfilled that is written about me in the Law of Moses, the Prophets and the Psalms" (24:44). He then goes on to interpret the Old Testament around the facts of His death and resurrection and the subsequent proclamation of repentance and forgiveness to the nation by His witnesses (vv. 45-49).

Two things are remarkable in light of these words. First, Jesus reminds the disciples of the fact that He had taken just this same approach to the Old Testament in His previous ministry among them: "This is what I told you while I was still with you" (v. 44). And, second, the content of the apostles' preaching as recorded by Luke in his sequel to the Gospel, the book of Acts, follows precisely the contours laid down by Jesus in verses 44-49 (see Acts 2:14-36 and 13:16-41).

And there is still another line of thinking that indicates this hermeneutical shift as understood by the New Testament writers. It is the way they now speak of the Word of God. As we have already seen, the apostles and writers of the New Testament era view the Hebrew canon as Holy Scripture, with this corollary: "What Scripture says, God says." This is no more and no less than the perspective held by any faithful Jew in their day. But from this perspective these men move into new and uncharted territory when they begin to equate their new Story with the old one!

On the day of Pentecost, Peter can demand repentance toward the God of Israel by requiring compliance with the story of Jesus he has just preached to the crowds (Acts 2:38).

Later Peter declares that salvation (divine deliverance from sin and its effects) is now to be found in "the name of Jesus" and nowhere else (Acts 4:10-12; compare Ps. 3:8 and Jon. 2:9 along with Isa. 42—44).

Paul in Pisidian Antioch can warn his Jewish hearers that rejection of Christ's message is tantamount to the rejection of the prophetic oracles of the Old Testament and, like that rejection, will bring God's curse (Acts 13:40-41).

Paul can refer to the Gospel as "the word of truth," which amounts to an equating of the new message with the Torah (cf. Eph. 1:13 with Ps. 119).

The apostles equate their preaching with "the word of God" (2 Cor. 2:17; 4:2; 1 Thess. 2:13; Heb. 4:12; 6:5; 1 Pet. 1:23, 25).

Paul can now refer to the Word of God as "the word of Christ" (Rom. 10:17; Col. 3:16)—that is, the word about Jesus.

## THE NEW CANON

All of which speaks of a dramatic turning point in the thinking of these Jewish men. With a daring that equals that of Jesus in the Gospels, these New Testament men see themselves as the custodians of the old canon and the shapers of a new one!

On what grounds did these men assume this role? We are forced to consider still more claims of Jesus Himself. The key passage is John 14—16, the so-called "Upper Room Discourse." Woven throughout this narrative of Jesus' last word to the apostles is His promise to send the Holy Spirit to enable them to perform His ongoing work in the world (see 14:16-17, 26; 15:26-27; 16:7-15). Integral to this ongoing work is the Spirit's work of bearing witness to Jesus in the witness of these men (15:26-27). This witness will prove to be a vindication of Jesus from all the false accusations made against Him during His ministry (16:7-11). Furthermore, this witness will take place in conjunction with the teaching of Jesus that will be conveyed and confirmed to the apostles through the ministry of the Holy Spirit. This will take a twofold form. First, as "the Spirit of truth" he "will teach you all things and will remind you of everything I have said to you"(14:17, 26). Second, "He will guide you into all truth. . . . He will tell you what

*Jn 14:26*

is yet to come. He will bring glory to me by taking from what is mine and making it known to you" (16:13-14).

What is intimated in these words is the process whereby the Story is conveyed and preserved for those who will believe in Jesus through the apostolic testimony (cf. John 17:20 with 15:26-27). This process has been described by Hermann Ridderbos as "the ongoing work of the history of God's saving acts."[3] And the ultimate effect or result of the ministry of the Spirit and the apostles working jointly in this role are the documents that came to make up the New Testament. The process is a divine one whereby the Story begun in the Old Testament reaches its climax in the testimony of the early Christian church to the life, the words, and the works of Jesus of Nazareth, the Messiah! In this Story the divine purpose and goal of human life and history are reached in the person and work of Jesus. And the Story is not without a denouement. This final unfolding of God's purpose revealed in Jesus is to take place under God's command and enduement *in the preaching and teaching of Jesus Christ as Lord.*

## KEEP THE MAIN THING THE *MAIN THING*

It is this distinctly Christian view of the Bible and its central theme that was the basis for apostolic practice in the years immediately following Jesus' ascension. Jesus was the theme of their ministries (see Acts 3:11-26; 8:26-35; 10:34-43; etc.). But how does this all relate to *pastoral practice,* to preaching and teaching within the churches? Doesn't all this have to do with evangelism, and more specifically to Jewish evangelism in the first century? And once the evangelism is taken care of, aren't we free to move on to other things, practical things, deeper things? Isn't there a fundamental distinction in the New Testament between preaching and teaching?

Each of these questions has a modicum of truth in it. Evangelism and pastoral practice, preaching and teaching, milk and solid food are all distinguished from one another in the New Testament. But the apostles, prophets, and elders in the New Testament churches were well aware of the facts that become apparent when these categories are placed side-by-side as they are in my previous sentence. They can be distinguished, but they may never be separated. Look at evangelism and pastoral practice in light of Colossians 1:28-29. The teaching and warning ministry to the church is not separated from the preaching of Christ. Look at preaching and teaching in light of 2 Timothy 4:2. It is in the pastoral work of "teaching" (3:16) and "careful instruction" (4:2) that Timothy is to "*preach* the Word." Look at milk and solid food in light of 1 Corinthians 3, Hebrews 5, and 1 Peter 2. It is the Word of Christ that is in view in each case, not the Gospel for the weak but something else (deeper things?) for the strong.

Such dichotomies rest upon a basic fallacy. It is the fallacy that the Gospel is a simple, even simplistic, set of facts necessary to get people into the kingdom of God. But once they're in, this mistaken notion claims, the Gospel as an elementary teaching about Christ must be left behind in the interests of Christian maturity; they must move on to other things.

Again, this fallacy is founded upon a very narrow and simplistic definition of the Gospel. For the writers of the New Testament, *the Gospel* is a virile term embracing the whole counsel of God viewed from the standpoint of the Jesus Story. It is the foundation of the building, but it is also the blocks the building is made of. It is the foundation of both theology and ethics, of belief and conduct. And it is precisely this inseparable connection that makes the Christian position, the Christian life, *Christian.*

Let us consider this first from the standpoint of Christian theology. (In a very real sense the New Testament never considers theology apart from conduct. Doctrine in the New Testament must be "sound doctrine," i.e., teaching connected to a healthy Christian life.)

What is involved in the Christian proclamation of God? The classical answer to this has been an attempt to define God in philosophical and abstract terms: omniscience, aseity (self-existence), immutability, etc. An example of this approach is found in the *Westminster Shorter Catechism.* But as I have argued elsewhere,[4] what we have here is a philosophical theism that is not distinctively Christian at all. The reason for this is to be found in a theological method that attempts to change the story form of the Gospel into a philosophical shape that is foreign to it. This is why the tendency of this method, especially in scholastic Calvinism, is to swallow up the personal God into a transcendent, infinite Deity.

The God of the Bible is, to be sure, a God of attributes. But these attributes are revealed in the historical context of God's covenant and promise. This is too easily forgotten. Even the opening chapters of the Bible, which present God, the Creator, in his otherness, power, etc., are a revelation of God given to a people in covenant with that God, to equip them to live in faithfulness to Him before the reality of the rampant polytheism of the culture they are about to encounter. Furthermore, the high-water mark of the Old Testament revelation of God (a revelation that will inform every subsequent disclosure on His part and reflection on the part of Israel [Exod. 34:6-7]), is a disclosure of God's character in the context of this same covenant and covenant people. Only this time the revelation is made in the face of their breaking the covenant. What will God do with them? He will deal with them in a manner that is consonant with His character, His name. In fact, when God discloses Himself He never uses terms like *attributes*. He tells us who He is by telling us His name. This takes us back, not to philosophical terms, but to the constituent elements of the story form.

In the New Testament parallel to Exodus 34, John 1:1-18, we find John doing the same thing. The God who reveals Himself in Jesus Christ is not the philosophical *Logos* of Philo, but the God who speaks in a new creation, the One who reveals His name in terms of covenant grace and truth. And He does this in the most concrete and least abstract way. He does this in the enfleshment of Himself, by taking on weak, frail, mortal human nature!

Christian preaching about God, then, will be guided by considerations like these. God is not known through abstractions, nor through a collection of abstractions. He is known in the name He has revealed in the history of Israel found in the Old Testament and in the history of Jesus of Nazareth found in the New Testament. This is a covenant-history, a salvation-history, and it is within these delimitations that he can be known at all. Beyond this history, this Story that he has chosen to tell, He is and remains the hidden God.

But what a revelation it is! The sense of thrill and excitement that permeates the whole New Testament signifies this. Here are these men, inheritors of the traditions of Israel, breathlessly rethinking, realigning, and restating that tradition in light of the fact of Jesus. One concrete example is found in Paul's restatement of Israel's *Shema* (Deut. 6, in 1 Cor. 8:4-6). The oneness of God that is foundational to Jewish (and Christian) faith is reframed to include the lordship of Jesus. The name of God is thus redefined in Christian terms. In a similar way "the God of Abraham, Isaac, and Jacob," a common form of God's self-revelation in the Old Testament, is "the God and Father of our Lord Jesus Christ" in the new language of faith. There is no suggestion of a repudiation of the Hebraic tradition, but only a radical reinterpretation of that tradition.

Christian preaching must grasp and be able to communicate this. Communication that seeks to convey truth about God in philosophical abstractions, in a manner that obscures or dismisses the story form of the Gospel, that views the God of the Old and New Testaments as in any sense dissimilar, is not Christian and is not preaching at all. "Anyone who has seen me has seen the Father" (John 14:9).

Similar things must be reckoned with in our ethical and practical preaching. Several years ago I was invited to speak with several other preachers at a summer family conference. One of my colleagues spoke each night on the Christian family. What became more striking with each installment in this series was there was nothing distinctively Christian about any of it! We were given, night after night, good advice, sound wisdom, entertaining anecdotes, but we were not told what made the Christian family unique and distinctive from, say, a pious Jewish or Muslim family. This example could be repeated infinitely on a large variety of subjects.

One of the most remarkable things about the New Testament is the way that its writers deal with thorny ethical issues. *Every ethical requirement, every matter of conduct, is rooted in the redemptive accomplishment of Jesus Christ.* We will consider a few general examples and then focus on a particular one.

This fact is implicit in the commonly recognized division between the doctrinal and practical sections of the major New Testament epistles (Rom. 1—11, doctrinal; 12—15, practical; Eph. 1—3, doctrinal; 4—6, practical; etc.). What is often missed is the organic unity between these sections. It is not: "Christians believe these things, and Christians behave like this." It is rather, "Christians believe these things, and *because they believe these things*, some conduct is unthinkable, while other behavior is the natural result of knowing and believing the truth as revealed in Jesus Christ." This is Paul's manner of dealing with sin in the life of the justified believer in Romans 6. It is the way he approaches the whole Christian life in Ephesians 4:17-24. It is the basis of Christian husbands and wives relating properly to one another in Ephesians 5:22ff. It becomes in 1 Peter the rationale for Christian suffering (2:20-25). A host of other examples could be marshaled forth in proof of this thesis. But let us consider a particular case, that of 1 Corinthians 1:10-17.

Paul had learned that, among many other problems, the church at Corinth was riddled with divisions. An ugly spirit of partisanship had risen in groups of church members who were separating from one another under their allegiance to various preachers—Paul, Apollos, Cephas, and Christ. These divisions, based as they always are on a spirit of superiority and one-upmanship, were having a pernicious effect on the everyday life of this church (cf. 1 Cor. 11:17-34). Paul's pastoral method in addressing this problem shows in the clearest possible way the difference between ethics and Christian ethics.

A purely ethical approach would have, no doubt, pointed out the moral inferiority and the destructive effects of arrogance, partisanship, and selfishness. It would have shown how inconsiderate and counter-productive such behavior is in our personal relationships. It might have emphasized the self-destructive tendency of such conduct. It might even (if it were a theistic ethics) have stressed that God (or the gods) frowns upon such conduct and rewards its opposite. Paul's method is a radical and dramatic departure from this.

Paul's approach is to show them that such conduct is, pure and simple, a contradiction of the Gospel. The cross of Christ is a display of the weakness and foolishness of God in contradistinction to the present age's models of power and wisdom. Since it is the cross that is the method of God's saving work in their lives, a return to worldly ideas of wisdom and power in such things as partisanship is a worldly, fleshly, and infantile mentality. Indeed, it is tantamount to conducting themselves as "mere men," that is, like non-Christians (1 Cor. 3:1-4). As subplots to this theme, Paul reminds them they were nothing when they first became recipients of God's grace. So how can they now behave as if they are something special (cf. 1 Cor. 1:26-31 with 4:6-7)? Furthermore, Paul's ministry among them at the beginning was itself a model of the weakness and foolishness of God, of "Christ crucified." So how could they have understood the nature of that ministry and then moved on to the proud superiority of comparing themselves with and separating from others? All of this points to a complete failure on their part to understand the essence of "Christ crucified." This is the apostolic and Christian method of insisting upon a certain kind of conduct from Christians. And it is this method that Paul especially is adroit in employing in his pastoral ministry to the churches. "You must be true to the Christian Story" is the essence of this method. Such a method is most suggestive to the contemporary preacher-pastor.

## THE SUM AND SUBSTANCE OF THE MATTER

If we are to keep the main thing the main thing, if we are to preach and teach Jesus Christ, the following principles must hold us in their muscular grip.

We must see our role as preachers from the vantage point of being behind the cross. That is, we must understand ourselves as "servants for Jesus' sake" (2 Cor. 4:5), "servants of Christ Jesus" (Phil. 1:1). We are bound to Jesus in our lives, our thinking, and our proclamation. We must labor to bring every thought, within ourselves and others, captive to Him. We are not moralists, we are not ethicists, we are not theistic or moral philosophers. We are simple, humble proclaimers of the Christian Story.

We must see the Story as the central thing, the fundamental thing. Christian theology is not basically a complex philosophical construct, even a construct that uses biblical texts as its building materials. It is basically a richly textured and varicolored Story of Israel's Creator-Covenant God who has revealed Himself fully and finally in the life, death, and resurrection of Jesus of Nazareth.

*we must
love the way*

We must see Christ as the living, beating, life-giving heart of this Story. We must be enamored and preoccupied with Jesus. This has immediate bearing on the way we live, think, preach, and pastor. We must be, in Spurgeon's terse word, "Jesus-men."

We must see the indivisibility of theology and conduct and must see each in its vital relationship to Jesus Himself. There is no Christian theology without the God-Man. There is no Christian practice that is separated from the implications of who He is and what He has done and will yet do in the world.

Preaching must reckon with these things, and that reckoning will take our complete concentration, will demand all our powers, and will go a long way in keeping the main thing the main thing.

## NOTES

1 What I intend here is to emphasize the *priority* of experience over theological conception and articulation. In other words, we come to faith in Jesus through apostolic *testimony* validated by the ministry of the Holy Spirit, Acts 2:14-40; I Thess. 1:4-10; I Cor. 2:1-16; et al. Theological constructs are built upon this foundation of apostolic testimony. For more on this idea see C. Stephen Evans, "Methodological Naturalism in Historical Biblical Scholarship" in *Jesus and the Restoration of Israel: A Critical Assessment of N.T. Wright's Jesus and the Victory of God* (Downers Grove: InterVarsity, 1999), Carey C. Newman, ed., pp. 202-204.

2 This point is made, albeit in different ways, by D. A. Carson, *The Gagging of God* (Grand Rapids, MI: Zondervan, 1996), Part 2, and N. T. Wright, *The New Testament and the People of God* (Minneapolis: Fortress, 1992), Parts 1 and 2. See also Hans Frei, *The Eclipse of Biblical Narrative* (New Haven, CT: Yale University Press, 1974), and George Hunsinger, Chapter 9, "What Can Evangelicals and Postliberals Learn from Each Other?" in Timothy R. Phillips and Dennis L. Okholm, eds., *The Nature of Confession* (Downers Grove, IL: InterVarsity, 1996), pp. 134-150.

3 Herman Ridderbos, *Redemptive History and the New Testament Scriptures* (Phillipsburg, NJ: Presbyterian and Reformed, 1988).

4 *Reformation and Revival Journal*, Vol. 8, No. 4 (Fall 1999), "The Full and Final Revelation of God," pp. 27-36.

# 6

---

# FROM FAITH TO FAITH:

## *What Makes Preaching So Vital for Reformation?*

■

### Wilbur C. Ellsworth

A few weeks ago a new high-tech radio arrived at our home. A letter in the box explained the superiority of our purchase:

> We strive to reproduce the musical sounds as closely as possible to those of the original performance. And we strive to avoid flashy sounds such as those associated with accentuated bass and/or treble frequencies. While these sounds may be initially attractive to the novice, they are not real and are not enduring.[1]

In preaching as in music, the objective is to get as close as possible to the original performance. In the tidal wave of change that we call the postmodern world, the ability to represent the original performance of God's saving grace in our generation has raised unsettling questions about the importance of preaching. Some of the proposed changes and substitutes for preaching seem to be falling into the category of what is initially attractive but not real and enduring. Understanding the importance and nature of preaching has never been more important to the life and ministry of the church than it is today.

In describing the role of preaching in the baptism of the Holy Spirit at Pentecost, Frederick Dale Bruner writes:

> It is in Luke's interest as he develops the Pentecostal events in Acts 2 that the meaning of Pentecost be found not in the interior spir-

itual life of the disciples nor even in the gift of the Holy Spirit, but in the preaching of Jesus Christ. In the center of Luke's attention at Pentecost—even quantitatively—is not what we usually think when we say "Pentecost," i.e., the Spirit, it is Jesus Christ; not spiritual ecstasy, but a Christian sermon.[2]

Romans 10 continues to assure us that faith comes by hearing, hearing comes by the Word of Christ, and that Word comes to people through preaching. Contrary to shallow dismissals of many critics, preaching has enormous appeal to a generation that is crying out for someone to simply talk to them. The deluge of technology has enhanced rather than diminished the importance of a real person talking to real people. People living in the culture of postmodernity are in desperate need of relationship. As marriages, families, friendships, and business relationships become less stable and secure, the human heart cries out for someone to understand and to speak with hope and with help.

Several times recently people have expressed appreciation that when they call our church they do not encounter a machine that plunges them into the impersonal maze of buttons to push for more options than many people can even remember. They appreciate talking to a person who relates to them. True talking is not cheap today. Personal, honest, helpful talking has never been more valuable, and the preacher must not let anyone make him think otherwise. This is a time for churches and preachers to keep their heads about the importance of biblical preaching and not to be intimidated with claims that the role of preaching has diminished in its importance.

Part of the importance of preaching is the unique quality that distinguishes it from teaching. This distinction is more a matter of emphasis than of exclusive definition because any true Christian teaching has much in common with Christian preaching, and Christian preaching must be deeply rooted in the disciplines of teaching. With this caution established, I propose that the chief quality of teaching is *faithful accuracy*. The spiritual and intellectual disciplines of exegesis and hermeneutics are foundational to the work of teaching the Bible. What a text says and what it means are the concerns of the teacher. But the preacher, while being committed to the accuracy of the biblical text, goes beyond the work of the teacher, for preaching has as its ultimate goal *redemptive penetration*. In describing the nature of God's Word, Hebrews 4:12 provides a working vision of preaching: "The word of God is living and active. Sharper than any double-edged sword, it penetrates even to dividing soul and spirit, joints and marrow; it judges the thoughts and attitudes of the heart."

While teaching concentrates on the mind, preaching penetrates to the heart, and in that penetration it describes reality in God's kingdom and appeals to the conscience of God's creatures. A preacher confident in Holy Scripture, concerned about the well-being of his listeners, and committed to submitting all of life to this redeeming truth is a mighty weapon in the hand of God. Preaching God's Word in the power of the Holy Spirit does more than merely connect with listeners. It penetrates the listener so that the soil of the heart is broken up and the seed of God's true Word is planted deep in the life, so that the gracious work of God may produce the fruit of grace.

*what preachers do*

Donald Bloesch describes the spiritual nature of preaching well:

> Communication of the gospel involves not simply the imparting of information but the transmission of meaning and power. Unless the truth we present is appropriated by the understanding and received by the heart, it falls short of being effectively communicated. Full appropriation of the truth involves assimilation as well as commitment.[3]

Bloesch's description may help us distill a working definition: Preaching is "the transmission of meaning and power."

*true repentance comes in here*

The issue of power in preaching raises the question of how the Holy Spirit relates the divine work of inspiration of the Scripture and the filling of the preacher. We should exercise caution when describing the mystery of the Spirit's work. "The wind blows wherever it pleases. You hear its sound, but you cannot tell where it comes from or where it is going" (John 3:8). Nonetheless, it seems to me that there are at least three landing places for the preacher that are essential for spiritual power in preaching. These landing places are points in the preacher's inner life where the Spirit penetrates the preacher with living power—the imagination of the intellect, the conscience of the will, and the passion of the heart. To put it another way, the preacher's inner vision, moral confidence, and deep desire must be enlightened and focused for the preacher to be the instrument of the Holy Spirit for the congregation.

Regarding the preacher's inner vision, the Spirit works in the preacher to make the statements, descriptions, stories, and commands of Scripture move beyond words and abstractions so that they become living images in the mind of the preacher that create a vision of life as God intends it. Scripture itself is full of this spiritual work of intellectual imagination. Paul's reflection on Deuteronomy 25:4, "Do not muzzle an ox while it is treading out the grain," applies this seemingly small detail of life to the larger issue of financial support of Christian workers (1 Cor. 9:9). This imaginative use of Old Testament case law expands a simple statement of Scripture into a life-impacting description of an attitude of responding to all the good that others do for us. That response may appropriately be money or it may be simple gratitude, but response for the good done to us is an issue of imagination allowing God's truth to run through our lives. The Holy Spirit most likely will help a congregation "see" this truth when the preacher has seen it first.

The Spirit also uses the Word in the moral conscience of the preacher to make the Word personally penetrating and probing. Preaching targets the conscience, and a preacher's clear conscience is as important as a surgeon's clean hands. Paul's letters to the Corinthian church are full of allusions to the conscience, both Paul's and the Corinthians'. Paul is careful to emphasize that his clear conscience is not a matter of self-righteous superiority but a product of God's grace (2 Cor. 1:12). In other words, Paul's moral achievement does not give him the stance of the judgmental accuser. Rather, his own moral freedom as a repentant and forgiven sinner gives him the quality of spirit that can probe and challenge the conscience of his flock without causing needless offense that a stained conscience always produces in others.

Anything we preach must be applied to our own conscience first, and whatever conscience condemns must experience God's cleansing

sower of repentance comes in if you're not
glowing in His love
"Help me, show me an area of my life
that I don't glow w/ your love"
Jm 1:9
Fall on it real quick

"1 what is God showing us?   2d para
spiritual check up
ds msg is to you first, others second
   Ask Him  re, humility for me or someone else

des conforming us into the very image
   of God's Son; Pray as Jesus did
le are accountable to what we're doing
ray, be quiet, listen to God's Word
          p89  pathos
hat is spiritual msg from His Word
end time ᾱ God —
d, from His Spirit, knows what the people
eed.

so — no passion, no preaching
      goal:
P See† crucified, not the preacher
15 teaching penetrates

Defects the best out of you !

p.84 2d - causes dead to live again;
        the Word is alive in you

● <u>Believe</u> God's Word & keep moving
        Don't be afraid - pray the Word
        Your steps are ordered by the Lord
            He ordains it

spirit & We are the reforming church
Word - Breath & speech to each other
Exposition - p 85
    1 Preach text
    2 Never fret about what to preach

●

    ethos - p 86        Spend time c̄ God
    pathos - p 89

God equips you - you cannot fail,
God's Word is full of creative power

placing fear in people's heart is the devils dea
is manipulation & control
● Love of God in you will will them to
        obedience
We must be tempered in love
Your love s/b like steel, not cast iron
        (Bendable) ↑
when
preaching, use inspiration, not intimidation

grace before we can hope to preach for moral transformation in others. This Spirit-empowered conscience never claims or implies perfection or having "arrived" (cf. Phil. 3:12-13), but it freely admits being in the process of the transformation of grace. A cleansed conscience toward the past, moral sensitivity in the present, and the pursuit of holiness for the future constitute key weapons of grace in the arsenal of the servant of God's Word.

When the Spirit has worked deeply in the preacher's imagination and conscience, the deep desire of the heart is naturally affected. When the eye of faith "sees" God's truth (Heb. 11:1), and the conscience is made clean by the blood of Christ (Heb. 9:14), the heart overflows with desire for God's glory to be lived out in the lives of the pastor's flock. Just as the heart of a godly husband focuses exclusively on his wife, so the heart of a godly pastor focuses exclusively on God's glory expressed in the lives of his people. Passion comes from the joy and gratitude of grace experienced, the sorrow for sin that still destroys, and the hope of the greater glory of God that grace will yet reveal. When the Spirit of God penetrates the preacher with the Word of God in this way, the preacher is a Spirit-filled vessel primed and ready to be a servant of Christ with God's sovereign mighty power. We are wise to be cautious about expecting vague prayers over unprepared preachers to accomplish what God intends and what people need from Christian preaching. This deep penetration of the Word by the Spirit reflects the apostles' priority: "We will give our attention to prayer and the ministry of the word" (Acts 6:4). It is prayer that drives the Word into the preacher's imagination, conscience, and passion and creates the preparation for the ministry of the Word.

Not only is the Word's penetration of the preacher the work of the Spirit, but the penetration of the listener is His sovereign work as well. This sovereign, uncontrollable, and unpredictable work of the Holy Spirit in preaching is a sobering, thrilling, and urgent reality for the preacher that should drive him to pray for the flock—asking that when the Scriptures are preached, the Spirit will do His work of penetration. Techniques of communication and cultural realities will play a part in the humanity of effective preaching, but only the Holy Spirit's work will bring the gracious gift of repentance and faith to the listener. Calvin presses the work of the Spirit through to the very end of the work of preaching:

> For as God alone can properly bear witness to his own words, so these words will not obtain full credit in the hearts of men, until they are sealed by the inward testimony of the Spirit. The same Spirit, therefore, who spoke by the mouth of the prophets, must penetrate our hearts, in order to convince us that they faithfully delivered the message with which they were divinely intrusted.[4]

Humble dependence never leaves the preacher in the humanly impossible task of preaching with the goal of raising people out of spiritual death. But how does the divine authority of Scripture extend to the fallible words of the preacher? Is it too much to claim that when the preacher speaks, his words are the Word of God to the listening church? In a world appropriately skeptical of human authority, how do the words of fallen preachers relate to the flawless word from the Lord? John Leith draws a helpful analogy that touches on this mystery:

> The Holy Spirit uses the words of the preacher in the same manner that the Holy Spirit uses the water or the bread and wine as occasions for the very presence of God. In this sense the word of the preacher—indeed the word of a poor sermon—may become the very word of God. By the same token, the word of a brilliant sermon may simply be the word of a very clever preacher without being the word of God. The *Westminster Shorter Catechism* declared that the reading of the Bible, but especially the preaching of the word of God, is a means of God's grace.[5]

Henry Bullinger, the author of the *Second Helvetic Confession*, which asserted that "the preaching of the Word of God is the Word of God," offers a more carefully nuanced statement in a sermon on preaching:

Let us therefore beseech our Lord God to pour into our minds his Holy Spirit, by whose virtue the seed of God's Word may be quickened in our hearts, to the bringing forth of much fruit to the salvation of our souls, and the glory of God our Father.[6]

Rather than an absolutist view that equates all preaching of the Scriptures by fallible men, Bullinger helpfully draws on the organic process of the Word being given in Scripture infallibly by the Spirit and through preachers of the Word dynamically through the Spirit with His sovereign purpose and penetration maintained through the veil of its imperfect human instrument.

The joining of the Spirit to the Scriptures through the servant of the Word has several pivotal issues the preacher needs to consider.

## THE FOCUS OF PREACHING: THE CENTRALITY OF CHRIST

*For I resolved to know nothing while I was with you except Jesus Christ and him crucified.*

*—1 Cor. 2:2*

Christocentric proclamation is at the core of Christian preaching. Christ must be at the core of preaching both because of God's intention and because of human need. God has no other purpose than to bring glory to Himself through Christ, and people have no other ultimate solution for their problems than God's gracious provision of Christ. Because of the glaring needs of contemporary culture and because many show either disinterest or antagonism to "religious answers," many preachers have turned to "therapeutic" preaching that often inadequately diagnoses the problem and offers shallow remedies as solutions. No human need is without a gracious resolution in Christ, but many human needs may be explained and relieved without Christ. Such limited visions of pastoral care must be firmly rejected by the Christian preacher.

Historically biblical preaching has always been confident in the therapeutic power of Christ. But psychologically oriented preaching without a strong biblical framework and a Christ-centered resolution will be guilty of Jeremiah's charge that "they dress the wound of my people as though it were not serious" (Jer. 6:14). Moralism, which merely tells people that what they are doing is wrong and tells them several practical steps to take that will correct that wrong, falls far short of preaching Christ. Preaching isolated biblical texts as examples of how to live without placing each story in the stream that leads to Christ falls short of preaching Christ. Empathetic descriptions of human struggle and psychologically oriented solutions that do not dig deep into the need for God's wisdom and redemption is something less than preaching Christ.

The church has always believed that God intends to heal His people through preaching! Preaching without the purpose of healing the hearer through the person of Christ is not Christian preaching. Christ-centered preaching will always see the problem of the human condition as a need for wisdom and redemption, and the provision for both of these needs is always Jesus Christ, who is given to us by the Father and made real to us through the Holy Spirit.

The preacher who determines to confine himself to "Christ and him crucified" will find himself wonderfully focused. Christian preaching must always move to a vision of the beauty, power, and authority of Jesus Christ. If a sermon does not take its listeners to Christ, it shouldn't be preached as a Christian sermon. This discipline of focusing on Christ must constantly be the confidence that keeps the preacher's heart warm toward Christ and the anchor that keeps the preacher's mind from drifting away from Christ. The preacher is wise to write a statement on every sermon's worksheet stating specifically how this sermon portrays the person and work of Christ as God's provision for the need the sermon addresses. Every sermon should bring the preacher to ask how Christ is introduced and offered to the hearer. This unblinking focus on Christ will help the preacher stay centered on what this culture and each of its generations need at the core of life. Let others deal with the less central issues of life as they wish. These lesser matters should not be the concern of the Christian preacher.

At the same time, if a preacher determines to preach only Christ and His redeeming work, he will soon discover that his imagination begins to expand to grasp the greatness of Christ in new ways, for there is nothing in the universe that does not relate to Christ in some way. Rather than abandoning large areas of human concern to others, the preacher will find himself challenged to think in larger and deeper ways as he grasps the wonder of Christ who is Lord of all. Since the Lord Jesus Himself established the hermeneutical principle that all Scripture concerns Him, it is the first task of the preacher to discover that connection. It is the work of the preacher as the servant of the Spirit to lift up Christ so that the Spirit may draw the hearers to Christ. That is the one central goal of preaching. Preaching Christ is the dust of the ground from which God breathes the saving breath of life into the heart of sinful and dead humanity.

## The Fearlessness of Preaching: The Conviction of Faith

*It is written: "I believed; therefore I have spoken." With that same spirit of faith we also believe and therefore speak.*
                                                            —*2 Cor. 4:13*

Paul used a strange snippet from an obscure line of Psalm 116 to make a foundational statement about the nature of New Covenant preaching. It is worth working though the text to understand Paul's statement. Psalm 116 is a celebration of God's saving mercy and power. The psalmist had been in great danger: "the cords of death . . . the anguish of the grave . . . trouble, and sorrow" (v. 3) as well as "tears" and "stumbling" (v. 8) had been his companions. It was while he was facing all these terrifying threats that he came to this crisis: "I believed; therefore I said . . . 'All men are liars'" (vv. 10-11). These words strangely seem to intrude angry thoughts into a psalm of relief and gratitude. But Paul saw the psalmist's experience reflected in his own. Paul had described his own difficulties in serving his Lord: "We are hard pressed on every side, but not crushed; perplexed, but not in despair; persecuted, but not abandoned; struck down, but not destroyed. We always carry about in our body the death of Jesus, so that the life of Jesus may also be revealed in our body. . . . So then, death is at work in us, but life is at work in you" (2 Cor. 4:8-10, 12). In other words, Paul had paid a price for being faithful to Christ.

In the present atmosphere of spiritual confusion where much contemporary Christian ministry has mistakenly exchanged cultural immediacy for Christian rootedness without seeing where the end of that trajectory will lead, preaching can be an intimidating prospect. The danger of a market-driven approach to preaching is that the desire to avoid rejection either of the preacher or his message will corrupt the integrity of the preacher in subtle ways. Paul's reflection on Psalm 116 and his own experience gave him a fearless conviction that he had something he believed in so passionately that he must say it no matter what the consequences might be. People who make a difference take risks! And part of the risk for the preacher is that suffering is an inevitable part of gospel ministry. This fearlessness makes the preacher able to discern more effectively the difference between success and fruit. "Our gospel came to you not simply with words, but also with power, with the Holy Spirit and with deep conviction" (1 Thess. 1:5). Any preacher looking for a favorable cultural consensus that gives him acceptance will be sadly disappointed and will need to cry to God for this spirit of faith.

The book of Acts frequently describes the speech of the early church as "bold." This word has in it the idea of freedom of speech that conceals or passes over nothing because of fear. The ministry of the Holy Spirit brings deep conviction and gracious confidence that overcomes fear and is essential to preaching. Even those who are not aware of fearfulness in preaching need to reflect on this. Most, if not all of us, are afraid of something. The preacher who seems to be abrasive and insensitive in his preaching may be covering a deep fountain of inner fear that hinders the spirit of faith and Spirit-given boldness. John Reed offers a fascinating description of what happens when a person speaks without the spirit of faith.

> A Christian psychologist, Frank Wichern, once told me that he could tell whether a client was lying to him in a counseling session. When a person was lying the counselor couldn't see a picture of the event being related in his head. If the experience being related actually happened the picture of the event appeared on the visual screen in the mind of the psychologist.[7]

Reed goes on to describe an experience in a public speaking course when a woman was reading a very emotionally impacting poem. He was deeply moved until about two-thirds of the way through the poem, and then his mind went blank and he could no longer engage with the poem. The entire class later related they had the same experience. When the woman was asked what she had experienced at that moment, she explained that because the poem was beginning to overcome her own emotions, she "turned it off" inside although she continued to read without any outward change. Her inner distance impacted all her hearers. When fear or uncertainty or inner confusion clouds our own inner vision, the effect will be sensed if not understood by our listeners. Fearless conviction that grips our hearts is an indispensable quality if we hope to engage the hearts of our listeners.

There is another side of this fearless conviction of faith, and we need to hold it in redemptive tension in our preaching.

## THE FRIENDLINESS OF PREACHING: THE COMPASSION OF SERVANTHOOD

*For we do not preach ourselves, but Jesus Christ as Lord, and ourselves as your servants for Jesus' sake.*

—*2 Cor. 4:5*

Postmodernity has planted pluralism deeply and firmly into the mind of today's listeners. Conflicting messages no longer trouble people as they once did. They expect them and resist those who require loyalty to one view to the exclusion of another. The postmodern listener has great tolerance for conflicting messages so long as the messenger has no expectation that the hearer will accept the message for himself. The philosophical foundations of postmodernity conceive all language to be a play for power. While communication that entertains does not appear to create resistance and resentment, any serious effort to impact a hearer's belief or way of life does not generally find the same level of acceptance. This resistance to an authoritative and exclusive message is not new in the history of Christian preaching, but today it has a new intensity and extent. It is the task of the preacher to seek the help of God to understand what is behind this wall of resistance and at the same time give room for the Holy Spirit to do His unique convicting work concerning sin, righteousness, and judgment (John 16:8-11).

At the same time the preacher, being dependent on the Holy Spirit, needs to see beyond the skeptical resistance to absolute truth to the underlying brokenness this resistance to God's reality has produced. Cornelius Plantinga, Jr. describes the postmodern generation as people who are living off their disinheritance, and they commonly show it by blending detachment and longing.[8] Dealing with this ambivalence is the great work of the preacher. Overcoming the detachment and nurturing the longing is the preacher's mission, and it requires nothing less than the grace of God working in the preacher to accomplish this. David Mills understands the present postmodern mood as that of "domesticated despair."[9] He describes an atmosphere of little hope, little confidence that life will reveal goodness and meaning. But rather than raging against such a bleak landscape, this generation has made some kind of skeptical peace with it.

That skepticism accounts for much of the dark humor in our entertainment culture. The preacher needs to feel the depth of this disenchantment and allow the shape of that inner world of unbelief and ignorance of God to mark his imagination and thought. A person who does not care about such a bleak inner world will not represent God faithfully to this generation. Jesus did not withhold Himself from people like this because "when he saw the crowds, he had compassion on them, because they were harassed and helpless, like sheep without a shepherd" (Matt. 9:36). Understanding the inner world of such a life to the point of being able to describe it imaginatively is a key to communicating Christ's truth with compassion to our culture.

I have been struck by a comment I once read from Helmut Thielicke on Charles Spurgeon. Thielicke had significant theological differences with Spurgeon, but he was powerfully drawn to his sermons. Thielicke simply said Spurgeon was no Savonarola. By that I take it to mean that while Spurgeon preached to the lower classes of a rather decadent city, he did so without a spirit of anger and condemnation. In other words, as a preacher he was friendly. He demonstrated the spirit of Christ, who was called "the friend of sinners." It is easy to rail against the sin and corruption in society today. It is even easier for the preacher to denounce the worldliness of the professing church. But the climate of our times calls for a deeper view of the failed lives around us. A thoughtful preacher with a carefully built biblical worldview and clear theological convictions will find it tempting to denounce our sinful society and the corruption of the church with the weak spiritual formation that marks the typical evangelical congregation. But if the preacher is to speak to these needs in the spirit of fearless faith, he must first love his people and be thoughtful in expressing godly goodwill and an attitude of generosity toward them. Humility and empathy are Christlike characteristics that God's Spirit will use to build a bridge of life toward the hearer. The message of Jesus Christ as Lord should always be accompanied by an authentic life revealing the messenger to be the hearer's servant for Jesus' sake.

## THE FRAMEWORK OF PREACHING: THE COMPASS OF THE STORY

*For I have not hesitated to proclaim to you the whole will of God.*

—*Acts 20:27*

Paul was not an obscurantist. He never lost sight of the forest because he could only see the tree he was dealing with at the moment. Our postmodern culture is in desperate need of seeing the forest, and that forest is "the whole will of God" (Acts 20:27). In other words, preaching today needs to be more theologically rooted and explicit than ever. Contemporary prejudice against the exclusive and authoritative message of Christ can best be addressed by helping people see the larger perspective of God's revealed truth and by explaining faithfully in each sermon how a particular Scripture or topic fits into the larger picture. Theological preaching does not mean that we begin with and emphasize unknown or technical terms, but it does mean that the preacher needs to develop and grasp a comprehensive theological framework by which he helps his hearers visualize and organize the mass of biblical preaching they hear.

The need for establishing the compass of the biblical story into a meaningful framework is not new to the church and this present culture. For years Christian colleges have been testing their incoming students from evangelical churches to measure the level of Bible knowledge they bring to their collegiate studies. The results are becoming more and more discouraging even as the church is spending more and more money, creativity, and effort to teach the next generation. Yet the most basic facts of Bible knowledge and the most elemental issues of theological understanding continue to elude the youth who have been nurtured in our churches. I suggest that the problem is a lack of clear mental organization and imagination in seeing how all the elements of biblical truth fit together.

As strange as it may seem, the problem partly is to be found in the emphasis on expository preaching that has so strongly marked America's more highly respected pulpits. Preaching the biblical text without a theological compass will often fail not only to be faithful to the Christocentric nature of the Bible, but it may also give the hearer no idea how the teaching of a particular text fits into the larger framework of the Christian faith. The further urgency of preaching a clear Christian biblical and theological worldview is found in the loss of confidence that there is a "big picture" or a "Great Story" through which all of life can be understood. The Christian preacher needs to grasp the philosophical concept of metanarrative as a foundational human need to find meaning and significance. The human mind and heart longs for story so deeply that we love to hear stories and enter into them even when we know they aren't true. So long as there is a shred of meaning or the thrill of adventure or the warmth of relationships or the suspense of the outcome, people are drawn to stories.

The great message of the Christian faith is that God has spoken and has told us as much of His story as we can comprehend. He is committed by His Word and Spirit to help us exchange our impoverished self-made stories for the glorious story of His Good News in Jesus Christ. Preaching that keeps giving descriptive details that fill in more and more of the Story will draw hungry Spirit-attracted hearts to God's truth. A carefully chosen catalog of theological concepts can form a framework upon which both the preacher and the hearers can hang the bits and pieces of biblical preaching. Such a framework is like a large piece of Velcro that will hold each sermon in the appropriate place in the listener's mind. Clarity of these pieces with vivid description of how these pieces are experienced in life will serve to build the faith vision of the congregation.

This is a wonderful time to be preaching God's Word to people. Preaching is the great work that encompasses teaching, encouraging, convicting, and correcting for a culture in great need. With all of postmodernity's skepticism, Jesus Christ still holds a magnetic fascination for people. Courage and compassion combined with a clear grasp of the Great Story come together as the means by which God will graciously give His Spirit to shine the light of the knowledge of His glory in Christ into the hearts of hearers today.

Peter Adam says it well:

> Perhaps the best way of describing it is to say that when human beings explain the Word of God, preach it, teach it, and urge people to accept it, then the Word of God achieves its purpose, and this is one of the normal ways in which God brings his Word to human beings. It is perhaps helpful to describe this in terms of the work of the Spirit. We must assert that the Spirit was involved in the creation of the Word of God, that is, Scripture. For Scripture is inspired by God (2 Timothy 3:16), and "no prophecy ever came by human will, but men and women moved by the Holy Spirit spoke from God" (2 Peter 1:21). We must also recognize the work of the Spirit in the activity of the preacher, and the activity of the Spirit in the minds, hearts and wills of the hearers. The Scripture itself is a product of the Spirit, and when the Spirit works in the preacher and in the hearers, the words of God are mediated and bear fruit in the lives of those who hear.[10]

Is preaching still important? It continues to be the Spirit-empowered way for faith to be passed from one generation to the next until Christ has built His Church and all creation sings of the glory of God's presence that fills it. Preach the Word, for God entrusts His cosmic purpose to it.

NOTES

1  A packing advertisement for the Bose Corporation, Framingham, Massachusetts.

2  Frederick Dale Bruner, *A Theology of the Holy Spirit: The Pentecostal Experience and the New Testament Witness* (Eugene, OR: Wipf and Stock Publishers, 1998), p. 165.

3  Donald Bloesch, *A Theology of Word & Spirit* (Downers Grove, IL: InterVarsity, 1992), p. 223.

4  John Calvin, *Institutes of the Christian Religion*, Vol. I, trans. Henry Beveridge (Grand Rapids, MI: Eerdmans, n.d.), p. 72.

5  John H. Leith, *Basic Christian Doctrine* (Louisville: Westminster/John Knox Press, 1993), p. 260.

6  See *The Decades of Henry Bullinger*, ed. Thomas Harding (Cambridge, MA: Cambridge University Press, 1849), pp. 69-70.

7  John Reed, "Visualizing the Big Idea," in *The Big Idea of Biblical Preaching*, eds. Keith Wilhite and Scott M. Gibson (Grand Rapids, MI: Baker, 1998), p. 150.

8  Cornelius Plantinga, Jr., "Dancing the Edge of Mystery," in *Books and Culture*, September/October 1999, p. 16.

9  David Mills, "Imaginative Orthodoxy," in *Touchstone*, November/December 1999, p. 30.

10  Peter Adam, *Speaking God's Words: A Practical Theology of Expository Preaching* (Downers Grove, IL: InterVarsity Press, 1996), p. 118.

# 7

---

# LEADING THE CHURCH IN
# GOD-CENTERED WORSHIP:

## The Pastoral Role

■

Jerry Marcellino

When a minister discovers the glorious truth of God's absolute sovereignty and its practical implications for all areas of life, other doctrines, as never before, seem to come alive and take on a beautifully different hue. Such foundational doctrines as Christ's imputed righteousness to the lost sinner's account and the evangelical act of offering true worth-ship[1] to the living God become more like the minister's long-lost friends. These new friends are really, of course, nothing more than a fresh conviction of God and His Word that soon move the minister to more joyful expressions of love and praise toward God. As a result, these emerging religious affections in his life, which are flowing freely from a much deeper apprehension of doctrines he has really always held, become his most precious ongoing experiential possessions. The minister has now come to know God as truly both transcendent and immanent toward His children, as both glorious in grandeur and graciously intimate with his beloved (Ps. 113; Prov. 3:32). God-sent friends like these doctrines are no better conveyed to us in Scripture than in the words of King David in Psalm 51:

> *Save me from bloodguilt, O God, the God who saves me, and my tongue will sing of your righteousness. O LORD, open my lips, and my mouth will declare your praise.*
>
> —*vv. 14-15*

In this brief portion of Scripture, which is an unveiling of David's heart upon the occasion of his repentance for his immoral actions with Bathsheba, we learn of the inseparable union of both doctrine and devotion.[2] The psalmist's few words of petition reveal to us that the foundation of David's joyful singing and declarative praise (or his God-centered worship) was his awesome contemplation of and joyful response to God for making him the recipient of Christ's own righteousness (Rom. 1:16-17; 2 Cor. 5:21). This joyful response is to be the believer's continuous spiritual response to the living God throughout the whole of his life. True worship, then, is our grateful response to all that God is and has become to us in Christ. John MacArthur has aptly put it this way: "Worship is all that we are, reacting to all that God is." Is this not what the writer of Hebrews was saying in chapter 13 of that epistle?

> Through Jesus, therefore, let us continually offer to God a sacrifice of praise—the fruit of lips that confess his name. And do not forget to do good and to share with others, for with such sacrifices God is pleased.
>
> —vv. 15-16

Notice how this wonderful passage further contributes to our thinking. We learn that the words "through Jesus" and "sacrifice of praise" are the basis for our responding to God with thanksgiving and adoration. In addition, this response to God (worship) produces a life that is marked by worship ("with such sacrifices God is pleased"). May God be pleased to grant us such tokens of His grace in enabling us to live the whole of our lives predominantly in this blessed way.

## WISDOM IN REFORMATION

The way to begin this reformation process of leading our churches into such a God-centered climate and culture[3] is not by an immediate editorial assault upon our church's worship bulletin. Neither should we begin by issuing a memo to our worship leader and our various choir members and/or musical ensembles for the purpose of exhorting them about their corrupt habit of offering God strange fire. Rather, we must begin this effort of biblical reform by rethinking why we suddenly desire such God-honoring worship in our church. In other words, we must ask ourselves why we believe such reforms are now necessary in the life of our particular flock. Hopefully our desires for these changes are motivated by clear scriptural reasons (1 Tim. 3:15), not by our desire to be accepted by other reformed ministers as truly reformed men.[4]

Therefore, leading our flocks in the offering of true worship to the living God, in both spirit and truth (John 4:24), with Christ's gathered church, is surely to be the aim of every authentic minister of the new covenant (2 Cor. 3:6). Such a minister is continuously marked by setting before his heart the salvation of lost sinners and the maturation of Christ's sheep, especially on each Lord's Day, for the purpose of building a God-centered climate and culture. Recently I had the privilege of reading a Third-World missionary church planter's prayer letter that echoed similar aims: ". . . longing for a God-centered, Christ-exalting, vibrant Biblical church . . . may we go on to become not merely a legally recognized church, but one recognized in heaven for consistently worshiping God in spirit and truth!"

As a result, leading your church toward a more God-centered worship service is easier said than done. Great patience with God's people and much prayer, coupled with sound and pertinent exposition, must be your overall general guiding rules for such reformation. There are numerous reasons for this approach, and the purpose of this chapter is to discuss them and then point the way ahead.

## We Were Created to Worship

Let us begin, then, with a brief overview of the scriptural understanding that God has made all human beings with a capacity for offering worth-ship to someone or something (Eccl. 3:11). This capacity is not at all satisfied with a contemplation of animate life here on earth. Man has an innate gnawing and continuous longing to know beyond what he can see with his naked eye. Augustine aptly described this yearning within man when he said, "Man is restless, until he finds rest in Thee."

Or as Bob Dylan once put it, "You gotta serve somebody." Now, when this innate capacity in a human being begins to gradually flower out of his totally depraved nature and unconverted state (Ps. 51:5; 58:3; John 3:19-21; Eph. 2:1-3), we begin to understand more clearly the origins of what Paul was describing when he penned these words in Romans:

> For although they knew God, they neither glorified him as God nor gave thanks to him, but their thinking became futile and their foolish hearts were darkened. Although they claimed to be wise, they became fools and exchanged the glory of the immortal God for images made to look like mortal man and birds and animals and reptiles. Therefore God gave them over in the sinful desires of their hearts to sexual impurity for the degrading of their bodies with one another. They exchanged the truth of God for a lie, and worshiped and served created things rather than the Creator—who is forever praised. Amen.
>
> —1:21-25

This age-old practice of exchanging the truth of God for a lie is not common among the irreligious alone. A brief perusal of Romans 2:1-16, and in particular verses 17 and following of that same chapter, reveal to us just the opposite. In fact, the latter reminds us that the original practitioners of this dark art were the religious Jews of Israel's wilderness wandering (Exod. 32), the parents of those whom Isaiah prophesied against in Isaiah 1:10-17, whose descendants Paul later addressed in Romans 2. Their posterity must now hear a word from us.

So then, when worldliness begins to infiltrate the church (as the Bible and history have so sadly testified to us), it's not surprising that its grievous offspring—man-made religion and its man-centered theology—begin to produce a type of worship that in time erodes, corrupts, and ultimately eliminates any vestiges of God-centered worship that had previously existed.⑤ This biblically unacceptable worship soon begins to reign supreme in the church, and it must be addressed by us, as our Lord once confronted it in his own day, as the following passage so clearly reveals: "They worship me in vain; their teachings are but rules taught by men" (Matt. 15:9). When we observe that this biblically unacceptable worship, so void of purpose as the original language indicates,[6] is becoming clearly embraced, let us unmistakably understand that all biblical authority in that particular realm has probably been lost. At such times ministers must wisely expose such departures from biblical truth and the subsequent vain worship and then begin to take the necessarily wise and scripturally accommodating steps toward reformation in leading their congregations toward God-centered worship.[7] One recent movement of reformation has authored the following incisive words in its *Cambridge Declaration*, which specifically addresses our present concern:

> The loss of God's centrality in the life of today's church is common and lamentable. It is the loss that allows us to transform *worship* into entertainment, gospel preaching into marketing, believing into technique, being good into feeling good about ourselves, and faithfulness into being successful. . . . We must focus on God in our *worship*, rather than the satisfaction of our personal needs. God is sovereign in *worship*; we are not. Our concern must be for God's kingdom, not our own empires, popularity or success.[8]

Further, the following words from Hebrews 10:19-22 remind us that such necessary reforms are worthy of our efforts:

> *Therefore, brothers, since we have confidence to enter the Most Holy Place by the blood of Jesus, by a new and living way opened for us through the curtain, that is, his body, and since we have a great priest over the house of God, let us draw near to God with a sincere heart in full assurance of faith, having our hearts sprinkled to cleanse us from a guilty conscience and having our bodies washed with pure water.*

God has called us to lead His people away from a grievous man-centered theology and its partner, an empty, shallow, man-centered worship. Such reforms must begin with us. The first step toward leading your church in God-centered worship is to look at yourself.

Are you a man of the Word? Is your personal life and ministry God-centered? Your example for good or bad will be followed by God's people.

## THE MAN OF GOD

Many centuries ago in ancient Israel, God's prophet Hosea pointed out to the people of God a wise maxim that must not go unheeded by any modern-day ministerial reformer. He said in Hosea 4:9, "And it will be: Like people, like priests. I will punish both of them for their ways and repay them for their deeds." The spiritual rule to apprehend at this point is that if the leadership in a local church goes astray, many will usually follow. In other words, if a minister is a man-pleaser, concerned about the approval of men (John 5:44; 12:43; Gal. 1:10; 1 Thess. 2:4), his congregation will be also with its attendant worship service. Likewise, when the leadership is faithful to its calling, the people usually follow after its example in the same manner. This is why the apostle Paul stated the following words in 1 Timothy 4:16 so soberly: "Watch your life and doctrine closely. Persevere in them, because if you do, you will save both yourself and your hearers." Further, this is why Peter echoed similar words in 1 Peter 5:3: "Not lording it over those entrusted to you, but being examples to the flock." Being scriptural examples to the flock is vital to its spiritual health. How you live personally, coupled with the content of your ministry publicly, will impact your people more than ministers often realize. As one minister stated years ago, "The minister's life is the life of his ministry." If you have children, you can more easily understand what I am driving at. Our children so often parrot more of their parents' ways than we really desire—both good and bad traits. The church in many ways is no different. Therefore, we must labor to so live before our flock that what they predominantly observe is a life that is marked by continuously offering true worth-ship to the living God.

In other words, aiming to model a truly biblical example of leadership must mark the true minister of our Lord Jesus Christ. Why? Because Christ's sheep have been fitted by Him to follow the spiritual conduct of His under-shepherds (Heb. 13:7). As a result, we must

*Gal 2:20* — Keep eye on Jesus / Stay in His presence

Be Jesus' pastor, ambassador

understand that a pastor's fitness to lead Christ's church does not begin and end with his primary duties of the pulpit and in overseeing the flock, but rather manifests itself in many of the secondary areas of his ministerial responsibilities, and chief among them is his leadership role in the weekly planning of God-centered worship services.[9] So his life and ministry play both a significant and an integral role in the formation of the spiritual climate and culture of his congregation. This means that the ministries of his flock, as the years go by, will essentially reflect eventually what he is both in and out of the pulpit. In addition, the corporate worship that flows out of and surrounds his ministry will inevitably sing the same song as both the pulpit and various ministries of his particular flock. So whether the pastor is musically inclined, trained, or inept, he cannot divorce himself from the ongoing responsibility of being a worship reformer.[10] His spiritual gifts and graces are his foundational reforming tools for leading Christ's church on the path toward God-centered worship.

## THE WORD OF GOD

Be a man/woman of the Word so sheep will follow

The man of God is to be first and foremost a man of the Word. Word-centeredness or its lack inevitably plays the most significant role in a church moving toward or away from a God-centered worship climate and culture. This is why the apostle Paul left Timothy with these final exhortations in 2 Timothy: Feeling pressure? You are on your own in the flesh

> In the presence of God and of Christ Jesus, who will judge the living and the dead, and in view of his appearing and his kingdom, I give you this charge: Preach the Word; be prepared in season and out of season; correct, rebuke and encourage—with great patience and careful instruction. For the time will come when men will not put up with sound doctrine. Instead, to suit their own desires, they will gather around them a great number of teachers to say what their itching ears want to hear. They will turn their ears away from the truth and turn aside to myths. But you, keep your head in all situations, endure hardship, do the work of an evangelist, discharge all the duties of your ministry.
>
> —4:1-5

allow time for worship

A minister who preaches the Word will do the work of an evangelist and thereby fulfill his ministry. His ministry will inevitably see men bow the knee because the end of the Gospel is worship. The Gospel makes pagans and heathens into worshipers (Ps. 96:9). This is the language of Psalm 84:4, "Blessed are those who dwell in your house; they are ever praising you." Therefore, knowing God is to worship Him (John 4:23). Being a Christian is to live a life of offering true worth-ship to the living God, putting no confidence in the flesh (Phil. 3:3). Romans 12:1-2 sums up this thought:   *His power*

> *Therefore, I urge you, brothers, in view of God's mercy, to offer your bodies as living sacrifices, holy and pleasing to God—this is your spiritual act of worship. Do not conform any longer to the pattern of this world, but be transformed by the renewing of your mind. Then you will be able to test and approve what God's will is—his good, pleasing and perfect will.*

Thus, as the pastor faithfully proclaims God's Word week in and week out, month after month, year after year, the complexion of his flock in due time, because of this Word-centeredness, begins to eventually reflect a God-centeredness in its corporate worship. The believers eventually become more Word-centered in their individual lives and therefore become more God-centered in their offering of true worth-ship to the living God. Note how Colossians 3:16 so clearly supports this truth: "Let the word of Christ dwell in you richly as you teach and admonish one another with all wisdom, and as you sing psalms, hymns and spiritual songs with gratitude in your hearts to God."

When the Word of Christ dwells in you richly, singing praise to God from the heart will eventually follow. True worship, at its most basic level, is seen to be our praise-filled response to a correct scriptural portrayal of God and His salvific work through His Son, Jesus Christ. This is what our Lord meant when He spoke about worshiping God the Father in spirit and truth (John 4:24)—worship that is neither all head and no heart, nor all heart and no head, but rather all head and all heart. Additionally, John tells us in that glorious chapter that the reason they are true worshipers is because God has sought and

*[handwritten margin notes: "awesome task / tremendous charge", "need to be in presence of God no matter what", "Prioritize / Simplify lives"]*

found them (v. 23; cf. Luke 15:1-7)! God has sought them through His Word—His Word faithfully proclaimed—and found them![11] The Welsh Baptist preacher Geoffrey Thomas elucidated this for us when he said, "When there have been great awakenings and multitudes of people brought to worship and adore God it has been under preaching that has told them clearly of their plight."[12] Such worship is essentially vertical and reverent (Eccl. 5:1-7). This church climate and culture is a living (Matt. 4:4), nourishing (1 Pet. 2:2), equipping (Eph. 4:11-16), and sanctifying (John 17:17) environment. Such worshipers are eager for (Acts 17:11) and responsible (1 Thess. 5:21) and submissive (Heb. 13:17) to the Word of God. This kind of a climate and culture always proves itself to be a worshiping community (Acts 18:11-13) that has a growing desire to be less concerned with what effect corporate worship services have on themselves and more concerned with what effect they have on God.[13]

Oh, brethren, God is seeking true worshipers! Do our worship services reflect that we are spiritually and truly seeking to worship Him alone? Such reforms are not the work of one man. There is wisdom in a multitude of counselors (Prov. 15:22; 24:6), and two are always better than one (Eccl. 4:9). This is why God in His wisdom has appointed that there be a plurality of spiritually qualified overseers in every church (Titus 1:5-9) who will lead Christ's sheep toward God-centered worship.

*[handwritten margin note: "Jesus; I always do what I see my Father does"]*

## THE MEN OF GOD

The pastor is not an island to himself! He is a leader among equals within the elder body. He is responsible to train his coleaders to understand what true worship is and then assist them in the implementation of a God-centered, scripturally-regulated, edification-oriented corporate worship service each time Christ's flock gathers, especially on the Lord's Day. This foundational approach toward leading your church in God-centered worship cannot be ignored. The proverbial saying, "Do not put the cart before the horse" cannot be overestimated here. Unless a pastor gains the hearts and consciences of his coleaders first as he tries to move their worship in a God-centered direction, almost all efforts that attempt to move one's worship services in such a direction will soon face sure opposition—if not by the leadership outright, assuredly by the congregation forthrightly. We must see the importance of the leadership of any evangelical church as being of one mind in its doctrine, methodology, and ministry. They must be, in actuality and before God's people, as one inseparable union of conviction about how Christ is presently leading their particular flock (Phil. 1:27).

Recently I read the bulletin of a church that is known for this type of leadership, and the following citation, approved by them for that printing, evidences this: "Out of reverence for the Lord and respect for those ministering to us, please arrive on time—ready for worship—so that everyone may benefit from all the Lord has prepared." Obviously this leadership had arrived at a unified position. The reason some leaders are able to take such action is because they are often with Christ's sheep (2 Cor. 12:15), that they might know well the condition of their flocks (Prov. 27:23). This enables them to teach them as they are able to hear the Word (Mark 4:33). In so doing they act wisely, not forgetting the typical makeup of most sheep (1 Thess. 5:14), and therefore aim patiently to labor among them for that sweet joy that comes to every child of God when he worships the living God in spirit and in truth (2 Cor. 1:24).

Now, this is not an easy task, and considering the diverse makeup of a typical congregation, much prayer as to how this end is to be realized must direct the leadership of every local church. As prayer and wisdom are operative and applied, volitional efforts beyond the preaching and teaching ministries of a particular church must also be pursued. Chief among these efforts must be a proper application of the 2 Timothy 2:2 principle—that is, the reproducing of themselves in the midst of the congregation. Hear Paul's words in this crucial text: "And the things you have heard me say in the presence of many witnesses entrust to reliable men who will also be qualified to teach others."

## THE PEOPLE OF GOD

As the pastor and the leadership of a local church are faithful to both model and proclaim biblical Christianity, God's people are soon in the

*Eph 4:11   what Paul meant*

process of being equipped for faithful service both to God and to one another. This is what Paul intended when he wrote in Ephesians 4:11-12, "It was he who gave some to be apostles, some to be prophets, some to be evangelists, and some to be pastors and teachers, to prepare God's people for works of service, so that the body of Christ may be built up." When God's people are being scripturally fed and led and are part of a growing church climate and culture that is increasingly Word-centered and thereby more God-centered, they want more of what God wants. They learn to think God's thoughts after Him. They desire more and more to conform to what God's Word has said about any area of their lives. This even applies to fresh evaluation of their church's worship services.

However, to equip our brethren to think more clearly about this tender matter of public worship and, in particular, to ask themselves if theirs is God-centered, we must begin by instructing them about the necessity of their personal heart preparation for the Lord's Day. We must teach God's people that it is vanity to come to God's house with a flippant and unprepared heart (Eccl. 5:1-7). They must understand that God is to be treated as holy by all who come near to him (Lev. 10:3). Further, they must be instructed that their church's worship must neither be man-centered, entertainment-driven, out-of-control, happy-clappy-slappy, nor, on the other side of the spectrum, dull, flat, or lifeless. Why? Because we are to "be thankful, and so worship God acceptably with reverence and awe, for our 'God is a consuming fire'" (Heb. 12:28-29).

In addition, we must teach God's people to discipline their minds in worship (2 Cor. 10:5), so that wandering thoughts will not disrupt them during their worship. However, if such thoughts do invade their worship, we must teach them that their response must be, "Praise the LORD, O my soul; all my inmost being, praise his holy name" (Ps. 103:1; see also Phil. 4:4). Finally, we must faithfully instruct the whole assembly on how to implement and maintain daily private (Ps. 5:3; 90:14a) and family (Josh. 24:15)[14] worship times in their homes. In so doing, we will teach them that their preparation for the next Lord's Day begins Monday morning and continues on throughout their week, in both private and family worship. One of the many great ways that daily family worship benefits public worship is in helping God's people to sing out with joy. A mark of a congregation's God-centeredness in public worship is how they sing from the heart with gusto.(15)

Let us never forget that where these spiritual disciplines are nonexistent or halfheartedly applied during the week, that congregation has learned to turn Sunday morning worship on and off! Of course, this is not worship at all but is none other than Sunday morning Christianity, at best. This is a frightening state for any church to find itself in. Finally, it can also be said that where God's people sing as they ought, they also attend to God in their worship as they ought. This is the powerful reminder that we receive when we read 1 Corinthians 14:24-25:

> *But if an unbeliever or someone who does not understand comes in while everybody is prophesying, he will be convinced by all that he is a sinner and will be judged by all, and the secrets of his heart will be laid bare. So he will fall down and worship God, exclaiming, "God is really among you!"*

May God help us to lead our congregations to such God-centered worship that not only our visitors but all who regularly attend our services in an unconverted state may fall down and worship God!

## THE WORSHIP OF GOD

With the foundation of a Word- and God-centered environment laid, and spiritual credibility having been earned, the minister may now attach the cart to the horse. That is, he now has a platform from which to more earnestly address the delicate matter of touching the typical elements to be found in any given church's worship services. Again, let us be much in prayer at this juncture.

*Aiming for a higher standard.* The following words of the ancient Greek philosopher Plato must necessarily be considered: "Let me write the songs for a nation, and I care not who makes its laws." This wise maxim is not only true for our own country, but also for Christ's holy nation (1 Pet. 2:9; cf. Matt. 21:43). That is, when we begin to aim for

*Goal - Keeps eyes on Jesus + worship God*

*Praising - chains fall off deliverance occurs*

a higher standard in our worship, we must not forget that our people are subject to all kinds of music in our American culture, as well as in our Christian subculture, which has caused them to adopt various tastes both good and not so good. Having said this, I am not saying that a number of good worship choruses did not come out of the Jesus folk-music movement of the 1960s; however, multitudes of those songs are better forgotten. In the same way, during the Reformation an estimated 100,000 hymns were written, out of which approximately 500 remain in hymnal use in our day.[16] In seeking to bring reform to the contemporary Christian music industry, the source for much of the material that churches are using today, pastor and music artist Steve Camp has outlined nine extremely hopeful, nonnegotiable guidelines[17] for doing God's work His way and according to His Word:

1) To produce an august view of God and do all to his glory.

2) To proclaim the authority of Scripture.

3) To pursue the accountability of the local church.

4) To protect the affections of our lives.

5) To do all things in the power of the anointing—The Holy Spirit.

6) To purpose to not partner in the advancement of the gospel with the unbelieving world.

7) To purpose to be above reproach in all business activity.

8) To make our products available, unrestricted solely by financial viability.

9) To partner with Christian artists in assisting them to fulfill their God-given duty and calling in the Arts.

Now, I realize that these efforts (and many more I have not cited[18]) of reforming an industry that greatly impacts our people are very encouraging, but obviously they are not the final answer for leading our churches in God-centered worship. Nevertheless, we can see that the standard must be raised. We must aim to do so. God and His people are worth pursuing such an aim! Let's take, then, an even sharper aim at this goal with the following four categories for our consideration.

*Aiming for a regulative principle.* Ernie Reisinger has said, "One of the things that will soon appear in any reformation of the church is some changes in worship and witness. When these changes begin to take place there will be some differences among good men who agree on the fundamental doctrines of Christianity."[19] This statement is especially true in regard to the regulative principle of worship. I am not aware of any true evangelical who would say that he desires to worship in his church contrary to the Word of God. All believers would agree that the written Word of God is sufficient to regulate their public worship. However, what they find in Scripture to justify their practices is as varied as the countless facets of prisms on a chandelier. How can we find the way ahead in this labyrinth? Let us begin by defining terms as the Reformers originally defined them when they spoke in terms of the regulative principle and the normative principle. The latter taught that if Scripture does not forbid it, it is allowed. The former said, in essence, that the only proper way to worship God is as He has commanded, instructed, and prescribed in His Word.

There is no problem with this definition of the regulative principle (especially if you add "supported" after "prescribed"). However, we must realize that it is easier to state this principle than to apply it. This is where the debate rages—in its detailed application. So what do we see in Scripture about New Covenant worship? We see that it clearly has seven elements to it: preaching/teaching the Word of God; singing psalms, hymns, and spiritual songs; sharing testimony; prayer of all types; baptism of professors/confessors; communion of the saints; and the offering of tithes and gifts. The sticky part in this debate has really centered on only one of those elements—the singing of psalms, hymns, and spiritual songs. Let us now look at how we can improve this element.

*Aiming for better lyrical content.* Our concern here is to communicate biblical truth. Why? Because if worship is our response to a correct scriptural portrayal of God, then we must be concerned that our lyrics reflect doctrinal and theological truth. Are our words clearly understood as they are set to music? Oh, brethren, they must be! Calvin was correct when he said, "Only pure doctrine can guide us to true worship." Therefore, do our lyrics adhere to biblical doctrine, or are they fuzzy and feely? Evaluate the lyrics of every hymn or chorus that your congregation is to sing. This responsibility is also interconnected with your call to feed the flock. Finally, such lyrics must not be drowned out by the music—they should be heard clearly. Our music, then, must cooperate with our doctrinally clear lyrics.

*Aiming for more God-centered music styles.* The area of public worship with its element of music styles is not an untouchable area in the work of reformation, even though it might still be the most powerfully delicate area in any local church anywhere on this globe. Martin Luther demonstrated that he understood the power that music has to be greatly used for the good of God's people when he said:

> . . . next to the Word of God, music deserves the highest praise . . . whether you wish to comfort the sad, to terrify the happy, to encourage the despairing, to humble the proud, to calm the passionate, or to appease those full of hate—and who could number all these masters of the human heart, namely, the emotions, inclinations and affections that impel men to evil or good?—What more effective means than music could you find?[20]

The best way to help God's people in this vital area is to ask ourselves two questions: Does our music cooperate with the words in making an artistic whole? Is our music, in all its elements (rhythm, harmony, melody, and style in general) essentially free of strong worldly associations?[21] I understand that this will not be an easy thing to ascertain. Further, we must not simply say that all musical forms other than the traditional styles played on a piano and organ are taboo in our church. We must avoid cultural bigotry here.[22] A final question: Does the combination of music and words in our hymns and choruses conform to the "true . . . noble . . . right . . . pure . . . lovely . . . admirable . . . excellent . . . praiseworthy" criteria of Philippians 4:8?[23] May God grant us music ministries that are not predicated upon fleshly enjoyment, but upon our people's need to grow into the likeness of Jesus.[24]

*Aiming for more God-centered worship services.*[25] The end of all our prayers and labors toward God-centered worship in our churches will be worship that is shot through with form and freedom—God-centered form and thoughtful structure as the Scripture commands us (1 Cor. 14:33; 1 Tim. 3:15), coupled with bright, non-stuffy freedom

(2 Cor. 3:17; Gal. 5:1, 13)—the freedom to compose the seven elements of New Covenant worship in a variety of ways. This freedom will also allow for more congregational participation than many would sadly grant today. Such congregational freedom was a part of Calvin's worship in Geneva. Calvin scholar Robert Kingdon, in commenting on the worship service in sixteenth-century Geneva, said, "Unlike the mass the worship service in the Reformed church involved direct participation by the entire congregation. They recited creeds, offered prayers, and sang from the Psalter in French. In every worship service they were expected to be active participants and not just observers" (cf. 1 Corinthians 14:26).[26] Let us then lead our churches in God-centered worship—worship that mirrors the words of the psalmist:

> *Come, let us sing for joy to the* LORD; *let us shout aloud to the Rock of our salvation. Let us come before him with thanksgiving and extol him with music and song. For the* LORD *is the great God, the great King above all gods. In his hand are the depths of the earth, and the mountain peaks belong to him. The sea is his, for he made it, and his hands formed the dry land. Come, let us bow down in worship, let us kneel before the* LORD *our Maker; for he is our God and we are the people of his pasture, the flock under his care.*
>
> —*Ps. 95:1-7a*

NOTES

1   Our English word *worship* is derived from the Anglo-Saxon word *weorthscipe*, which means honor, dignity, worth-ship. Thus, to worship God is to render proper worth-ship to Him. We do this practically, reverently, and devoutly by attributing worth to both His character and name.

2   R. G. Rayburn agrees that true worship (devotion) flows from a correct apprehension of who God is (doctrine): ". . . the activity of the new life of the believer in which, recognizing the fullness of the Godhead as it is revealed in the person of Jesus Christ and His mighty redemptive acts, He seeks by the power of the Holy Spirit to render to the living God the glory, honor, and submission which are His due" (*O Come Let Us Worship* [Grand Rapids, MI: Baker, 1980], p. 21).

3   What I intend by the use of these two nouns is to prompt you to consider that we must aim for a God-centered realm in our church that can be both felt (cli-

mate) and observed (culture, from *cultus*, meaning worship). This is what I believe Paul was describing to us in 1 Corinthians 14:23-25.

4 It is important that ministers, at such times, do not change their church's worship services as quickly as John Knox did the Church of Scotland's. They must move beyond being enamored by the Reformers and Puritans and other men who believe that they are their present-day heirs and in a scripturally objective fashion begin taking wise steps toward such blessed change.

5 An example of where churches in this type of state might degenerate to in their worship services is displayed for us in an article from the Southern Baptist Convention's Home Mission Board magazine about Second Baptist Church of Houston, Texas. We read in this article that their worship services have included a ". . . 20-float Electric Light Christmas parade which has become the envy of the Disney staff that served as advisors, and the 1986 Super Sunday presentation of the Super Bowl at the church which drew an estimated 2,200 worshippers—the most people to see the Super Bowl in one site other than the field it was played on" *Missions USA* (May-June 1993).

6 The Greek word used here in Matthew 15:9, *maten*, which also appears in Mark 7:7 and 1 Timothy 1:6, means "to no end, without purpose, or empty prattle." For a helpful description of this word, see *A Greek-English Lexicon of the New Testament and Other Early Literature*, eds. Bauer, Arndt, Gingrich, Danker (Chicago: University of Chicago Press, 1979 [second edition]), p. 495; and *New International Dictionary of New Testament Theology*, ed. Colin Brown, Vol. 1 (Grand Rapids, MI: Zondervan, 1975, 3 vols.), p. 552.

7 Ernest R. Reisinger, *Thoughts on The Regulative Principle in a Reforming Situation* (Cape Coral, FL: Christian Gospel Foundation, 1982).

8 The Alliance of Confessing Evangelicals, 1716 Spruce Street, Philadelphia, Pennsylvania 19103; *The Cambridge Declaration*, pp. 9-10. Their phone number is: 215-546-3696; their web address is: www.AllianceNet.org.

9 Recently I received an E-mail from a friend whose church had been searching for a pastor who could not only live and preach soundly before them but could "effectively plan and lead worship." Thankfully they did not compromise their conviction, and God soon granted them the desire of their hearts. Sadly, many churches have not been as wise as my friend's church in the selection of a pastor and have instead chosen a man who has soon disconnected himself from responsible involvement in this vital area of the church and has incurred the following rebuke of *The Cambridge Declaration*: "Pastors have neglected their rightful oversight of worship, including the doctrinal content of the music" (ibid., p. 4).

10 For some excellent counsel for such an overwhelming task, see Leonard Payton's practical suggestions on pp. 203-205 of *The Coming Evangelical Crisis*, ed. John Armstrong (Chicago: Moody Press, 1996).

11 Of course, the ultimate reason why they responded to this Word-centered environment is, as Jesus has said, because He "calls his own sheep by name" and "My sheep listen to my voice; I know them, and they follow me" (John 10:3, 27).

12 "Worship in Spirit," *Banner of Truth* magazine, # 281, August-September 1987, p. 5.

13 Rayburn, *O Come Let Us Worship*, p. 28.

14 See my booklet titled *Rediscovering the Lost Treasure of Family Worship* (Laurel, MS: Audubon Press, 1996).

15  John Wesley's *"Rules for Methodist Singers"* is still a helpful pattern for most congregations to follow. His seven rules are: "(1) Learn the tunes. (2) Sing them as printed. (3) Sing all. If it is a cross to you, take it up and you will find it a blessing. (4) Sing lustily (passionately) and with good courage. (5) Sing modestly. Do not bawl. (6) Sing in time. Do not run before or stay behind. (7) Above all, sing spiritually. Have an eye to God in every word you sing. Aim at pleasing Him more than yourself or any other creature. In order to do this, attend strictly to the sense of what you sing, and see that your heart is not carried away with the sound, but is offered to God continually."

16  Armstrong, ed., *The Coming Evangelical Crisis*, p. 200.

17  *Grace Today* (the newsletter of Grace Community Church of Panorama City, California), Vol. 2 No. 20, May 16, 1999.

18  One such movement that I must mention is Church Music at the Crossroads. They can be reached at: 807-A S. Orlando Avenue, Winter Park, Florida 32789 or by E-mail at: terry@stpaulpca.org.

19  Reisinger, *Thoughts on the Regulative Principle in a Reforming Situation*, p. vi.

20  *Luther's Works*, 55 vols., American Edition, Pelikan (vols. 1-30) and Lehman (vols. 31-55), eds., Vol. 53 (St. Louis: Concordia; Philadelphia: Fortress Press, 1955-1986), p. 323.

21  Terry Yount, "A Letter to Henry," in *The Presbyterian Journal*, February 26, 1986, pp. 8-9.

22  Richard L. Pratt, Jr., *He Gave Us Stories* (Phillipsburg, NJ: Presbyterian and Reformed Publishing, 1990), p. 367.

23  Terry Yount, "Why Should the Devil Have All the Good Tunes?" *Reformation Today*, September/October 1993, pp. 31-32.

24  Calvin Johansson, *Discipling Music Ministry: Twenty-First Century Directions* (Peabody, MA: Hendrikson, 1992), p. 168.

25  For some good models of worship services that can assist you in formulating your own, contact Dr. Gregg Strawbridge by E-mail at strawbridge@olsusa.com or by writing to him at 6779 Overlook Drive, Fort Myers, Florida 33919 for copies of his books, titled *Toward a Theology of Worship and Worship Services* and *Concerts of Praise Sourcebook*.

26  *Calvin Courier* (the newsletter of the H. Henry Meeter Center for Calvin Studies at Calvin College in Grand Rapids, Michigan), Spring 1999, No. 23, pp. 3-4.

# 8

# THE CURE OF SOULS:

## The Pastor Serving the Flock

■

Jim Elliff

*"The hired hand is not the shepherd who owns the sheep. So when he sees the wolf coming, he abandons the sheep and runs away. Then the wolf attacks the flock and scatters it. The man runs away because he is a hired hand and cares nothing for the sheep."*
—*John 10:12-13*

I used to hear a Christian radio program years ago as I would go to work. The announcer called himself "the old hireling." I do not know whether he was demeaning himself in order to minimize responsibility for his mannerisms or whether he was even knowledgeable of the text we are discussing, but he did unwittingly embody an increasingly acceptable model of pastoral leadership. The model is of a pastor who somehow has the right to speak to the sheep's life-needs and even manage the sheep's activities—a figure, a caring voice, an authority of sorts—but without an actual shepherd's bond to the sheep.

Not all members of churches correctly perceive the immensity of the relational distance between the sheep and the hireling because pastors often have the ability to transmit a semblance of love that is absent of content. In one of the churches I pastored, a lady began to experience delusion. She listened to the radio late at night as a warm-voiced Christian radio host played soothing songs for the listener with sympathizing comments between numbers. The woman at first benefited from feeling loved as a believer. However, it was not long until she literally "fell in love" with the man, believing that he was speaking directly to her. We had to intercept her in the Chicago suburbs at the man's studio! She thought she was loved by him, but in reality she was not. As pastors, it is important to convey as much genuine *Christian* love as possible in our public speech, but is creating a mere perception of love, however intense, enough?

It may seem severe of me to say that I believe the care of souls is in such a deplorable state in otherwise orthodox (and often growing) churches because of this failure to love on the part of pastors. There are, thankfully, notable exceptions. Nonetheless, I will lay this out as a general observation worth contemplating: Many of the sheep are being led off into aberrant religious convictions and are turning away from us to secular counselors whose value and belief systems are adverse to ours. They are ravaged by sins that will forever damage them and are stymied by unresolved conflicts with people, largely because pastors do not love sufficiently. The trans-chronological language of Jesus in the John 10:12-13 passage above demands that we face this as a disturbing possibility, and the evidence of battered and scattered sheep admits our culpability. A hireling leaves his sheep defenseless before the wolf because he "cares nothing for the sheep."

Note that Jesus said that such a neglectful leader is really no shepherd at all ("The hired hand is not the shepherd"). Since the word *pastor* is literally the word *shepherd*, we must assume that what we are seeing in so many of our churches is a "pastor" who is not a pastor. He may be concerned for truth; he may be concerned for preaching; he may be concerned for growth; he may be concerned for evangelism. *But if he is not concerned about the sheep, he is only a hireling.*

If pastoral care is in any way distinct from that which nonbelievers can offer, it is because it flows as love derived from God as a supernatural characteristic of the regenerate. And because the minister is a pastor of sheep, this quality should be resident in him in liberal supply. The capacious and earnest nature of his love is that which should mark him as a pastor. We have confidence in him because we know that love will drive him to do anything necessary to protect and care for the sheep. On the other hand, nothing reveals the selfish and unloving nature of a hireling like the approaching footsteps of a wolf!

Jesus was urging love. In the description of the judgment of Matthew 25:31-46 (the sheep and the goats), Jesus brings forward the concept of compassion as determinate. In this judgment the criteria of compassion working itself out in deeds (feeding the hungry, giving drink to the thirsty, showing hospitality to strangers, clothing the naked, visiting the sick and the prisoners) in fact provides the *sole* basis of judgment. Though He depicts the future judgment of all men, the distinctive pastoral nature of the evidence to be examined should make every pastor fear. Compassionate deeds are such an emphatic evidence of true conversion that no mention of justification, propitiation, conversion, regeneration, repentance, or faith is required in the text. We are to understand that compassion tells the whole story. If this is true, and it is, many pastors will be revealed as impostors at the judgment.

Think of all that can be done in the field of church superintendence without love. We may speak eloquently with "the tongues of men and of angels," and we may have insight into Scripture and "fathom all mysteries and all knowledge." We may be people of vision and "have a faith that can move mountains," and we may sacrifice to the point of giving up our own salary and our possessions to feed the poor. We may even be martyrs on the stake, and yet have no love (see 1 Cor. 13:1-3). Ability and method do not ultimately qualify a man before God. Though love will *make* a man passionately eloquent, visionary, full of faith, prophetic, sacrificial, and self-denying, motive is critical.

Love from pastors can be detected by the sheep, but sooner or later so can pretense. The lips of the pastor may speak of love, but the whole person eventually conveys a message of its own. Bushnell, with all his errant theological views, correctly connects the body with the human spirit when he says:

> And if the Divine nature can use the organ [the human body] so effectively to express itself unto us, if it can bring itself, through the looks, tone, motions, and conduct of a human person, more close to our sympathies than by any other means, how can we think that an organ so communicative, inhabited by us, is not

always breathing our spirit and transferring our image insensibly to others.[1]

Perhaps the reason there is so much movement from pastorate to pastorate is this failure to love. A hireling finds it easy to abandon the sheep, but a true pastor is so bound that moving away is difficult, even when he knows the Lord has instructed him to go. As was true of Christ, the very seeing of persons in need moves him (Matt. 9:36); but not so with the hireling who is first of all concerned for his own skin.

It was authentic pastoral love that was the conspicuous component in the ministry of John Fawcett (1740-1817). He was converted through the instrumentality of George Whitefield. At age twenty-six he was ordained as a Baptist minister. His life was one of significant achievement. In 1777 he opened a school for young preachers; he wrote a number of books on practical Christianity; and in 1811 Brown University in the United States awarded him a doctorate in light of his accomplishments. His field of service, however, had no prestige. He served in an impoverished village named Wainsgate in northern England.

On the day he was scheduled to leave Wainsgate after some years of pastoring there, the saddened parishioners gathered around the wagons. Mrs. Fawcett finally broke down and said, "John, I cannot bear to leave. I know not how to go!" "Nor can I either," he said. The order was given to unpack the wagons! Fawcett stayed with this simple church for fifty years until a stroke caused his death on July 25, 1817. In one of the ensuing sermons Fawcett shared the words to a hymn he composed that have been meaningful to us for two centuries: "Blest be the tie that binds our hearts in Christian love! The fellowship of kindred minds is like to that above." This is the affection of a genuine pastor.

## THE CURE OF SOULS

The term *cure of souls* emerges principally from the Catholics and Anglicans. John Angell James (1785-1859), in his noteworthy book *An Earnest Ministry*, believed that Dissenting ministers of his day should learn something from the term. In explaining his position he unfolds some of the meaning of the concept:

> It has long appeared probable to me, that we, as Dissenting ministers, have something to learn in reference to this part of our duty from the clergy of the Church of England, and even from the priests of the Church of Rome. We do not perhaps sufficiently enter into the meaning and functions implied in that very expressive phrase, "the cure of souls"; a phrase which comprehends far more than the preaching of sermons, and the duties of the Sabbath and the sanctuary, however well performed. There is a definiteness, an explicitness, in this beautiful expression, into which we have need more deeply to enter. It is true we have our word "pastor," which in the impressive Saxon term "shepherd," implies a great deal; but it is neither so specific nor so solemn as the description conveyed by "the cure of souls." Nor do I think we have all the functions which this phrase implies, so much within the range of habitual contemplation as those by whom it is employed. In leaving college, and entering upon the sphere of our ministerial labour, our attention is perhaps often chiefly fixed upon the pulpit, without taking sufficiently into consideration the various private duties of which this is but the centre: while the [Anglican] clergy, though not altogether neglecting the work of preaching, enter upon their parishes with a wider range of view, as regards the duties of their offices. The visitation of the sick, the catechizing of children, and an attention to private exposition of the Scriptures and individual cases, enter more into their plans of clerical activity than into ours.[2]

By *cure of souls* it is generally meant that there is a pastoral responsibility outside of preaching. We may and should argue that preaching or "feeding the sheep" is essential for the sheep's health and therefore should be included in the term *cure of souls*. It is true that such a separation of concepts may cause people to say, "He is not a preacher, but he is a fine pastor." In my view one cannot be a fine pastor without being a fine preacher. Whatever may be said for the reasonableness of including or excluding preaching under the concept of curing souls, we are here going to take the word in its typical usage as indicating such responsibilities as fall to the pastor when he works with individuals or small groups outside of the preaching task. It will concern the more personal and individual care of Christians rather than the public ministrations of the pastor. We will take the term to denote such activities as biblical counsel, catechetical instruction, sickroom care, personal or small group biblical instruction, discipling persons in the biblical disciplines, discipline of church members, etc.

Puritan Richard Baxter (1615-1691) of Kidderminster, England, is perhaps the first name that comes to the mind of those who know their Christian history when considering expert pastoral ministry. He also distinguished the preaching aspect of the minister's work from what he called the pastoral aspect.

> I know that public preaching of the Gospel is the most excellent means of ministry because we speak to so many at once. Other than that single advantage, it is usually far more effective to preach the Bible's message privately to a particular sinner. In public we may not use the more homely expressions, and our speeches are so long that we overrun our hearers' understanding and memory. Thus they are not able to follow us. But in private we can take them at their own pace of understanding and keep their attention by argument, answers, and objections as they raise them. I conclude, therefore, that public preaching is not enough. You may study long, but preach to little purpose, unless you also have a pastoral ministry.[3]

What makes a complete pastor as related to this issue of curing souls? There are six integrant components:

1) *Pastoral intimacy*: Developing the relationship that undergirds all other ministry toward the individual.

2) *Pastoral tutelage*: Providing personal biblical instruction for increasing character, skills, or knowledge.

3) *Pastoral guidance*: Offering objective biblical direction through conflicts, reversals of life, distortions in thinking, and decision-making for those overwhelmed by them.

4) *Pastoral consolation*: Giving spiritual comfort during trials.

5) *Pastoral guardianship*: Watching out for the enemy's assaults on the weakness of the sheep and warning and disciplining the sheep when they are rebellious.

6) *Pastoral intercession*: Praying with believers.

## THE INTIMACY ELEMENT

The passage that is driving this chapter is that of the hireling and his relationship with the sheep. But we should consider this passage in the larger context. In that context we see that if we are going to be like the good shepherd, we must *know* the sheep.

> *"I am the good shepherd. The good shepherd lays down his life for the sheep. The hired hand is not the shepherd who owns the sheep. So when he sees the wolf coming, he abandons the sheep and runs away. Then the wolf attacks the flock and scatters it. The man runs away because he is a hired hand and cares nothing for the sheep. I am the good shepherd;* I know my sheep and my sheep know me—*just as the Father knows me and I know the Father—and I lay down my life for the sheep."*
> —*John 10:11-15*, emphasis added

Jesus, the Good Shepherd, the model shepherd, "knows" His sheep, and his sheep "know" Him. If a pastor would be like Christ in his shepherding, efforts must be made to know the sheep and to allow the sheep to know him. In other words, shepherding is not just about good management of the sheep, or just about reaching more sheep, or about merely teaching the sheep; it is intrinsically about being intimately related with the sheep. A man does not—cannot—pastor sheep without knowing them.

To be practical, there is a growing concern about how we carry out this simple task of pastors knowing the sheep. The body of believers may do much for other sheep in their mutual concern and interaction; however, the ultimate responsibility of caring for sheep is still the pastor's. This obviously poses a problem for the larger church. But even in smaller churches pastors find themselves neglectful of pursuing this duty with any kind of planning and relish. What can be done?

For one thing, a congregation intentional about clear pastor/sheep relationships should pursue the securing of a plurality of elders. It is going to be debated among us just what these men ought to be called, but it is abundantly clear that the early churches had more than one man pastoring them. How many people can one man know and know well? Alexander Strauch states, "In the exercise of this authority from Christ the apostles uniformly and universally enjoined and supervised the establishment of elderships in the local churches under their care (Acts 14:23; 15:2; 16:4; 20:17; Philippians 1:1; Titus 1:5; 1 Peter 5:1)."[4]

Pastors who take seriously the pastor/sheep relationship must also consider the implications of a large, possibly unregenerate membership exceeding the number of active members. In most cases, a sizable non-attending membership is impossible to adequately know, making for low-quality shepherding. Since genuine believers are those who love the brethren and the atmosphere of true Christian fellowship, it must be assumed that many of this inactive sort are actually unregenerate. But this may not be clearly known until attempts are made to know them. Therefore, a wise pastor will pursue the non-attending members until they are either "in" (attending with signs of being regenerate) or "out" (non-attending with signs of not being regenerate). In the final analysis, he will do all that is possible to make his membership roll as close to the actual attending membership as possible. In fact, considering unregenerate children and visiting people, it should be his goal to have more attending than on the membership roll. To fail in this would not only be to misconstrue the meaning of *the church*, but to not take seriously the fact of the future judgment of leaders found in Hebrews 13:17. Each pastor will give an account for all the sheep under his charge.

Finally, it goes without saying that knowing the sheep cannot be left to happenstance. There must be some planning in most situations to make sure that each of the sheep knows and is known by a pastor. This plan may include several aspects but should at least include one of the most notable characteristics of pastors—hospitality (1 Tim.

3:2). It is a reasonable course of action for pastors to have members in their home often. If it is impossible for a pastor to show hospitality to those under his charge in a suitable period of time, then there are not enough pastors for the sheep, or there is insufficient love in the heart of the pastor.

## THE TUTORIAL ELEMENT

In the early church the Word was taught not only from the temple area, but from house to house (Acts 2:46). Paul said, "I have not hesitated to preach anything that would be helpful to you but have taught you publicly and from house to house" (Acts 20:20). He admonished Timothy with this command: "And the things you have heard me say in the presence of many witnesses entrust to reliable men who will also be qualified to teach others" (2 Tim. 2:2). In these passages and numerous others, Paul is establishing a difference between public and private ministry of the Word. He also reveals a particularly relevant plan of taking along disciples like Timothy as he speaks publicly. The implication is that following those public messages was much private explanation. This is the same plan Christ used with His disciples (see Matt. 13:10-11). And He also established the concept of training faithful men to pass on the teachings to others as a means of perpetuating the teachings. The pastor's private biblical instruction relates to all members, but with a special sensitivity to leaders or developing leaders.

A faithful pastor who teaches others will attempt to develop others in three areas: character, skills, and knowledge. There is some danger in proceeding in one area without bringing up the others. For instance, the person who has a great deal of knowledge without sufficient character will often offend. If he has knowledge without skills, he will be impotent. If he has skills in working with people, but no knowledge, he is dangerous and may lead people astray by his leadership abilities. The Scriptures speak to all three of these areas.[5]

Though it might seem archaic in our day, a pastor can take advantage of opportunities to teach by simply carrying his Bible or New Testament into every home he visits, even if for a merely social evening. The believers will come to expect that sometime in the evening he will discuss something he is learning in the Bible. In other words, the people will come to see the pastor's place as a teacher and will know that he is going to do that job whenever, with grace and thoughtfulness, he can possibly do so. Imagine what you would discuss if the apostle Paul came to visit. I tried to create such a sense of the pastor's divine mandate to teach the Word that the people actually would expect the Bible to be part of every visit.

J. I. Packer explains Richard Baxter's way of fulfilling his tutorial role in relation to the church as a whole.

> What Baxter refers to here is the practice which he describes and commends in *The Reformed Pastor* . . . of systematically interviewing families for the purpose of personal spiritual dealing. Baxter met families in this way at the rate of seven or eight a day, two days a week, so as to get through all 800 families in the parish every year. "I first heard them recite the words of the catechism [the *Westminster Shorter Catechism* was the one he used] and then examined them about the sense, and lastly urged them with all possible engaging reason and vehemency to answerable affection and practice. I spent about an hour with a family." His testimony to the value of this practice is emphatic. "I find we never took the rightest course to demolish the kingdom of darkness till now. . . . I find more outward signs of success with most . . . than of all my public preaching to them."[6]

Pastors may think that their people are not yet willing to learn a catechism. If there is some question about the practicality of this approach, one could modify the visit by saying that reciting of the catechism will only be done if the member desires, but the catechism will nonetheless be used by the pastor as a platform for teaching some vital truths. Also, use of a catechism may be focused only toward children rather than the whole family if desired, meaning that children would be asked to recite in the visits to the home. The parents would be connected to the catechism by teaching their own children. Or a suitable Scripture memory plan may be used if the plan helps the believer sense a progression in his learning. Catechetical instruction may be augmented in the church by having Bible study teachers take ten minutes or so of their Sunday Bible study period for review of a portion of the catechism. This combination produces the best results.

I suggest that leadership training take place in small groups on the model of Jesus and the disciples. An excellent resource related to Christ's work with men is found in the classic study on discipleship by Robert Coleman, *The Master Plan of Evangelism.*[7] I have found nothing on parallel with this. Many pastors re-read this book periodically in order to help them retain a proper focus on leadership development. I suggest the same.

## THE GUIDANCE ELEMENT

A sustained, sensitive pastoral ministry will concern itself with the inner turmoil of the people. Pastors are to be available to the sheep for counsel in times of stressfulness, depression, and confused thinking that may come from difficult decision-making, reversals of life, conflicts, etc.

Chrysostom believed that such issues in the lives of believers were impossible to solve unless the person was willing to be helped.

> Shepherds have full power to compel the sheep to accept the treatment if they do not submit of their own accord. It is easy to bind them when it is necessary to use cautery or the knife, and to keep them shut up for a long time when that is the right thing, and to introduce different kinds of food one after another, and to keep them away from water. And all other remedies the shepherds think will promote the animals' health they apply with perfect ease.
>
> But human diseases in the first place are not easy for a man to see. "For who among men knows the thoughts of a man except the man's spirit within him?" (1 Corinthians 2:11). How, then, can anyone provide the specific remedy for a disease if he does not know its character and often cannot tell whether the person is even ill? When it later becomes apparent, then it has become all the more intractable. You cannot treat human beings with the same authority with which the shepherd treats a sheep. Here too it is possible to bind and to forbid food and to apply cautery and the knife, but the decision to receive treatment does

not lie with the one who administers the medicine but actually with the patient.[8]

For the above reason, pastors must make additional efforts at building the kind of relationship with the members that encourages the members to talk with him. Not every pastor does this well. Some are reticent because they know what it means to be dominated by a person addicted to receiving sympathy. But pastoral counsel has an answer for this also.

The pastor has really one responsibility in giving counsel. He is to objectively apply the Bible to the problem. He will listen, attempt to comprehend the situation with an objective ear, then give the troubled member the biblical perspective on the problem. He will then help the person work out how he may learn to fully adopt that perspective as truth and will lay out any steps to carrying out the commands involved. If the person does not want God's answers to the problem he or she faces, then coming to a pastor is not going to be helpful. Just because the pastor's job is simply stated does not make it simple to carry out, however. The deceitfulness of sin makes the job sometimes daunting. In the final analysis, the troubled person either believes the truth or he does not and will either obey the truth or will not.

In our day of specialization and attention to therapy, the more typical pastor will turn all the "really big problems" over to some other counselor. Many pastors are grateful for the option of giving another person, sometimes a person who has no biblical insight at all, the job of caring for their sheep. However, I think this notion is generally neglectful and dangerous. Even with purely physical problems, the Lord's counsel is to be sought first, a lesson King Asa had to learn (2 Chron. 16:12). With some obvious caveats, let me assert that as pastors we do have what the sheep need, provided they are willing to receive it (2 Tim. 3:16-17).

Perhaps chronic problems encountered in the process of soul care need to be thought of differently. An unacceptable method of dealing with such a problem is to leave the church member in the care of someone else without any further concern on a pastor's part—i.e., to turn over complete care to a therapist. A better model in chronic cases is to consider that some people may be in need of multiple helpers, with a pastor at the center of the helping process. If a pastor needs to send the person to a family physician to check for blood problems, sleep disorder, unhealthy eating patterns, etc. that might relate to the person's condition, he could do so. And if a pastor needs to refer the individual to another person or two in the church who had earlier experienced similar problems, then he can direct that connection.

If there are needs for an outside professional who is a believer practicing a biblical counseling technique that the pastor values, then a pastor may refer the individual. But his pastoral involvement is not over. I believe it is mandatory for a pastor to have an agreement with an outside counselor that assures that the relationship is triangular. He must retain his pastoral leadership. In other words, nothing should take place in the counseling room that the pastor will not be fully apprised of through regular communication with the counselor and the struggling church member.

One possible benefit of outside assistance in counseling is savings on time. The time issue is one the pastor will have to weigh since any one person may take all of his available hours. But an outside counselor's time may be too available. As long as a patient is able to provide payment for his services, some professional counselors will continue to offer their help indefinitely. There is an ethical issue here that each counselor and referring pastor has to deal with.

Some therapists with recognized credentials have the ability to offer drugs to their patients also. If the problem is indeed physiological, then drugs are a possible but only partial answer. However, drug use has become too convenient a tool for some therapists. The words, "The doctor says my problem is a chemical imbalance and has put me on this medicine" are heard far too often. Though I am not willing to completely rule out the use of drugs for rare cases, I would not encourage their use without considerable consultation and prayerfulness. We may assume that patients are generally relieved to hear that their problem is physiological, since that shifts the blame for their behavior. But the patient's readiness to hear those words may cause therapists to recommend drugs too often. My experience is that once a person starts down the road of taking drugs for mood alteration, the use of them will continue for years, if not his entire life, along with the need to consult the physician repeatedly to make adjustments. On the other hand, we can be thankful for drugs that are helpful to those who desperately need them. Most people who deny their necessity totally have never been hopelessly depressed or had family members in that condition.

In addition, if a pastor is relatively inexperienced in facing certain problems, a counselor's experience might be of help also. But again the pastor should not forfeit his pastoral concern or involvement even if inexperienced. Pastors must realize that a large number of patients who see therapists are not permanently helped and that temporary relief is not the same as a right standing with God.

One of the main issues in pastoral counseling is the examining of the soul to see if there is life there at all. The Puritans were masters at this kind of soul surgery. I believe that we often assume too quickly that a person has life in Christ and would be much more effective by pointing out that aberrant and apathetic lifestyle over time often is indicative of an unregenerate state. Failure to get at the root of the problem often prolongs the counseling process endlessly, wearing out both the pastor and the member and serves finally to assist that soul toward hell. There is a sorrow that leads to death (2 Cor. 7:10).

At all times the pastor must seek to turn the individual to the Lord and should adamantly resist being the person's rescuer. The Lord is his helper.

## THE CONSOLATION ELEMENT

Paul expresses the immense value of consolation toward those who suffer in 2 Corinthians 1:3-7. The encouraging message there is that God is interested in our human suffering and our spiritual comfort. After all, he is "the God of all comfort" (v. 3). Suffering expands the capacity we have to comfort others. It should not be surprising to pastors if they receive a measure of suffering themselves in order to be able to minister effectively to others. Pastors are instruments of the Holy Spirit, who comes alongside the believer in times of difficulty to offer hope. Paul's advice to the Thessalonians concerning those who had "fallen asleep" is a model of hope-giving (1 Thess. 4:13-18). In their case, facts altered grief. In other words, good theology extends hope. Do not, therefore, fail to offer both the touch of your love and the truth of your love.

## THE GUARDIAN ELEMENT

In the passage that has gotten our attention (John 10), the Master Shepherd assumes the role of guide to the sheep, as mentioned above. The sheep follow. Their following assumes the intimacy that we have already discussed.

"His sheep follow him because they know his voice" (v. 4). Christ also said that the sheep "will never follow a stranger; in fact, they will run away from him because they do not recognize a stranger's voice" (v. 5). "All who ever came before me," he said, "were thieves and robbers, but the sheep did not listen to them" (v. 8). Christ tells us that the genuine sheep we must lead are *prone* to follow Him. Our job is to help them know Christ well and to guide them in the right direction as Christ's undershepherds. With all being said about the sheep's attraction to the Shepherd's voice, we still face the issue of the wolf who is capable of catching and scattering the sheep (see v. 12).

Conflict awaits the sheep, and the pastor's job is to "see the wolf coming" (v. 12) and to protect the sheep no matter what it costs him. The apostle Paul puts it like this, addressing the elders of the church in Ephesus:

> *Keep watch over yourselves and all the flock of which the Holy Spirit has made you overseers. Be shepherds of the church of God, which he bought with his own blood. I know that after I leave, savage wolves will come in among you and will not spare the flock. Even from your own number men will arise and distort the truth in order to draw away disciples after them. So be on your guard! Remember that for three years I never stopped warning each of you night and day with tears.*
> —*Acts 20:28-31*

Paul goes beyond his public ministry in the church and claims that he did not cease to warn everyone "night and day with tears" (v. 31). He made the sheep's protection a full-time occupation for three years because of his concern for them. He warned everyone night and day. He warned them with tears of concern. I wonder how many pastors have such an interest in the sheep.

His great concern was for the "savage wolves" who come from both the outside and the inside of the professing church. Their intention is to "draw away disciples after them" (v. 30). Ephesus was a cosmopolitan city that boasted of being the refuge for the great temple to Artemis. No doubt some of Paul's concern was in keeping the Ephesian believers clear of that place and its prevailing doctrines. But Hymenaeus and Alexander (1 Tim. 1:3, 20) also introduced false teaching from within that led to "controversies" (v. 4). Eventually John would tell this church that they had left their "first love" (Rev. 2:4).

In our day the shepherd must be alert for foolish mysticism. A believer who watches hours of religious TV, for instance, is prone to be moved away from the simplicity of devotion to Christ. Recently, as an illustration, faith healer Benny Hinn, on the TBN *Praise the Lord* program, October 19, 1999, told TBN's Paul Crouch that the time is coming when thousands of dead will be raised when their bodies are put in front of television sets while TBN is broadcasting.[9] Other illustrations would be more subtle, but this serves to alert us to the kind of subjectivism to which our people expose themselves, sometimes daily. We have responsibility to warn them of such false teaching.

The believer is subject to internal lusts as well as contrary teaching. Because Satan "prowls around . . . looking for someone to devour" (1 Pet. 5:8), the shepherd must never allow himself to be inattentive to the sheep. Again, a plurality of elders allows one man to stand watch while another takes a rest; but like a mother with her child in a china shop, there should never be a moment when the sheep are not being watched.

The guardian function also includes that of severely reprimanding, admonishing, and disciplining church members when their sins begin to dominate them or produce relational difficulties. Church discipline, though ultimately involving the church as a whole, is a process guided by pastoral care. It is loving to discipline and negligent to fail to discipline.

## THE INTERCESSORY ELEMENT

There is one mediator between God and man, and pastors are responsible to carry out an intercessory function of prayer for believers in His name. This is particularly easy to see in James 5:13-18 where elders are called upon to pray for the sick. They are told to "pray over him and anoint him with oil in the name of the Lord" (v. 14). Without attempting to address the difficulties of this passage, let me at least point out that this concept of praying for the sick is in the job description of the pastor and should not be neglected. The pastor's praying with others may cover much more than their sicknesses, but this aspect must not be forgotten.

## THE PASTORAL OBJECTIVE

The above facets of the pastor's ministry toward the individual are focused on a single objective: to present that man or woman or young person to God perfect in Christ.[10] Paul made it clear that this requires labor and striving, premised on faith:

> *We proclaim him [Christ], admonishing and teaching everyone with all wisdom, so that we may present everyone perfect in Christ. To this end I labor, struggling with all his energy, which so powerfully works in me.*
>
> —Col. 1:28-29[11]

There is no sense in Paul's view that he will fail to be adequate for the task. God works in him mightily to accomplish this goal. You should think the same way (and this is our hope). However, Paul is not so foolish as to assume that the work of presenting people perfect in Christ is accomplished while incessantly relaxing in the study or in front of the television. He is laboring and striving, warning and teaching "everyone." In context, Paul means that even the Gentiles are included in the "mystery" (v. 27) hidden for previous ages. But there is an individual aspect to his words as well. No one is to be excluded. He is not only speaking of admonitions and instruction for the masses; his labors include the individual person. He will not be satisfied with any person who is not growing toward perfection in Christ. First they must be converted, but then they must mature. His aim is to present "everyone perfect [mature] in Christ." This statement should be framed and put above your desk for a daily reminder!

I must stress the intentionality of the statement, "everyone perfect in Christ." There are pastors who do not see this. They are driven to add to the church, but not to mature the individuals in the church. Others are content when there is peace in the church, but do not make any plans for the maturity of the people. They are not against maturity in Christians—after all, they need leaders. But for the most part they are not going to take any responsibility to "labor" for that end. They love it when mature Christians join their church, but they cannot be said to have added to the number of the mature in any significant way themselves.

I contend that a man must consider himself a failure in pastoral ministry if he does not labor for the maturity of individuals in Christ and in some obvious way see the fruits of his labors in godly lives. Therefore I ask this question: Are you maturing saints? And if so, are you conscientiously reaching "every man" (KJV)?

## WHY DO IT?

We all know that we can pastor like a hireling but look like a humble servant. But Jesus invites us to lay down our *lives* for the sheep—those foolish, sin-craving, distracted, and dirty sheep—even the sheep that don't show progress and perpetually do the wrong and even the ugly thing. The soul care we must give them will cost us something dear. It will, in fact, cost more than most of us would want to pay if it were not for the prying and persuading and mental reengineering work of the Spirit. None of us wants this job because we love to get our hands dirty. And God forbid that we should want it for pride. We do it because we cannot do anything else when God calls us to Himself—that is, when we enjoy Him in the doing of it.

Once a friend said to me that marriage was the source of his greatest joys and his greatest heartaches. So it is with the cure of souls. The agony and effort of the care of souls batters the best of men, but the joys are unlike any known on earth. What pastor among us has not felt that inner gust of joy blow across his spirit when he sees a broken man or woman or child come out of addiction to sin to be something noble in Christ? And if that moment of reflection about such a person causes joy, what will heaven be like for the man who loves men and women and children so much that he brings them to maturity in Christ?

*For what is our hope, our joy, or the crown in which we will glory in the presence of our Lord Jesus when he comes? Is it not you?*
*—1 Thess. 2:19*

## NOTES

1 Horace Bushnell, "Unconscious Influence," *The World's Great Sermons* IV (New York: Funk and Wagnalls, 1909), pp. 254-255.

2 John Angell James, *An Earnest Ministry* (Edinburgh: Banner of Truth, reprint 1993), pp. 164-165.

3 Richard Baxter, *The Reformed Pastor*, abridged edition (Portland: Multnomah, 1993), p. 114. In an unabridged edition of this seminal pastoral ministry book, Baxter included the following aspects of ministry in his set of pastoral duties toward individuals: (1) Knowing them, (2) Instructing the ignorant, (3) Advising them that seek advice, (4) Looking to particular families, (5) Resisting seduction, (6) Encouraging the obedient, (7) Visiting the sick, (8) Comforting, (9) Privately admonishing offenders, (10) More public discipline. (By the later, he meant that public admonition follows, at some point, the private aspects of church discipline.) (Ligonier, PA: Soli Deo Gloria, reprint 1991), pp. 384-390.

4 Gregory Nichols, "Parity and Diversity in Eldership, Part I—Parity," *In Defense of Parity*, eds. Samuel Waldron, et. al. (Grand Rapids, MI: Truth for Eternity Ministries, 1997), p. 10.

5 When Paul writes to the Colossians (1:9-10), for instance, he stresses that he is praying that they may be filled with the "knowledge of his will through all wisdom and spiritual understanding" (knowledge), that they "may live a life worthy of the Lord" (character), and that they would be "bearing fruit in every good work" (skills).

6 J. I. Packer, *Among God's Giants* (Kingsway, Eastbourne, England: 1991), p. 53ff., as found in Wallace Benn, "The Baxter Model, Guidelines for Pastoring Today," *Orthos*, Vol. 13, 1993, pp. 2-3.

7 Robert Coleman, *The Master Plan of Evangelism* (Old Tappan, NJ: Revell, 1977).

8 John Chrysostom, *On the Priesthood*, chapter II, sec. 2, pp. 55-56, as found in Thomas Oden, *Classical Pastoral Care*, Vol. I (Grand Rapids, MI: Baker, 1987) p. 43.

9 Trinity Broadcasting Network, *Praise the Lord* program, October 19, 1999.

Hinn said, "But here's first what I see for TBN. You're going to have people raised from the dead watching this network. You're going to have people raised from the dead watching TBN. . . . I'm telling you, I see this in the Spirit. It's going to be so awesome—Jesus, I give you praise for this—that people around the world—maybe not so much in America—people around the world who will lose loved ones, will say to undertakers, 'Not yet. I want to take my dead loved one and place him in front of that TV set for 24 hours.' I'm telling you, I can feel the anointing talking here. People are going to be canceling funeral services and bringing their dead in their caskets, placing them—my God! I feel the anointing here—placing them before a television set, waiting for God's power to come through and touch them. And it's going to happen time and time—so much it's going to spread. You're going to hear it from Kenya to Mexico to Europe to South America, where people will be raised from the dead. So much so that the word will spread that if some dead person be put in front of this TV screen, they will be raised from the dead and they will be by the thousands. I see rows of caskets lining up in front of this TV set and I see them bringing them closer to the TV set, and as people are coming closer I see loved ones picking up the hands of the dead and letting them touch the screen and people are getting raised as their hands are touching that screen."

10 Curtis Vaughn explains the word "perfect," using other versions of the Scripture as commentary.

The word "perfect" suggests the attaining of the proper end and goal of one's existence. Other versions use such terms as "complete" (NAB), "full grown" (Montgomery), "mature" (Williams, RSV). The reference is to maturity in faith and character (cf. Eph. 4:13), and it is a prospect held out for "every man." Such maturity is possible "in Christ," that is, by virtue of the believer's union with Christ. (*Colossians—A Study Guide* [Grand Rapids, MI: Zondervan, 1973], p. 62)

11 This passage may speak of a maturity of *concept* in the minds of believers. That is, Paul may be laboring to get the Colossian people to believe the truth about their union with Christ and something of the fullness of their being "qualified . . . to share in the inheritance of the saints in the kingdom of light" (1:12). Those who understand this are the mature ones. After all, Paul goes on to say that Christians are *already* complete in Christ (2:10). Maturity is comprehending the riches of what they already have in Him. Without being complicated in my explanation, it is possible simply to say that Paul could be teaching that those who are brought to a correct understanding of their relationship to Christ and are not being led away by contrary philosophy (2:8) are the ones who are complete or mature. Pastorally, he labors to bring them to this maturity.

# 9

## REFORMING THE CHURCH
## THROUGH PRAYER:

### The Pastoral Contribution

■

### Arturo Azurdia

Arturo Azurdia

| THE *SINE QUA NON* OF SPIRITUAL ADVANCEMENT

> What a man is alone on his knees before God, that he is, and no
> more.

According to this stunning statement of Robert Murray
M'Cheyne it cannot be denied that the biblical record, in its portrait
of Nehemiah the cupbearer, furnishes us with a model worthy of emu-
lation. As the story goes, he was a man driven to accomplish a great
work for the glory and honor of Yahweh: the reconstruction of the
shattered walls of Jerusalem. For several decades the walls had laid in
ruins, a lingering testimony to the earlier Babylonian appetite for dom-
ination and the subsequent Persian anxiety concerning revolution.
Consequently the nation of Israel had become an object of international derision and contempt. This humiliation so aroused Nehemiah's
zeal for the covenant people that he secured a leave of absence from
his position at court and traveled to Jerusalem where he personally
directed the rebuilding of the walls, a herculean task completed in just
fifty-two days.

In the face of such a task, it is noteworthy that the omnicompe-
tent Nehemiah did not commence his endeavors by drawing upon his

own inherent powers of leadership (an almost involuntary reflex action endemic to leaders). Instead, he purposefully bowed his knee and took hold of the outstretched hand of God in prayer, readily acknowledging the sovereignty of his covenant Lord.[1] Moreover, a simple reading of the text reveals that this prayer was no anomaly in the experience of Nehemiah. To the contrary, prayer was the steady and definitive characteristic of his leadership methodology. The fact and frequency of his praying, therefore, leads the biblical reader to an obvious deduction: The outworking of Nehemiah's ministry was governed by a theological presupposition that recognizes prayer to be the *sine qua non* of spiritual advancement, the means through which the sovereign God most commonly effects His purposes in the world. If M'Cheyne is right that prayer is the spiritual measure of men and women in a way that nothing else is, then Nehemiah the cupbearer was a leader among God's people evincing a profound spirituality.

Why is it that such authentic spirituality is lacking in our time, particularly among those set apart for gospel ministry? Other than those found within the pages of Scripture and Christian biography, most of us would sadly acknowledge that we have known few *pastoral leaders* whose practice of ministry could be defined, at least in part, by a vibrant and thoroughgoing experience of prayer. Such a disturbing observation, however, cannot be the sole consequence of neglect on the part of those who occupy pastoral office. Rarely, if ever, does a pastoral job description articulate the congregation's expectation that the practice of prayer be among the primary expressions of pastoral ministry. Rather than expecting a priest-prophet whose primary concern is to develop a life of prayer among the people of God, the tacit implication is that a pastor will be hired to serve as the moral errand-boy of the congregation, performing those good deeds the parishioners deem appropriate but have little time to undertake. Seminaries, as well, have done little to convince theological students of the primacy of prayer in relation to pastoral ministry. Though privileged to enjoy nearly ten years of theological education, I cannot recall any intentional contribution made toward my understanding of prayer as a principal expression of pastoral labors.[2]

Stated simply, a glaring defect is painfully evident in the lives and ministries of evangelical pastors: the lack of a devotional habit, of which the neglect of consistent and serious prayer is most notorious. For pastors who affirm an affinity for theological Calvinism, this deficiency is even more condemning in that it exposes a grievous lack of integrity, evidenced by a practice of ministry that effectively denies our theological distinctives. In his creative style, Eugene Peterson has rightly captured this inconsistency:

> We are, most of us, Augustinians in our pulpits. We preach the sovereignty of our Lord, the primacy of grace, the glory of God: "By grace are ye saved . . . Not of works, lest any man should boast" (Ephesians 2:8-9, KJV). But the minute we leave our pulpits we are Pelagians. In our committee meetings and our planning sessions, in our obsessive attempts to meet the expectations of people, in our anxiety to please, in our hurry to cover all the bases, we practice a theology that puts our good will at the foundation of life and urges moral effort as the primary element in pleasing God.
>
> The dogma produces the behavior characteristic of the North American pastor: if things aren't good enough, they will improve if I work a little harder and get others to work harder. Add a committee here, recruit some more volunteers there, squeeze a couple of hours more into the workday.
>
> Pelagius was an unlikely heretic; Augustine an unlikely saint. By all accounts Pelagius was urbane, courteous, convincing. Everyone seems to have liked him immensely. Augustine squandered away his youth in immorality, had some kind of Freudian thing with his mother, and made a lot of enemies. But all our theological and pastoral masters agree that Augustine started from God's grace and therefore had it right, and Pelagius started from human effort and therefore got it wrong. . . . How did it happen that Pelagius became our master?
>
> Our closet Pelagianism will not get us excommunicated or burned at the stake, but it cripples our pastoral work severely . . . it is catastrophic to the church's wholeness and health.[3]

The dark consequences that have resulted from the unequal yoking together of an Augustinian confession of theology with a Pelagian practice of ministry calls us to the pressing need for reformation; not, at this point, a reformation of theological orthodoxy, but a reformation of pastoral ministry. Essential to the renewal of evangelical congregations is a return to the practice of an authentically biblical ministry, a ministry that not only acknowledges the sovereignty of God by affirmation but portrays this conviction in the outworking of its life. This will insure the restoration of the centrality of prayer to the devotional habit of pastors, ultimately manifesting itself in the corporate prayer life of congregations. The wedding together of pastoral methodology with theological affirmation means that our ministries must be governed by the same presupposition that owned the heart of Nehemiah. We must recognize prayer to be the *sine qua non* of spiritual advancement.

## A DISTINCTIVE OF THE SACRED CALLING

Some time ago I received an invitation to have lunch with a ministerial colleague who lived in another city. Though I was aware of who he was, our acquaintance with one another could be characterized as nothing more than casual, defined by two or three personal meetings and a handful of telephone conversations, all of which had related to the subject of pastoral ministry. After our meal had been served, his agenda became clear, taking me quite by surprise. "Brother," he began somberly, "I need to be honest with you. You've not been a good friend to me. You've taken my calls and been helpful in response to the various concerns I have brought to your attention, for which I am thankful. But you have done nothing to pursue a personal relationship with me."

To say the least, I was at a severe loss to know how to respond. It was obvious I had been a source of disappointment to this man. His assessment, however, was accurate. Though always cordial, our contacts had been exclusively professional. I had never given consideration to the intentional development of a more personal friendship. Throughout the remainder of the meal his expressions of dissatisfaction with my lack of initiative continued. Finally, as his remarks drew to a conclusion, he posed the inescapable question: "So, Art, what do

*Gal     Walk in the spirit*

*with yield to spirit of God in our relationships with people*

you think about what I have said?" To be sure, my initial reactions to his criticisms were characterized by anger and defensiveness. On this occasion, thankfully, they remained unspoken. It became evident, however, that I needed to be both compassionate and forthright with this brother. "I am sorry to have disappointed you," I replied. "I've never designed to avoid you. I will pray for God to grant you a supportive ministerial colleague. On the other hand, I must tell you that because of the responsibilities I have in relation to ministry and family, I cannot assume any more obligations to people. To the contrary, I need more alone time in my life."

Even now I recall how difficult it was to speak those words. Yet they *needed* to be spoken. They revealed the distinctiveness of my sacred calling. I am a minister of the Gospel. Consequently, if my divinely ordained responsibilities are to be executed in a fashion pleasing to the Chief Shepherd and beneficial to His people, that will necessitate the securing of protected and protracted periods of "alone time," including times for personal prayer. Realization of this fact is indispensable to any significant reformation of pastoral ministry.

First and foremost, the ministry of Jesus Christ Himself should cause this to become evident. Not only do the four evangelists record Jesus praying with great frequency and in diverse settings,[4] they are careful to cite specific occasions during His ministry when, by obvious design, He withdrew from all other company to pray for extended periods:

*Very early in the morning, while it was still dark, Jesus got up, left the house and went off to a solitary place, where he prayed.*
—Mark 1:35

*But Jesus often withdrew to lonely places and prayed.*
—Luke 5:16

*One of those days Jesus went out to a mountainside to pray, and spent the night praying to God.*
—Luke 6:12

*Once when Jesus was praying in private . . .*

*—Luke 9:18*

As has been rightly noted, "Our blessed Master's example is here much to be observed. As a man, he had most responsible concerns to transact with God. Nothing important was done without prayer . . . time was redeemed from sleep for this sacred employment."[5]

In the second place, it is apparent that the original apostolic leaders embraced Christ's preoccupation with prayer. When the demands of additional ministry threatened their narrowly focused priorities, these needs were quickly addressed by the appointment of a second group of spiritually mature men. "Brothers, choose seven men from among you who are known to be full of the Spirit and wisdom. We will turn this responsibility over to them and will give our attention to prayer and the ministry of the word" (Acts 6:3-4). This delegation of responsibility was not indicative of laziness on the part of the original apostles. Nor did it betray a sense of spiritual superiority. It was a division of labor calculated in part to protect the centrality of prayer.

Prayer, then, is not to be regarded as a postscript to pastoral ministry, a mere token expression of dependence that in actuality exposes one's own conviction of self-sufficiency.[6] Nor is it quite accurate to describe prayer as "the atmosphere" in which one carries out his pastoral labors. Practically speaking, such ethereal terms do not foster the kind of prayer rigor displayed by Jesus and the apostles. Rather, it emasculates the significance of prayer by relegating it to something that can be done while performing other functions. Pastors must embrace the fact that prayer *is* their work, the defining function of their pastoral ministry.[7] To this end Charles Spurgeon exhorted his students:

> Of course the preacher is above all others distinguished as a man of prayer. He prays as an ordinary Christian, else he were a hypocrite. He prays more than ordinary Christians, else he were disqualified for the office he has undertaken. "It would be wholly monstrous," says Bernard, "for a man to be highest in office and lowest in soul; first in station and last in life." Over all his other

relationships the pre-eminence of the pastor's responsibility casts a halo, and if true to his Master, he becomes distinguished for his prayerfulness in them all.[8]

Charles Bridges poignantly lends his affirmation: "Prayer is the ornament of the priesthood, the leading feature of our character . . . and that man ceases, if I may use the expression, to be a public Minister from the time he ceases to pray.[9]

## THE PASTOR HIMSELF

What are the grand subjects that will occupy the private praying of the man of God? Like all other Christians, the pastor is a redeemed human being seeking, by grace, to overcome the effects of the curse in his life and in the lives of those nearest him. As such, his praying will encompass the concerns that are common to all Christians. Nevertheless, certain subjects distinct to his calling ought to be among the steady preoccupations of his prayers. One of these is his sacred responsibility with the inspired text, his weekly privilege to be a faithful interpreter of the Gospel to the people of God.

"Preaching is irrelevant." We recognize this as an all-too-frequent indictment leveled against the church in our time, one that often arouses contemptuous feelings, tempting us to marginalize those who convey it. But in our defensiveness we ought not to be quick to dismiss all such sentiments as expressions of irreverence. It accurately identifies the symptom (irrelevance) while simultaneously misdiagnosing the disease (preaching). To state it more directly, true gospel preaching is not irrelevant. *Preachers* are irrelevant. No deficiencies inherently exist within either the biblical message or method of communication. Preachers are frequently irrelevant, however, precisely because they have failed to experience the transforming relevance of the God-breathed Word. Men appointed to the task of weekly exposition stand in need of illumination that transcends textual criticism, diagrammatical analysis, and the technical insights of the most sophisticated commentators (all of which are essential to the work of faithful preaching). Experiencing the relevance of the sacred text necessitates that sermon preparation must always occur within the context of the psalmist's cry: "Open my eyes that I may see wonderful things in your law" (Ps. 119:18).[10] Karl Barth has said, "The first and basic act of theological work is prayer."[11] Pastors must pray themselves into the marrow of the biblical text if they are to experience its relevance in a penetrating fashion. Such Spirit-produced illumination, sought in fervent prayer, will profoundly contribute to preaching that is more than chilling analytical discourse.

> Without prayer, even the more spiritual truths will be very apt to be studied as a science merely, and our increasing acquaintance with them will not minister to our spirituality. With it, we shall acquaint ourselves more with the adorable and ever-blessed God, and with every view of him shall sink in the dust before him, and make his service our joy. It is not the view of the naked eye that discovers God's truth in its beauty; it is the view taken through the telescope of prayer, in which distant objects are brought near and magnified. Things unseen elsewhere are seen at the mercy-seat, and in new aspects, and in new beauty and loveliness. They stand out in their celestial brightness, they cluster like the stars in the Milky Way. The delighted eye dwells upon them, the swelling bosom feels them, and when we speak of them it is with glowing lips.[12]

To be sure, this praying ought not to be confined to the work of sermon preparation, but extended to beseech the gracious Spirit for empowerment when the moment of actual proclamation arrives. Again and again the man of God must return to the throne of grace, seeking the following qualities to be characteristic of his preaching: faithfulness to the biblical text, courage to proclaim without compromise, clarity of thought and speech, sensitivity to the assembled congregation, and effects that will redound to the honor of God. In the face of such lofty aspirations, the preacher weekly finds himself beyond his capacities and wholly dependent upon divine mercy. Recognizing the gravity of his task, the preacher must repeatedly return to the sole source of sufficiency through the means of private prayer. Effective exposition requires a form of preparation that only God Himself can effect.

> The oral side of our career is visible, but it is never the source of spiritual power. In fact, our devotional life . . . is the secret of real clout. A friend of mine long ago reminded me that I could not help people if I was always with people. . . . When Harold Fickett, Jr., says, "A preacher is the epic poet of his people," we must admit that the epic gains its form from silence. . . . Preaching from the silent center is the evidence that we who preach on trust are also living it. Preaching, in one sense, merely discharges the firearm that God has loaded in the silent place. The successful volley does not mean that we have passed homiletics but rather that we have been with God.[13]

Edward Payson has captured the issue most succinctly: "It is in the *closet* that the battle is lost or won."[14]

A second subject to which the pastor must give regular attention in prayer is the spiritual well-being of the congregation given to him by divine appointment.[15] The finest congregations are simultaneously characterized by the full spectrum of spiritual life and interest. Some in the congregation are authentically Christian, vitally engaged in the gracious pursuit of Christlikeness (cf. 2 Thess. 1:3-5). Some in the congregation are believers who have recently become ensnared in specific sinful habits (cf. 1 Cor. 3:1-4). Some in the congregation are becoming progressively vulnerable to the enticements of worldliness (cf. Jas. 4:1-5). Some in the congregation are new Christians in need of maturity (cf. 1 Pet. 2:2-3). Some in the congregation are lukewarm Christians in need of exhortation (cf. Rev. 3:14-20). Some in the congregation are defiant Christians in need of chastisement (cf. 1 Cor. 5:1-13). Some in the congregation are on the precipice of apostasy and in need of warning (cf. Heb. 2:1-3). Some in the congregation are not Christians at all but are spiritually deluded (cf. Matt. 7:21-23). Some in the congregation are decidedly not Christians (cf. Acts 20:29-30).

Can pastors engage in effective ministry on behalf of such a diver-

sity of people? We must answer in the affirmative, through the means
of intercessory prayer. But such will be the case only when our conception of pastoral labor finally transcends the corporate model and
assumes its full *priestly* dignity. Pastors must once again call to mind
the priority of intercessory prayer evinced by Samuel the prophet: "As
for me, far be it from me that I should sin against the LORD by failing
to pray for you" (1 Sam. 12:23). Peterson refers to this work as the
forgotten art of curing souls, "a term," he says, "that identifies us with
our ancestors and colleagues in ministry . . . who are convinced that
a life of prayer is the connective tissue between holy day proclamation
and weekday discipleship."[16] The epistles of Paul steadily reveal this
priestly emphasis:

> *God, whom I serve with my whole heart in preaching the gospel*
> *of his Son, is my witness how constantly I remember you in my*
> *prayers at all times.*
>
> —*Rom. 1:9-10a*

> *For this reason, ever since I heard about your faith in the Lord*
> *Jesus and your love for all the saints, I have not stopped giving*
> *thanks for you, remembering you in my prayers.*
>
> —*Eph. 1:15-16; cf. 3:14-19*

> *I thank my God every time I remember you. In all my prayers*
> *for all of you, I always pray with joy because of your partner-*
> *ship in the gospel.*
>
> —*Phil. 1:3-5*

> *For this reason, since the day we heard about you, we have not*
> *stopped praying for you.*
>
> —*Col. 1:9ff.*

> *We always thank God for all of you, mentioning you in our*
> *prayers. We continually remember before our God and Father*
> *your work produced by faith.*
>
> —*1 Thess. 1:2-3*

*I thank God, whom I serve, as my forefathers did, with a clear conscience, as night and day I constantly remember you in my prayers.*

—2 Tim. 1:3

*I always thank my God as I remember you in my prayers.*

—Philem. 4

To the church in Colosse Paul commends a fellow servant named Epaphras. About him the apostle writes, "He is always *wrestling in prayer* for you, that you may stand firm in all the will of God, mature and fully assured" (Col. 4:12, emphasis added). Intercessory prayer, then, is not a cavalier endeavor but an agonizing pastoral labor.[17] "All vital praying makes a drain on a man's vitality. True intercession is a sacrifice, a bleeding sacrifice."[18] Of course, it is the priestly ministry of the Chief Shepherd Himself that supplies us with the ultimate pastoral model. The writer of Hebrews says, "He is able to save completely those who come to God through him, because he always lives to intercede for them" (7:25), a fact powerfully illustrated in the preservation of Simon Peter (Luke 22:31-32) and in the high-priestly prayer of Jesus in John 17.[19] Even the most rudimentary conception of Christian ministry will identify intercessory prayer as a primary function of the pastoral office. Thus Spurgeon exhorts:

If you are a genuine minister of God you will stand as a priest before the Lord, spiritually wearing the ephod and the breastplate whereon you bear the names of the children of Israel, pleading for them within the veil. . . . The preacher who neglects to pray much must be very careless about his ministry. He cannot have comprehended his calling. He cannot have computed the value of a soul, or estimated the meaning of eternity. He must be a mere official, tempted into a pulpit because the piece of bread which belongs to the priest's office is very necessary to him, or a detestable hypocrite who loves the praise of men, and cares not for the praise of God. . . . He cannot be one of those who plough deep and reap abundant harvests. He is a mere loiterer, not a labourer. As a preacher he has a name to live and is dead. He limps in his life like the lame man in the Proverbs, whose legs were not equal, for his praying is shorter than his preaching.[20]

Third, the vitality of the pastor's own spiritual condition is a subject to which the man of God must give due preoccupation in prayer. The enemy of the church is mindful that sheep scatter when shepherds are struck down. We can recall that Peter was a unique target for the direct assault of Satan (Luke 22:31). John (Acts 4:1-3, 21), a group of unnamed apostles (Acts 5:40), Stephen (Acts 7:54-60), James (Acts 12:2), Barnabas and Paul (Acts 14:1-5), and Silas along with Paul (Acts 16:22-23) were also objects of severe persecution. Men occupying positions of spiritual leadership must expect to be the recipients of violent attack in various forms. The apostle Paul autobiographically cites the unique trials he faced as a minister of the Gospel:

> *I have worked much harder, been in prison more frequently, been flogged more severely, and been exposed to death again and again. Five times I received from the Jews the forty lashes minus one. Three times I was beaten with rods, once I was stoned, three times I was shipwrecked, I spent a night and a day in the open sea, I have been constantly on the move. I have been in danger from rivers, in danger from bandits, in danger from my own countrymen, in danger from Gentiles; in danger in the city, in danger in the country, in danger at sea; and in danger from false brothers. I have labored and toiled and have often gone without sleep; I have known hunger and thirst and have often gone without food; I have been cold and naked. Besides everything else, I face daily the pressure of my concern for all the churches. Who is weak, and I do not feel weak? Who is led into sin, and I do not inwardly burn?*
>
> —*2 Cor. 11:23-29*

A ministerial colleague recently made a humorous but poignant observation. "I've learned something from twenty-five years in pastoral ministry," he said. "I used to believe that 'PT' stood for *pastor-teacher*. Now I know that it stands for *primary target*."

Rigorous attention, therefore, needs to be given to the spiritual preparedness of the preacher. On the evening of His arrest in the Garden of Gethsemane, Jesus gave the following exhortation to His slumbering disciples: "Watch and pray so that you will not fall into temptation" (Mark 14:38).(21) The implication inherent in His words is clear: To divorce themselves from the means of grace (in this case, vigilant prayer), either by outright disregard or passive neglect, would render these disciples more susceptible to the temptation of spiritual compromise, a fact borne out by their experience a short time later (cf. Mark 14:50).

To be sure, the minister of the Gospel is vulnerable to trials and temptations distinct to his calling: *jealousy* ("why are his gifts more esteemed than mine?"); *bitterness* ("why does the congregation criticize everything I do?"); *fear* ("will they leave the church if I teach particular redemption?"); *depression* ("will this church ever grow?"); *grief* ("why have there been so few conversions?"); *frustration* ("why does the board appear to distrust my motivations?"); *doubt* ("why has God caused such suffering in the life of this family?"); *anxiety* ("how will we ever afford to send our children to college?"); *sexual indiscretion* ("why does it seem that my wife is not as responsive to me as other women in the church?"); *despondency* ("why doesn't the congregation love Jesus with greater fervor?"); *desperation* ("have I rightly discerned my call to ministry?"). It is imperative, then, for pastors to structure their lives in order to insure that ample time is given in prayer for the protection and promotion of their own spiritual condition. For this reason, barring emergencies, it has become my habit not to schedule appointments or receive telephone calls before 1:00 P.M. Certainly this kind of prioritizing can elicit initial accusations such as "Our pastor is not very approachable. He's not as accessible as I would like. It's difficult to get close to him." Over time, however, maturing Christians will appreciate the value of such discipline. And they will be the benefactors of it. Until such time the pastor must rest in the conviction that the development of his interior life is in the best interest of the congregation.

"Learn" (said Dr. Paley) "to live alone. Half your faults originate from the want of this faculty." . . . We have great need to watch,

lest public activity should be considered to atone for neglect of
private intercourse with God; and thus our profession should
become a snare to ourselves, and divested of all spiritual savour
to our flock . . . nothing will enrich or console us in the neglect
of intimate communion with God. We must "walk with God" *at
any rate,* or our souls will die. Even Christian communion will
form an empty substitute for this hallowed intercourse. The command is—"Enter into thy closet, and shut thy door." Shut out not
only vanity and the world, but even *for a time* "the communion
of Saints." The soul may lose its spiritual vigour in any company
but that of God—in the best as well as in the worst—in the
Church, as well as in the world—in the active engagements of the
Ministry, as well as secular employments.[22]

## THE PASTOR AND THE CONGREGATION

At this point a fundamental transition is necessary from pastor to congregation. If the woeful neglect of prayer among pastors necessitates
a call to reformation, is it not safe to assume that a similar sort of reformation will be needed among congregations? How, then, can a pastor
reform a congregation with regard to its practice of ministry, specifically related to the subject of prayer? How should the realignment of
pastoral priorities advocated above express itself practically in the life
of the gathered church? Once the man of God has embraced the
priestly dimensions of pastoral ministry, his redirection of the congregation ought to express itself through three principal means of influence: *instruction, modeling,* and *leadership.*

Ecclesiological issues are transformed in Christ under the authority of His revealed Word. Therefore, it is incumbent upon the man of
God to set before the congregation the biblical/theological arguments
for the priority of prayer in local church ministry. First, this must
include instruction regarding the place of prayer in pastoral responsibility.[23] Second, congregations should see the emphasis given to prayer
among the early Christians. "They devoted themselves to the apostles'
teaching and to the fellowship, to the breaking of bread and to prayer"
(Acts 2:42, cf. 1:14, 24; 4:23-31; 6:4; 8:15; 9:11, 40; 10:2, 9; 12:5;
13:3; 14:23; etc.). Third, the apostolic imperatives concerning prayer

need to be explicated (cf. Rom. 12:12; 15:30-32; Eph. 6:18-20; Phil. 4:6; 1 Thess. 5:17; 2 Thess. 3:1; 1 Tim. 2:1-2; Heb. 13:18). Fourth, congregations should be supplied with the biblical promises associated with prayer (cf. Matt. 7:7-11; John 14:13-14; 15:7; Phil. 4:7; Jas. 1:5; 5:16; 1 John 5:14-15). The work of reformation is dependent upon clear, biblical instruction. As such, the people of God need a scriptural apologetic for the priority of prayer in congregational life.

Consistent modeling powerfully reinforces careful instruction. To our knowledge, Jesus never conducted a weekend seminar focused upon the subject of prayer. Instead He prayed, and as a result the request was made of Him, "Lord, teach us to pray" (Luke 11:1). When a consistent ministry of intercession is heartily embraced as an essential expression of pastoral responsibility, the praying of the pastor can become a fulcrum within the community of faith, prompting the congregation to recognize with greater seriousness its responsibility to pray. Though care must be given to avoid all displays of ostentation, the pastor must nevertheless be recognized as a man of prayer. This can be made evident in several ways, two of which are: 1) a weekly schedule that reveals his devotedness to prayer; and 2) a greater attention given to his public praying. It is painfully evident that many pastors give little consideration to their public prayers. Thus these prayers often lack coherence. They frequently reveal no forethought. They belie a regard for the One being addressed. Some churches have altogether forsaken the pastoral prayer in their services. Of those that continue this expression of worship, the substance of their prayers is notoriously imbalanced. The adoration of God's perfections is not heard. Confession of sin is rarely mentioned. Thanksgiving is a lost art.

The sad consequence to this is that the pastor's public praying actually becomes *counterproductive*. His well-intentioned exhortations directed toward the congregation related to the priority of prayer are implicitly neutralized by his own obvious lack of attention to prayer. Are prewritten prayers the answer to this dilemma? Not necessarily. Certainly a read prayer, either on the part of the pastor or the congregation, can be genuine if recited from the heart. More often than not, however, when liturgical prayer is emphasized over that of a more spontaneous expression, the liberating movement of the Spirit is impeded.[24] At this point an exceedingly fruitful study for the pastor would be a careful consideration of the recorded prayers in the Bible (e.g., 1 Kings 8:22-53; Ezra 9:5-15; Neh. 1:4-11; 9:1-38; Dan. 9:1-19; John 17).

Finally, it is essential that pastors exercise the leadership granted to them by the Chief Shepherd. Instruction and modeling must eventuate in direct application. Meetings for prayer need to be scheduled into the life of the congregation. Edmund Clowney has said, "Whether in formal or informal gatherings, fervent corporate prayer is the life-breath of Christ's church."[25] Presently at Christ Community Church we have designated the following opportunities for prayer (this does not include Sunday morning and evening worship services):

> Tuesday: Elders' prayer meeting
> Tuesday morning: Women's prayer meeting
> Wednesday evening: All-church prayer meeting/Bible study
> Saturday morning: Men's prayer meeting
> Sunday morning: Elective prayer meeting during Christian education hour

Each of these meetings is given specific focus by those who direct them. For example, the Saturday morning prayer meeting is specifically structured to pray for evangelistic concerns, missionaries, and the services on the following Lord's Day. In addition to these weekly meetings, four or five additional evenings are scheduled throughout the year for corporate prayer, most often related to evangelistic endeavors. These are very carefully planned meetings with extended periods of directed prayer that are intentionally interspersed with the reading of related Scriptures and corporate singing.[26] What can be the benefits of exercising such pastoral leadership, the scheduling and planning of meetings specifically designed for congregational prayer? *The congregation may come to more deeply believe that their covenant Lord is a prayer-hearing God*: "O you who hear prayer . . ." (Ps. 65:2). *The congregation may come to more truly identify their dependence upon God*: "Give us today our daily bread" (Matt. 6:11). *The congregation may come to more fully appreciate the mediatorial accomplishments of Jesus Christ*: ". . . since we have confidence to enter the Most Holy Place by the blood of Jesus, by a new and living way opened for us through the curtain, that is, his body, and since we have a great priest over the house of God, let us draw near to God . . ." (Heb. 10:19-22). Through the means of biblical instruction, consistent modeling, and proactive leadership, a pastor can be used by God to teach his congregation to pray.

Nehemiah had it right: Prayer is the *sine qua non* of spiritual advancement. Any substantial reformation of pastoral ministry, then, must include three essential aspirations. First, pastors must seek to be *reformed pastors*, laboring to match an Augustinian practice of ministry with an Augustinian theology. This correspondence will express itself most intentionally in the renewed priority given to prayer as an indispensable component of pastoral work. Second, the reformed pastor must patiently use the Scriptures to develop a *reformed congregation*, one that recognizes the biblical weightiness of private and corporate prayer. Third, the reformed pastor and congregation must together seek the courage and discernment to wisely implement this *reformed ministry*. Traditions may be undone. Priorities may be overturned. Ministries may be invalidated. Such is the necessary work of *reformation*.

We hear the haunting words of M'Cheyne, with the slightest of alterations: What a *pastor* is alone on his knees before God, that he is, and no more. What a *congregation* is alone on her knees before God, that she is, and no more.

## NOTES

1 This is made evident in the ascription with which Nehemiah begins his prayer: "O Lord, God of heaven" (Neh. 1:5).

2 Though dated, Walter Wagoner's sad indictment of the prayer life of theological students is still valid: "Students suffer from the general syndrome of Protestant churches: they've become artful dodgers of a disciplined prayer life. They use social action, spiritual guruism—in the form of psychological counseling—and a scrupulously academic approach to the study of religion as a substitute to evade the problem of a totally religious prayer life." Walter Wagoner, "Can Modern Man Pray?" *Newsweek*, 72, No. 27, 1969, p. 38.

3  Eugene H. Peterson, *Working the Angles: The Shape of Pastoral Integrity* (Grand Rapids, MI: Eerdmans, 1998), pp. 73-74.

4  Jesus prayed during His baptism (Luke 3:21), prior to His selection of the disciples (Luke 6:12-13), shortly before feeding the 5,000 (Luke 9:16), on the Mount of Transfiguration (Luke 9:28), standing before the tomb of Lazarus (John 11:41-42), prompted by the coming of the Greeks (John 12:28), subsequent to the Upper Room Discourse (John 17:1-26), in anticipation of the crucifixion (Luke 22:39-45), and while hanging from the cross (Matt. 27:46; Luke 23:34, 46; John 19:30).

5  Charles Bridges, *The Christian Ministry with an Inquiry into the Causes of Its Inefficiency* (Carlisle, PA: Banner of Truth, 1991), pp. 149-150.

6  In contradistinction, we would do well to hear the words of one who rightly defines biblical prayer as "a renunciation of human means. It is not merely the point beyond which I could not go, the limit of my power which dissolves into impotence, but it is indeed a stripping bare, the abandonment of all human apparatus in order to place myself, without arms or equipment, into the hands of the Lord, who decides and fulfills." Jacques Ellul, *Prayer and the Modern Man*, trans. C. Edward Hopkin (New York: Seabury Press, 1970), p. 30.

7  Of course, Acts 6:4 (along with many other New Testament texts) would compel us to identify preaching as an equally defining function.

8  Charles Spurgeon, *Lectures to My Students* (Pasadena, TX: Pilgrim Publications, reprint 1990), p. 40.

9  Bridges, *Christian Ministry*, p. 147.

10  It is noteworthy to consider the frequency with which David in Psalm 119 makes explicit petition to God for the illumination of divine revelation (vv. 12, 18-19, 26-27, 34-36, 64, 66, 68, 108, 124-125, 135, 169).

11  Karl Barth, *Evangelical Theology*, trans. Grover Foley (Garden City, NY: Doubleday, Anchor Books, 1964), p. 160.

12  Gardiner Spring, *The Power of the Pulpit* (Carlisle, PA: Banner of Truth, reprint 1986), p. 140.

13  Calvin Miller, *Spirit, Word, and Story* (Dallas: Word, 1989), pp. 25-26.

14  Attributed to Payson without reference in Henry C. Fish, *Power in the Pulpit* (Carlisle, PA: Banner of Truth, n.d.), p. 19.

15  Despite the frequency with which men change pastoral charges, it is essential for both pastors and congregations to be mindful of God's sovereign involvement in the establishment of these relationships. Cf. Acts 20:28, "Keep watch over yourselves and all the flock *of which the Holy Spirit has made you overseers*" and 1 Peter 5:2-3, "Be shepherds of God's flock . . . not lording it over *those entrusted to you*" (emphasis added).

16  Eugene H. Peterson, *The Contemplative Pastor: Returning to the Art of Spiritual Direction* (Grand Rapids, MI: Eerdmans, 1989), p. 59.

17  The term in Colossians 4:12, *agonidzomai*, means to engage in intense struggle, to strive to do something with great intensity and effort. "The supreme goal for which we fight and work and suffer is not our own salvation alone; it is the salvation of many . . . the form of battle is prayer. In prayer there is achieved unity between the will of God and that of man, between human struggling and action and effective divine operation. . . . In prayer one man becomes the representative of the other, so that there is here opened up the possibility of one

standing in the breach for all . . ." Ethelbert Stauffer, *"agonidzomai,"* *Theological Dictionary of the New Testament,* ed. Gerhard Kittel, Vol. 1 (Grand Rapids, MI: Eerdmans, 1965), pp. 138-139.

18  Attributed to J. H. Jowett without reference in J. Oswald Sanders, *Spiritual Leadership* (Chicago: Moody Press, 1980), p. 125.

19  In his great high-priestly intercession (John 17) Jesus prays for Himself (vv. 1-5), His immediate disciples (vv. 6-19), and finally all who will come to Him by faith through the apostolic witness (vv. 20-26).

20  Spurgeon, *Lectures,* pp. 46-47.

21  Though prayer is not mentioned specifically, spiritual leaders would do well to remember passages of similar emphasis (e.g., Acts 20:28, *"Keep watch over yourselves* and all the flock of which the Holy Spirit has made you overseers," emphasis added).

22  Bridges, *Christian Ministry,* pp. 150-151.

23  It has been common to avoid instructing congregations about the divinely ordained responsibilities of pastoral ministry, often owing to a misplaced fear of irrelevance. Unfortunately, the neglect of these profoundly relevant issues has effected tragic consequences within the church (e.g., approaches to ministry that are foreign to the Scriptures and thus detrimental to the maturity of both pastors and congregations). To the contrary, the author has found his congregation exceedingly responsive to biblical instruction regarding the role and responsibilities of pastors.

24  James Denney warns: "A liturgy, however beautiful, is a melancholy witness to the quenching of the Spirit: it may be better or worse than the prayers of one man, but it could never compare for fervour with the spontaneous prayers of a living church." Cited without reference in J. Oswald Sanders, *The Holy Spirit and the Gifts* (Grand Rapids, MI: Zondervan, 1970), p. 99.

25  Edmund P. Clowney, *The Church* (Downers Grove, IL: InterVarsity, 1995), p. 133.

26  It is a sad but honest acknowledgment concerning the evangelical churches in our time that meetings specifically set aside for prayer tend to be the most sparsely attended. This is due, at least in part, to the fact that most often these meetings are the least stimulating. But they are often the least stimulating because they have been the most poorly planned.

# 10

## ALL THINGS IN COMMON:

### The Pastoral Role in Building Real Fellowship

■

David W. Hegg

One of the privileges of living in Southern California is having fresh fruit from trees in our own backyards. Freshly squeezed orange juice, lemons for tea or pies, and fresh guacamole have become delightfully commonplace. So when our lemon tree failed to produce the fruit we expected, we took action. First we examined the leaves and the branches, the bark and the blossoms, and set about to clip, snip, and spray our way to a successful harvest. We spent both time and money and worked hard doing good things for our tree. But the next year— no lemons! Then we called in an expert. After taking a look at our tree he announced, "Healthy fruit comes from healthy roots." We took his advice, fertilized the roots, and now have enough lemons to share with the neighbors.

In too many ways our churches resemble that fruitless lemon tree, especially in the area of authentic fellowship. What the New Testament describes as fellowship—souls knit together in love, having all things in common, considering others as more important than oneself, trusting one another's protection enough to allow for mutual, personal confession of sin, preferring one another as forgiven brothers and sisters, and working diligently to enhance the perfecting work of the Holy Spirit in one another unto love and good deeds—is today described in terms of social events, friendly greeters, punch and cookies, name tags, meals-on-wheels, and creatively named affinity groups. While all of these have a place, they don't begin to fill up the biblical measure of fellowship. But we don't seem to notice. Somehow we are increasingly satisfied with defective fruit. Worse, we may have forgotten how sweet and necessary the authentic fruit of fellowship is to our souls.

To be sure there are many today who argue strongly that fellowship is essential to church health, and especially church growth. Usually this is expressed as a need for "community." "People today need to belong," we're told. And the church must devise ways to create fellowship opportunities and assimilate individuals into the fellowshipping community before they fall through the cracks or slip out the back door. This concern to integrate people into the group has spawned a whole new area of church expertise, and Pastors of Assimilation have begun springing up everywhere. In many places this intentional development of a caring community that offers the individual a sense of belonging has become the primary purpose of the church. In this context, acceptance and connection with others become the necessary prerequisites to transformation. Unfortunately, while much of this thinking stems from a heart of love for people, it is really nothing more than an attempt to produce healthy fruit by clipping, snipping, and spraying. Simply put, true fellowship cannot be programmed, packaged, or produced through even the most creative energies focused on people. Healthy fruit comes from healthy roots, and in the case of true fellowship, the root is Christ.

By now you're wondering where this article is going. So here it is: *Fellowship among believers is the fruit of fellowship with Christ.* To produce the first, you must fertilize the second. What elevates true fellowship far above what the world would call friendship and belonging is simply this: Our relationship with fellow believers is a demonstration of our union with Christ, and the dynamics of this fellowship with others are dictated and defined by the fact that we are new creatures—loved, chosen, redeemed, forgiven, justified, and adopted into the family of God by God Himself through our Lord Jesus Christ. The rest of this chapter is my attempt to prove this and to encourage you in your pursuit of authentic fellowship in the church.

## TODAY'S CHALLENGES

Growing the healthy fruit of authentic fellowship today is hard, very hard. But the fact that Scripture encourages and demands believers to persevere in faithfulness presupposes ongoing, active opposition. To grow healthy lemons you must understand the enemies that put the root and fruit at risk. Any attempt to reform fellowship in the church must begin with a look at the forces that threaten deformity. Of all the challenges we face in ministry today, three stand out as those that present the greatest opposition to true fellowship.

*Consumerism.* One of the most daunting realities I face as a pastor is the challenge of turning religious consumers into humble servants. The consumer mentality, where the customer is king, has set the church back on its heels. What pastor does not feel the pressure to give religious consumers what they are shopping for so they will become steady customers? In many churches everything from preaching and music to child-care and parking is reexamined almost monthly to ensure that the church meets the ever-changing needs of the religious consumer.

Like any good marketing organization, these churches realize that the more attachments a customer has with the company, the harder it will be for him to take his business elsewhere. This is where personal relationship becomes a key factor in retention and growth. If we want to attract people and keep them, we must offer them a sense of belonging, a connection with others through shared needs and interests. And so we make it a priority to offer the people what they will enjoy and what we know will help us keep them. We strategize and then program connecting opportunities, creatively packaged and advertised as ways to become part of a caring community—all in the name of fellowship.

Unfortunately, sooner or later we have to tell them that, actually, Christianity is not man-centered but God-centered. The customer isn't the king—God is. The church exists for Him and is called to exalt Him above all else, in humility and fear. We have to take those whom we have attracted and assimilated by meeting their needs and tell them that Christian maturity demands that they now subordinate their needs to the needs of others, their wants to the wants of Christ. But consumers don't appreciate disappointment. All too often they will opt to take their budgeted religious resources of time and money and spend them elsewhere.

For our purposes here I only want to call attention to the effect consumerism has on true fellowship in the church. Consumerism tempts the church to substitute group acceptance for the more demanding investment of true fellowship. The first offers you a place in the group, while the second puts you at the foot of the cross. A sense of belonging may improve your quality of life, your enjoyment of church, and even your sense of spiritual obligation; but ultimately a consumer mentality will rebel when things don't go as planned. When feelings get hurt, when views collide, when stylistic changes occur, when leadership moves on, or when sinful behavior is uncovered and confronted, mere group acceptance will seldom be enough to maintain relationship. Simply put, a shared sense of felt needs will never preserve relationship when pride and selfishness mar the idealistic picture of community that pervades the mind of the religious consumer.

True fellowship, on the other hand, begins with a common understanding that you and I are sinful, but that our sin has been nailed to the cross, fully charged to Christ, and forgiven. Consequently, the foundation of our relationship is that we share a common weakness. Neither of us is ideal. But what *is* ideal is that we share a perfect Savior whose grace has captured us, and in whom we find the only acceptance that really matters. Your lack of perfection, far from being unexpected, does not rupture our relationship, for it only reminds me of my weaknesses and chases me back to the cross where the ground is level and the forgiveness complete. As we will see, it is this utter reliance on Christ that the Spirit uses to knit believing hearts together in a relationship so mutually dependent and satisfying that Paul likens it to the unity of the human body. What is deformed by the selfishness of consumerism is only reformed by the sacrifice of the cross.

*Independence.* In California, independence is a virtue. In fact, we are more and more prone to define success as self-sufficiency. If we had it our way, we would never have to depend upon anyone for anything any time. And I fear we are not unusual among the people of America, and perhaps most of the world. While the freeways are jammed, the carpool lanes are largely open—a telling testimony to the stubborn insistence that we all want to preserve our ability to go and come at will, even if it costs us hours of frustrating delay.

But then again, such is the spirit of man. The psalmist represented this thirst for independence well in Psalm 2:1-3 where, in opposition to the Great King who sovereignly rules over all and to His Anointed One, mankind defiantly says, "Let us break their chains and throw off their fetters." From the beginning man has wanted to live his life with no strings attached.

In the middle of an increasingly independent society, where affluence has made independence even more commonplace, the church is called to fashion independent individuals into an interdependent body. The challenge here is real and formidable. Even among believers, whose hearts and minds have been realigned according to the truth of the Gospel, independence is a powerful force that works against the very essence of biblical fellowship.

Independence may allow for cordiality, but it usually resists intimacy. As such, this trend toward independence and self-sufficiency presents a problem at the opposite end of the spectrum from consumerism. While consumers come looking to get, those who prize their independence proudly assert that they don't need anything. Sadly, the believing community is not without these independence-minded brothers and sisters whose ardent self-sufficiency is diametrically opposed to the heart of biblical fellowship. When Paul, in 1 Corinthians 12:20-21, points to the absurdity of an eye's saying it does not need the hand, the case is closed. True fellowship among believers is the opposite of independence and self-sufficiency. True fellowship resonates through our humble admission that we are in over our heads, are not well-suited to go it alone, and are desperately in need of "each part [doing] its work" (Eph. 4:16).

As with consumerism, the challenge of independence will never be met by treating the fruit. Those who take pride in their independence and self-sufficiency will not come to prize a fellowship of interdependence until the myth of their independence is reformed according to the truth of Christ. The fruit of true fellowship, demonstrated through mutual dependence among believers, comes only as we acknowledge our mutual dependence upon Christ. It is Christ whose grace has demolished our sinful independence and drawn us into eternal relationship with Him. It is Christ who dwells in our hearts by faith and enables us to see that our need for spiritual intimacy with others is a delightful necessity. It is our relationship with Christ that is the root of true fellowship, for it is to Christ that we belong (Gal. 5:24).

*Networking.* In the middle between the ardent consumers and the self-sufficient independents are the networkers. This growing group of people view the church as a vast resource pool, and they prize relationships with people not merely to meet personal needs but to enhance achievement of personal goals. The challenge of the church today is to turn goal-centered networkers into God-centered worshipers.

In a networking context, people are ranked according to how their resources, position, knowledge, or influence can help you reach your goals. During my years in the world of corporate finance I learned firsthand the necessity and value of building a network of acquaintances whose experience, influence, knowledge, or generosity could help me succeed. But I also came to see the dehumanizing effects of this self-focused activity. The obvious negative in the pursuit of a network is that people who seemingly offer you no advantage are passed over. We become elitists. We have no time to pursue relationships with those below our station, those we do not believe can help us.

The networking mind-set presents great challenges in the church. First, it makes the purpose of the gathered community the promotion of the individual rather than the exaltation of God. And second, it undermines true fellowship. Unfortunately, many in the church today have honed their networking skills and insights so well that they have largely lost the ability to appreciate people as people. We have become programmed to pursue those who can help us, who are like us, or who offer us some advantage. We only value those we consider valuable. But this is quite the opposite of true church fellowship. In his letter James strongly criticized his readers for preferring the rich over the poor, saying they had become "judges with evil thoughts" (2:1-4). The church of the Crucified One—the Body of Christ—is not a place where people are first appraised and then ranked according to their earthly importance. Rather, the church is a company of redeemed equals called into united worship of God Himself. All attempts to insert earthly distinctions actually eat away at the very foundation of the church's distinctiveness and muffle the church's central call to worthy worship.

Here then is the third great challenge the church faces in our attempt to establish true fellowship. As with the challenges of consumerism and independence, the power to turn networkers into worshipers will not come from programming alone. To appreciate the lowly, to delight in the humble, we must learn to look at others through the eyes of the Savior. We must come to understand that the greatest thing that can be said of anyone has nothing to do with their bank account, their position, their experiences, their abilities, or their influence. It has everything to do with the fact that, as believers, they are gifted dwellings of the Holy Spirit, covered with the righteousness of Jesus Christ; and as children of God Himself, they offer to us a privileged opportunity for intimate, eternal relationship.

## BIBLICAL COUNSEL

In order to pursue reform, we have to recognize the forces that bring deformity in order to identify ways to combat them. But that is not enough. We must also settle on what the governing pattern will be, what the standard is to which we will "re-form" what has become twisted and broken. The Reformers of the sixteenth century spoke often of the need to be "reformed according to the Word of God." Certainly in the area of true fellowship in the church, this must be our only standard as well. The task of reforming fellowship is first and foremost the task of bringing it into conformity with the truth of Scripture. And to be sure, this is not a onetime task. It is an ongoing challenge that calls us to reform what is deformed and to adopt as part of our mission the vow to be ever reforming all that we are and do according to the pattern of God's Word.

When we survey the New Testament texts that touch on fellowship, we find that they often rely on the term *koinonia.* Seventeen times the New Testament authors use this word to describe events of sharing, participation, and interaction. Most of these texts assume the reality of fellowship; few describe it. We first meet the term in Acts 2:42, where fellowship is listed as one of four marks of the Jerusalem congregation. The term takes on more definition when we see it used to describe financial contributions (Rom. 15:26; 2 Cor. 8:4; 9:13) and the sharing of possessions with one another (Heb. 13:16). And yet *koinonia* also represents an even deeper, more essential bond than the sharing of resources might indicate. Paul describes fellowship as a partnership in which two parties are "yoked together" (2 Cor. 6:14). Such a relationship is a mutual participation in a common life that gives rise to shared enjoyment and responsibility. Consequently, Paul sternly warns his readers not to be "yoked together with unbelievers," for there can be no mutuality between "light [and] darkness" (2 Cor. 6:14).

This state of being "yoked together" may seem, at first glance, something to avoid. After all, who ever wanted to be bound, tied down, restricted? Yet this is actually the beginning of a true understanding of fellowship as the New Testament describes it. The relationship that exists between believers is <u>one of shared life</u>, not merely the sharing of the things that fill our lives. To be sure, this relationship of interdependence, of interlocking lives, necessarily gives rise to overt demonstrations of love and concern. These are represented in the New Testament by means of the many "one another" passages (see, for example, Rom. 12:10; 15:7; Eph. 4:2, 32; Col. 3:16; 1 Thess. 5:11; Heb. 3:13). But while these actions represent the necessary actions arising out of true fellowship, they do not define the essence of it. Fellowship speaks specifically to that sense of bondedness—the interlocking of lives, each having a participatory responsibility—among believers that distinguishes us from the unbelieving world. It is a willing investment of my life in yours.

This essential connectedness and interdependence is so dynamic that there is a shared sense of being: When one rejoices, all rejoice, and when one grieves, all know grief (Rom. 12:15). Paul describes believers as having been "united in love" (Col. 2:2) and as a result enabled to be "like-minded, having the same love, being one in spirit and purpose" (Phil. 2:2). In this fellowship it is to your advantage to be "<u>like-minded</u>" and <u>not to be "proud, but . . . willing to asso-</u>

ciate with people of low position" (Rom. 12:16), for the joys of the lowly will be enjoyed by all. In the same way, all of the scriptural injunctions to accept, admonish, build up, comfort, forbear, pray for, and give preference to one another (see Rom. 12:10; 15:7, 14; 14:19; Eph. 4:2; 1 Thess. 4:18; Jas. 5:16) only have real meaning and importance if we truly believe that "we who are many form one body, and each member belongs to all the others" (Rom. 12:5). If my life is joined to yours, then your well-being matters, and it matters to me. Your spiritual maturity matters, and it matters to me. Your joy, your accomplishments, your losses, and your gains all matter, and they matter to me, because my life is knit to yours and we share a common life and future. These descriptions of fellowship in the church describe much more than the familiarity or friendship that may be facilitated at potlucks. They describe a mysterious yet actual fusing of individual lives into one body so that the many may act and feel as one.

Even as I write these words I shudder with great misgivings. What I see in Scripture and what I know to be true in my own experience just don't match. At times it seems I am only nibbling at the edges of this thing we call true fellowship. Certainly in my marriage I have come to know a fellowship that obscures the line where my life ends and Cherylyn's begins. And to be sure, I have known the joy of risk-free relationship and soul-to-soul participation with brothers and sisters in Christ with whom I have shared ministry and life. But I confess that the greater part of my involvement with people—fellow believers, true laborers for the kingdom—has often not gone beyond the cordial, the friendly, the expected actions of the non-threatening brand of Christianity that makes few authentic demands on us. As James said, "My brothers, this should not be" (Jas. 3:10).

When we hold our practice up to the light of Scripture, we recognize our great shortcomings. But greater still can be the joy of knowing that the same Word of power is able to bring us back into alignment with God's gracious design.

Let's go back again to the Scripture's use of *koinonia*. While the word *fellowship* is used in the New Testament to describe the relationship between believers, it is also regularly used to describe the participation believers have in Jesus Christ. As sons of God by faith, we have peace with God through Christ (Rom. 5:1). But the relationship we enjoy is more than that of a pardoned criminal. We have been made partakers of the divine nature (2 Pet. 1:4) and mysteriously joined to Christ Himself (Gal. 2:20; Col. 1:27-29; 2:9-12). Paul describes this to the Corinthians by saying that they were "called into fellowship with his Son Jesus Christ our Lord" (1 Cor. 1:9). John describes the same sense, declaring that ultimately "our fellowship is with the Father and with his Son" (1 John 1:3). This relationship with Christ is labeled "the fellowship of the Holy Spirit" (2 Cor. 13:14), for it is through the Spirit that we have been "born again" (John 3:3-8) and brought into union with Christ (1 Cor. 12:12-14). What becomes apparent is that our union with Christ is the root from which the fruit of fellowship with other believers springs.

John clearly and forcefully demonstrates the divine priority and order of fellowship in 1 John 1:3-7. First he reminds us that our fellowship is with the Father and the Son (v. 3). Then he declares that there is a relationship between our fellowship with God and our fellowship with one another. He first defines "fellowship with him" (v. 6) as "walk[ing] in the light, as he is in the light (v. 7). Then the apostle states that the great fruit of walking in fellowship with Him is fellowship with one another. Don't miss the point here. That which brings forth true fellowship among believers is the reality of our fellowship with God in Christ Jesus. If it is the fruit of fellowship in the church that you want, fertilize the root of union with Christ. The first grows from the second. The only effective energy for a fellowship among believers that truly shares a common life is a recognition that that common life is the life of Christ. Show me a group of redeemed laborers who find daily delight in their union with Christ, whose one goal is the glory of Christ, whose only boast is in the cross of Christ, and I will show you a group of people whose love and preference for one another is radiant and inviting. That love is the fruit of their deep understanding that they have been joined to Christ through faith and thus share a unity that transcends the natural and previews heaven. They love because they first were loved. The fruit of their fellowship is rooted in Christ Himself.

## Reflective Fellowship in the Church

The idea that our life *for* Christ ought to be a reflection of our life *in* Christ is one of the great themes of the New Testament. Jesus Himself exhorted those on the hillside that the light of their lives ought to reflect their Father in heaven (Matt. 5:16). Later he told the Twelve that their love for each other was to reflect His love for them (John 13:35). Elsewhere we see that our lives are to reflect the life of Christ, including His holiness (1 Pet. 1:15), His faithful endurance (Heb. 12:1-3), His humility (Phil. 2:5-8), and His submission (1 Pet. 2:21-25). But how is this possible? How can the fallen ever mirror the perfect? The answer is found in the union of the believer with Christ the Savior. It is this fellowship, this sharing, this participation the believer has with Christ that stands at the core of all Christian ability and obedience. Even as Paul exhorted the Philippian believers to "work out [their] salvation with fear and trembling," he punctuated his command with the radical reminder that ultimately it is "God who works in you to will and to act according to his good pleasure" (Phil. 2:12-13). All we are to be and do as redeemed sons and daughters can be traced back to who God is and what He has accomplished for us through Jesus Christ.

All of this speaks to the truest way to motivate or increase Christian obedience. How do we grow in grace? How do we motivate believers to walk in righteousness? How do we grow the fruit of true fellowship in the church? If our standing before God is only because of Christ, and if the power to obey is only through our fellowship with Christ, and if we stand transformed only by the love of Christ, then the primary motive for every Christian virtue must be our love for Christ. Our glorious ongoing challenge as believers is this: to grow our love *for* Christ in response to our expanding understanding of the love *of* Christ that has been graciously lavished upon us. Out of this will come a reflective life, a reflective holiness, a reflective obedience, a reflective fellowship that is the fruit of our fellowship with the Lord Himself. Paul summed it up beautifully: "Be imitators of God, therefore, as dearly loved children and live a life of love, just as Christ loved us and gave himself up for us as a fragrant offering and sacrifice to God" (Eph. 5:1-2).

## REFORMING FELLOWSHIP IN THE CHURCH

If I have made my case, by now you understand that the question of reforming fellowship in the church is really better asked this way: How can we increase our understanding of the favored position we have in Christ and thereby deepen our love for Christ? When we ask the question this way, we are acknowledging that true fellowship in the church is only a by-product of hearts that are thrilled with Jesus! How should we begin our attempt to increase the capacity of believing hearts to delight in Christ?

## PREACH THE WORD

God has so constructed His world that the preached Word comes with great power when delivered in truth and in the power of the Spirit. God has always led and fed His people through His Word, and that is still true today. All attempts to move the heart of the church in obedience to the commands of Christ must include passionate, prayerful preaching. I suggest the following as overall themes necessary to increase love for Christ.

### Preach Christ as Sovereign Savior

> So do not be ashamed to testify about our Lord, or ashamed of me his prisoner. But join with me in suffering for the gospel, by the power of God, who has saved us and called us to a holy life— not because of anything we have done but because of his own purpose and grace. This grace was given us in Christ Jesus before the beginning of time, but it has now been revealed through the appearing of our Savior, Christ Jesus, who has destroyed death and has brought life and immortality to light through the gospel.
> —2 Tim. 1:8-10

In all of your preaching, stress the fact that salvation is all of grace. Don't be ashamed of that. While the heart is by nature adverse to the sovereignty of God in salvation, ultimately nothing humbles the pride of man like the knowledge that his salvation is not at all of his own doing. Those who consider themselves better than others must come to know the joy expressed by the hymn writer: "Nothing in my hands I bring; simply to thy cross I cling." And when we come to see that our standing before God is due only to His eternal love extended to us in Jesus Christ, we begin to see the Savior in a whole new light. No longer is He a consultant we have hired with the currency of our faith. No longer is He an adviser whom we have put on retainer. No longer does Jesus exist to help further our agenda and increase our importance. Rather He is the mighty Redeemer, the King, the Sovereign who has chosen us as sons and daughters not because of our ability or merit, but only because it so pleased His loving heart. Further, He is the one who has cleansed our criminal record and clothed us in righteousness. On our best day we stand accepted before the Almighty only because of the righteousness of Christ; on our worst day we stand accepted before the Almighty only because Christ died in our place and for our good. Knowing this, how can we ever become cold toward Him? How can we ever cease to wonder at His grace, His love, His power, His humility, His wisdom? Contrary to what many may think, it is the fire of God's sovereign selection and redemption of the sinner that warms the heart and drives the mind deeper and deeper into the mysteries of Christ.

The biblical understanding of salvation humbles the heart, and this has two marvelous consequences. First, as sinners see their own unworthiness in light of God's great grace, they will be moved in love for their gracious and loving Lord. And second, so moved, they will begin to look with love and affection on those who enjoy full acceptance along with them as they live in the shadow of the cross.

### Preach Christ as Suffering Servant

In Jesus Christ we are afforded the greatest picture of one who, out of love and loyalty to the divine redemptive plan, willingly gave up that which He had every right to hang on to, in order to serve others. Paul highlights this in Philippians 2:5-8:

> *Your attitude should be the same as that of Christ Jesus: Who, being in very nature God, did not consider equality with God something to be grasped, but made himself nothing, taking the*

*very nature of a servant, being made in human likeness. And*
*being found in appearance as a man, he humbled himself and*
*became obedient to death—even death on a cross!*

This text, so important to a proper Christology, is actually just an illustration Paul uses to motivate his readers to a proper relationship—fellowship—with one another. The theme of the chapter is righteous Christian living in the church, and Paul puts forth three examples of persons who, out of great love and humility, gave up privilege for sacrificial service. To motivate the Philippians to live together in a manner worthy of their fellowship with Christ, he reminds them of Timothy and Epaphroditus, both of whom had served the church from the heart. But first he points the readers to Christ and powerfully depicts the radical nature of Christ's humility. To increase their obedience in fellowship, Paul praised the Suffering Servant.

With Paul we must preach the glories of the Suffering Servant who came to save. An appreciation of the humiliation Christ joyfully endured for us can have powerful influence in our lives. First, it puts to death the myth that spirituality and arrogance can ever peacefully coexist in the believer. Second, it demonstrates the priority God places on loving service to others. Third, it offers specific details on what Jesus expects of all who would follow His command, "As I have loved you, so you must love one another" (John 13:34). If believers are to live in righteous relationship with one another, they must be continually presented with the glories of humble service as seen in the life of the Savior.

## Preach Christ as Loving Shepherd

A good friend once told me that if he had his ministry to do over again, he would spend more time considering and proclaiming the love of Christ for His own. What I dismissed as a curious reflection I since have come to own as a guiding principle. The love of Christ, which Paul says "surpasses knowledge" (Eph. 3:19) and is the model for our earthly existence (Eph. 5:1-2), is even more grand than these verses alone depict. The love of Christ is that arena in which, as chosen and beloved children of the King, we exist in unconditional and eternal acceptance. Paul puts it this way:

*Who shall separate us from the love of Christ? Shall trouble or hardship or persecution or famine or nakedness or danger or sword? As it is written: "For your sake we face death all day long; we are considered as sheep to be slaughtered." No, in all these things we are more than conquerors through him who loved us. For I am convinced that neither death nor life, neither angels nor demons, neither the present nor the future, nor any powers, neither height nor depth, nor anything else in all creation, will be able to separate us from the love of God that is in Christ Jesus our Lord.*

—Rom. 8:35-39

Since true fellowship is an extension of the love of Christ for us, our people need to hear about His love. We need our hearts to be impressed by it, and then let the overflow water the hearts of our people. The love of Christ is irrevocable. As Matheson wrote from the depths of personal anguish, His is the love "that wilt not let me go." It is there in comfort when I am distressed. It is there in grace and conviction when I sin. It is there in mercy and healing when I repent. And it is there, pervasively and faithfully, in all of the tragedies and traumas as well as the joyful experiences of life.

As a pastor I have come finally to understand that I cannot fix people. I can't heal their diseases or mend their brokenness. But I can extend the love and grace of Christ—in word and action—and call them to return to the Shepherd and Guardian of their souls (1 Pet. 2:25). And when they do, they will find that His boundless love brings rest to their souls (Matt. 11:28-30). But even beyond that, those who come to drink their fill at the fountain of Christ's love become carriers of that water to the lives of others. Paul draws this connection in 2 Corinthians 5:14: "For Christ's love compels us . . ." Regardless of whether this is taken as an objective or subjective genitive, the final thought is the same. It is Paul's great love for Christ, which is only the fruit of Christ's love for him, that moves Paul in obedience toward others. Peter makes it even clearer in 1 Peter 1:22: "Now that you have purified yourselves by obeying the truth so that you have sincere love for your brothers, love one another deeply, from the heart, for you have been born again . . ." It is the love of Christ *for* me that grows love for Christ *in* me and moves me to extend the love of Christ *from* me to the world.

## TAKE FULL ADVANTAGE OF THE LORD'S SUPPER

In our graphically dominated world we may lament that ours is a word-based faith. But in His great wisdom Christ has given us a dramatic, living enactment of true fellowship by which we can reinforce the central truths of true fellowship.

### Promote the Christ-centeredness of the Communal Meal

Mealtime is family time. It is all about sharing life with those you love. But in this sacramental meal, Christ is central. Don't neglect the opportunity to demonstrate that our fellowship with one another is first and foremost a fellowship with Christ.

### Promote the Equality of Those Partaking

The simple acts of eating and drinking are meant to remind everyone in the room that their standing in grace is only through grace. No matter the position, all must be nourished by Christ unto life eternal. Rich and poor, small and great—all are equal around this table. All are equally accepted by Christ and dependent upon Him.

### Promote the Unity of Christ in His Church

When we eat and drink, we are signifying to our own hearts that we are joined to Christ. We live only as He grants us eternal nourishment. Yet, is it not also a beautiful reminder that we are united to all who are so united to Christ? Surely the table of the Lord is meant to awaken our slumbering hearts to the fact that we are a family, called out of darkness into light in order to demonstrate our unique position as God's own possession by the way we participate together in true fellowship.

## A LAST WORD

During the tyrannical days of Hitler, seminary students were forced into hiding to continue their training. It was during his time as a teacher in one of these underground seminaries that Dietrich Bonhoeffer came to consider the very fabric of Christian community. May his words and final question move us to true fellowship:

> Because God has already laid the only foundation of our fellowship, because God has bound us together in one body with other Christians in Jesus Christ, long before we entered into common life with them, we enter into that common life not as demanders but as thankful recipients. We thank God for what He has done for us. We thank God for giving us brethren who live by His call, by His forgiveness, and His promise. We do not complain of what God does not give us; we rather thank God for what He does give us daily. And is not what has been given us enough: brothers who will go on living with us through sin and need under the blessing of His grace? Is the divine gift of Christian fellowship anything less than this, any day, even the most difficult and distressing day?[1]

NOTES

1 Dietrich Bonheoffer, *Life Together* (San Francisco: HarperCollins, 1954), p. 28.

# 11

## PASTORAL MINISTRY AND
## THE PLACE OF THE SACRAMENTS

■

### T. M. Moore

Not long ago it was my privilege to administer the sacrament of baptism to one of my grandchildren, at the gracious invitation of her pastor. This was not a church in my tradition but one that, by virtue of its evangelical convictions, shared much in common with my own communion. I followed my normal procedure, taking the time to explain the sacrament and its place in the history of redemption, the life of the child of God, and the mission of the church before securing testimony of faith in Christ and administering the element, using the words of institution as the Lord gave them to us. After the service I was struck by how many of the members of the congregation approached me, thanking me for explaining the nature of baptism and for taking what seemed to them a most thoughtful and deliberate approach to the sacrament. Several expressed how much it meant to them to be encouraged to recall their own baptism and to seek the grace of the Lord in improving it and remarked that this was one of "the most meaningful baptisms" they had ever witnessed.

I was pleased, but not surprised, by their responses, which emphasizes not so much my skills as a pastor as the routine way that the sacraments tend to be regarded in churches in the evangelical tradition. Evangelicals have placed much emphasis on such matters as the preaching of the Word, discovering more relevant styles and approaches to worship, the importance of fellowship and growth in

Christ, customized approaches to ministry, and improved facilities. At the same time we have, whether wittingly or not, remanded the sacraments to something of a secondary role in the life of the church. In one congregation of which I am aware, baptisms are not even performed in the gathering of the saints for worship, but in a side room between services, with only friends and family in attendance. In perhaps the vast majority of evangelical churches, the Lord's Supper has been relegated to a quarterly observance that is carefully systematized and choreographed to ensure that it can be accomplished in the minimum amount of time. Is it any wonder that the profound significance of these ordinances tends to become lost on the minds of many church members? Or that they seem to have so little to do with what is really important in the life and work of the church?

Yet the very nature of baptism and the Lord's Supper makes them of vital significance for the church, regardless of size, cultural setting, or historical context. The failure of the church's ministry dramatically to impact the lives of postmodern men and women and to transform the culture and society of which they are a part—a point well-argued by many, though with little in the way of perceptible results thus far—suggests that, for all the indications that evangelical churches are enjoying great success, we are not fulfilling the mandate that has been given to us to go and make disciples in all the nations. While a number of explanations could be proffered for this as-yet-unacknowledged failure of mission, certainly the sad state of the sacraments among congregations of evangelical conviction must not be overlooked. The sacraments were intended to establish, strengthen, and distinguish the church and to equip her for kingdom life and mission in every age and context. Indeed, they were intended to be foundational to this calling; so when we reduce them, even unintentionally, to mere routines devoid of substance and deep conviction, the church and her ministry suffers, as does the dying age in which we live.

The very idea that the sacraments have anything much to do with the mission of the church may strike some readers as strange. In this chapter I will argue that recovering a proper sense and use of the sacraments can help put the evangelical church back on track for turning the world upside-down for Christ. After a brief overview of the importance of the sacraments, I will focus on three aspects of their contribution to the life and work of the church before concluding with some suggestions as to how evangelicals can begin to recover a proper use of the sacraments in their kingdom callings. We will look first, then, at a brief apologetic for the sacraments in the life of the church.

## THE IMPORTANCE OF THE SACRAMENTS

The importance of the sacraments derives only secondarily from the benefit they bring to the churches of Christ, which benefit we will shortly explore. Rather, their value, indeed their utter importance to the church, stems from two explicitly biblical facts—the command of Christ and the practice of the apostles①

There can be no denying—and certainly no evangelical would wish to do so—that our Lord Jesus Christ commanded the use of baptism and the Supper as integral aspects of life in the kingdom community of the church. His mandate in Matthew 28:18-20 is clear: We are to make disciples among all the nations, baptizing them in the name of the Trinity, and teaching them to obey the words of Christ. Here the sacrament of baptism is placed alongside the ministry of the Word as of supreme importance for building the church. So also His instruction concerning the Supper: We are to observe it as often as we will, remembering as we do the work that He has accomplished for us (Luke 22:19) and looking forward with joy to His glorious return. Clearly, in Jesus' mind one of the distinguishing marks of the community He would bring into existence was faithful and careful obedience in carrying out these commands.

I stress the words *faithful* and *careful*. Let us agree that most evangelical churches are *faithful*, after a fashion, in administering the sacraments. That is, the sacraments are in use on a somewhat predictable basis—baptism at the end of a new member cycle and the Supper at regularly established intervals. Thus evangelicals would at least seem to have a foundation to build on. But without *careful* attention to their administration, these sacraments can become mere routines, mindless, meaningless exercises that accomplish little in

*bread or wine — prayer, worship, repentance*

preparing the church for kingdom living in the world. Are we careful in the administration of the sacraments when we rush through them for the sake of saving time in an already-crowded service? Are we careful when we fail to explain their distinctive nature and unique contributions to the life of the church? Are we careful when the sacraments are used either as mere tokens of belonging or a convenient reminder or proof of church membership rather than for the purposes for which they were given?

The first church leaders understood the importance of the sacraments, and the evidence is clear that they held them to have a central place in the life of the church. Peter's command to the seekers in Jerusalem on that first Christian Pentecost was to "repent and be baptized" (Acts 2:38), making it clear that a new beginning awaited all who truly turned to the Lord in obedience to His explicit instructions. Paul reminded the Corinthian believers that their schismatic practices ran contrary to the "one baptism" into which they had entered through the Lord Jesus Christ (see Eph. 4:5; cf. 1 Cor. 1:11-13). The same was true of the Lord's Supper. The report from the Jerusalem church is not entirely clear as to whether the common meal that was frequently enjoyed was the Lord's Supper or some other joint undertaking (Acts 2:46). However, the seriousness with which Paul approached the use of the Lord's Supper (see 1 Cor. 11) suggests that it must have been held in a similar regard by all the churches for which he had responsibility, as well as by those congregations—including the church in Jerusalem—that had rallied to the defense of his ministry at the Council in Jerusalem (Acts 15). Apostolic practice followed the commands of Christ in a faithful and careful manner, thereby demonstrating the importance of the sacraments in the life and work of the church, according to the Lord's will.

The sacraments are important to the church. Their faithful and careful observance fulfills the command of Christ and continues the tradition of the early church. They identify the particular community of which believers are a part. They unite that community in one Spirit, on the basis of one finished work, and for the purposes of one world-transforming end, the glory of God. But how does their importance relate to the church's work of ministry in the world—that is, her kingdom calling?

## THE SACRAMENTS AND THE MINISTRY OF THE CHURCH

I should clarify what I mean by "the ministry of the church" before examining the role of the sacraments therein. By this phrase I mean the everyday activity of the saints of God as they live for Christ in their own peculiar life settings, worshiping Him, showing His love to one another, caring for the needs of their neighbors, and calling the lost to repentance and faith in Christ. The role of church leaders is so to prepare the members of the congregation through all the tools at their disposal—including the sacraments—that they can go forth in a lifestyle of ministry among the people in their unique mission fields (Eph. 4:11-12). The result of this faithful ministry on the part of God's people is that the church is built up and grows increasingly to express the fullness of the stature of Christ in its community (Eph. 4:13-16). We must not limit the idea of ministry either to what the pastor or church leaders do or to the programs we sponsor in the Lord's name. All believers are called to ministry—to service—following the example of Christ (Mark 10:42-45). And since ministry does not come naturally to us, we must be carefully and continuously equipped for it by the leaders of the church. What part can the sacraments play in this effort?

Let me suggest three contributions to the ministry of the church for which the sacraments are uniquely suited. First is their ability to focus the people of God for *a heightened consciousness of Him and of the work He has done on our behalf.*

Evangelical Christianity has become a highly individualized endeavor, in which "ministry" is that which the church sponsors for and in the name of her members, rather than a way of life for which all members are being continuously equipped. Any typical evangelical congregation will feature a wide range of programs targeted at individual needs, normally defined within some kind of group context—children, youth, single adults, married couples, the divorced, and so on. In the midst of this frenzy of activity what often gets lost sight of is the centrality of God to the life of the covenant community and the utter necessity for the work of ministry of *knowing Him*. God's focus throughout the history of redemption has been on the creation of a *people* for His glory, on the march to embody and proclaim His kingdom—not just an assortment of spiritual self-seeking individuals huddled together under the shelter of a variety of church programs. In the process of calling that people into existence He has resolved to make Himself the center of their attention, admiration, and aspiration.

Indeed, the Scriptures give the impression that undue concentration on individual needs is not a healthy thing. In Psalm 43, for example, when the psalmist is whining about his need for vindication and slipping ever more deeply into despair, his solution is to reprove himself for this unbecoming focus on self and to recover his view of God and the hope that attaches to knowing Him. The apostle Paul, who experienced more in the way of trouble, opposition, betrayal, and inconvenience than most modern evangelical congregations, saw his weaknesses and afflictions not only as something to remedy, but as means by which to know the strength of the Lord and to have the power of Christ made more perfect in him (2 Cor. 12:9).

Precisely here the sacraments can help us recover our vision of God and His work on our behalf. In baptism and the Lord's Supper we join together in the gracious provision of God's covenant and the acknowledgment of His sovereign working in the lives of men. He is our common Father and has given us these ordinances by which to be born and knitted together into the family of His people.[2] He is the superintending (spiritual) physician at the waters of baptism, where duly-ordained (spiritual) midwives draw covenant children out of the darkness of the world of sin through the birth waters of the sacrament into newness of life.[3] He is the host of the banquet at which His children feast on the gracious meal He has provided. These ordinances are of His design, are carried out in His household and under His watchful eye, and speak to us of the unfathomable grace of God the Father who brings and binds us together into one new people in Christ.

The Lord Jesus Christ (and His work) is equally evident in the sacraments. In baptism He has both borne up under the water-judgment of the Lord[4] and washed our sins away through His blood. We are admitted in His name, by virtue of His credentials, to participate with Him in these sacraments, so that each time we observe baptism or celebrate the Lord's Supper we have the opportunity to be renewed and refocused in the Savior of mankind. In Him we are washed; on Him we feast; by Him we are admitted to each of these gracious institutions. The enormity of His grace and love are dramatically displayed in the sacraments, and they can inspire us to a greater consistency of loving ministry in His name.

So also with the Spirit, who is given to us from without, like the waters of baptism, and who provides the spiritual presence of Christ that binds us together as one and unites us with Jesus and the Father in the Lord's Supper (Eph. 1:3). He is the agent of our regeneration, symbolized by baptism (Gal. 4:6). He is the principal means, working with the Word of God, by which we are transformed from glory to glory and built together into a holy temple in the Lord (2 Cor. 3:17-18; Eph. 2:22) as we join together in the Lord's Supper. Without the work of the Spirit in our lives the sacraments are of no value whatsoever. Baptism will not save us unless He applies the work of Christ to our hearts and enables us to cry out, "Abba, Father." The Supper will not avail us unless He has renewed and cleansed us from our sins and keeps us in the presence of the Father and the Son (Ps. 51:10-12). The faithful and careful observance of the sacraments can remind us of the awesome, life-changing power of the Spirit of God and encourage us to trust Him to use us in gracious ministry to others.

We are not careful in the administration of the sacraments when we allow them to become a time either for celebrating the testimonies of men or the observance of a solemn but spiritually vapid ceremony. Careful use of the sacraments will equip us for ministry in the kingdom by leading us to a renewed vision of our God and a deeper appreciation of His work on our behalf, together with a growing confidence in His ability to use us as agents of grace in a dying world.

The second way the sacraments can serve to equip us for ministry is, as has already been suggested, *by reminding us of our oneness in Christ.* Recently, in a sermon on baptism, our pastor reminded us that for all our differences and disagreements, all Christian churches stand together on the importance of the sacraments. These ordinances are our common inheritance, defining our spiritual bloodlines to one another and to all the saints from every place and every age. They are exclusively for the people of God, and not to be intruded upon by unworthy pretenders. Through the sacraments the members of the Body of Christ have more in common—in heritage, outlook, spiritual essence, and prospect—than they have even with the members of their particular societies, races, or families. The oneness into which the sacraments usher us is the key to effective witness. When the world sees us celebrating together, joyously binding ourselves to one another in the sacramental love of the family of God, it will believe that the Father has sent the Son into the world, for it will not be able to point to anywhere else that such a singularity of heart, soul, mind, and strength exists (see John 17:21).

What a tragedy that we allow these ordinances, which are meant to bind us, instead to shatter our unity, disrupt the bonds of peace, and fracture the Body of Christ! It is to the great shame of Evangelicals, Catholics, and Orthodox alike that we have worked harder to emphasize and condemn our differences over these ordinances than to seek ways of overcoming these differences for the sake of our love for one another and our witness to our risen Lord. Even in individual congregations where strife, schism, backbiting, gossip, jealousy, and resentment breed and swarm like mosquitoes in a discarded tire, we have not yet figured out how to let the sacraments perform their bonding, binding work of making us one people in Christ.

Yet here, in the local church, is the place to begin recovering this sacramental dynamic. *All* members of local churches are admitted to the Body through the waters of baptism. *All* join together around the table of the Lord to share in His body and blood. Surely we can discover ways of focusing on this oneness that can provide healing, reconciliation, and mutual appreciation and affection among the members of our churches. What Thomas M'Crie wrote of the sacraments in 1821 is true yet today: "The institutions of the Gospel were intended as a bond of union among Christians, and by joint celebration their union is maintained and expressed."[5] The strength, joy, hope, and support that we experience through this renewal of our oneness in the sacraments will provide solid equipping for ministry in our individual lives.

_3_ Finally, the sacraments can serve the ministry of the church by continually refocusing us on our mission in the world. The sacraments are decidedly eschatological in nature.⑥ Baptism marks the beginning of a journey that ends gloriously in the presence of our Lord forever. Each time we participate in the Supper we are reminded that this is a temporary ordinance that will be done away with when the marriage supper of the Lamb becomes our perpetual feast. But as we journey toward that end we are a community of witnesses. Each baptism declares the saving work of Christ anew and calls those who do not yet know the Lord to consider their need of His saving mercy. Each celebration of the Lord's Supper declares the glorious work of His broken body and spilled blood for wretched sinners such as we. None but those who have come to know the Lord are admitted to either sacrament; thus all who are debarred from them may be left longing to participate in the rich fellowship, sublime joy, and mysterious presence they sense each time the sacraments are administered, while those who participate are reminded of their individual callings as witnesses for Christ (1 Cor. 14:24-25; cf. Acts 1:8).

In the sacraments each believer is reminded of his or her own reason for being left here—namely, to know the Lord and to make Him known (1 Pet. 2:9-10). The witness we enter into corporately in the sacraments should reinforce our commitment to living ministries of witness in the world, strengthening us in the presence of the Lord and the reminders of His work, encouraging us by our common commitment to the kingdom mission of the church, and sending us forth with new resolve and new strength for the task at hand.

Growth in the knowledge of the Lord, and in grateful attention to his work; deepened affection for our fellow believers; a firmer commitment to our mission in the world—these are the ministerial benefits the sacraments can provide, undergirding and reinforcing all our other efforts at equipping the saints with dramatic representations, careful explanations, solemn reminders, and heartfelt prayers through these mysterious institutions in which the presence of the Lord of glory is somehow wondrously intensified in our midst. As Simon Chan has written:

> If spiritual life is essentially life in the body of Christ, then spiritual direction must help individuals grow within the spiritual organism of the body. This means first initiated into the body by baptism and then feeding on the shared life in Christ through the sacrament of Communion.[7]

## RECOVERING THE MINISTERIAL POWER OF THE SACRAMENTS

How then shall we proceed to recover this ability of the sacraments to infuse new life into our churches and new power into our ministries? I have four suggestions.

First, *let us be certain to teach the sacraments in a faithful and careful manner*. This should be done through preaching and teaching by the pastor and other church leaders. It must also receive careful attention during new members' classes and in church materials prepared for the interest of the community. But we must also be willing to take the time to explain, if only briefly, the meaning and significance of the sacraments each time we observe them. We cannot assume that the deep significance, dramatic beauty, and ministry value of the sacraments will be picked up by some process of spiritual osmosis through simple observation over time. Only faithful, careful attention to teaching the sacraments as often as possible and at every opportunity will enable God's people to receive the benefit in ministry for which they were, at least in part, intended.

Second, *we should strive to increase the frequency with which we observe the sacraments*. It will do no good to teach the people how utterly important they are to the life and work of the church if we do not back that teaching up with real implications as to their observance. Is it necessary to wait until we have a group of people to baptize one believer? Or for the end of a new members' class? What might be the effect of a baptism, faithfully and carefully administered, each month, or even each week, in the lives of the people of God? And Jesus has given us a virtual *carte blanche* with his Supper: "As often as you will." Our problem is that we only "will" it quarterly or monthly at best. Some congregations have already begun to move toward a weekly observance of the Supper, and with good reports as to the response of the people. There are indications that some of the early Christians took the Supper daily, as even their enemies observed. While that may not be practical, and weekly may take a while to achieve, surely a monthly observance is not too much to expect. The objection often heard is that we don't want to water down the beauty of the sacraments or their significance by a too-frequent observation. Familiarity breeds contempt, you know. Shall we apply that standard to preaching? Or hymn-singing? Or corporate worship? The sacraments are as important as any of these and should be given greater frequency in the life of the local church.

Third, *we need to focus more on the spirituality of the sacraments—that is, the real presence of the Lord in them.* For most churches the sacraments are observed as mere routines occasionally intruded into our normal service. Little time is given for quiet, thoughtful reflection, careful instruction, or prayerful response to the Lord. Just as a too-mechanical approach to any of the spiritual disciplines robs them of their power to transform, so too the sacraments, unless they are observed in a deeply spiritual manner, will have no benefit in the lives of the people (cf. Ps. 50).

4 Finally, *let us use the sacraments to challenge the people of God in their mission for Christ.* Each member can be challenged to "improve" his or her baptism, to use the language of the *Westminster Standards*—that is, to recall Christ's saving work on their behalf, to introspect concerning areas of needed growth and change, and to seek the grace of the Lord in bringing forth the fruits of repentance that should issue from our baptism (cf. Luke 3:8). The Supper can be used to challenge us to consider afresh the greatness of Christ's love for us and to reflect on the implications of that for our own lives. As He loved us, so we are to love one another (1 John 4:11). This can include specific challenges in the areas of reconciliation, mutual encouragement and help, contributions for the needs of the poor, and witness for Christ, among others. We "show forth the Lord's death" not only in

the drama of the elements but by the outworking of that dying love in our own self-denying lives in relationship to one another. Specific challenges given at the appropriate time during the Supper can help the people of God to be better equipped for the work of ministry to which they are called.

CONCLUSION  *of sacraments*

The foregoing thoughts will be for most readers neither controversial nor new. They are intended primarily to remind us of what we all know very well: The sacraments matter in the life of the church, and as with all the gifts of Christ, they are intended to equip us for kingdom living in the world; but in our day their use has been allowed to degenerate into little more than a liturgical routine. As we prepare for the reviving winds of God to begin to blow once again, a more faithful and careful observance of the sacraments will help hasten the day of renewal.

NOTES

1   There is not space here to examine in detail a theology of the sacraments. Readers are encouraged to refer to relevant sections of such works as Edmund Clowney, *The Church* (Downers Grove, IL: InterVarsity, 1995); Simon Chan, *Spiritual Theology* (Downers Grove, IL: InterVarsity, 1998); and Miroslav Volf, *After Our Likeness: The Church as the Image of the Trinity* (Grand Rapids, MI: Eerdmans, 1998) among contemporary writers; and the works of Calvin, Bannerman, and Berkhof (among others) among classic theologians.

2   Chan, *Spiritual Theology*, pp. 111-112.

3   The language here is figurative and should not be taken to mean that the writer believes that baptism is the actual occasion of new birth.

4   Clowney, *The Church*, p. 279.

5   Thomas M'Crie, *Unity of the Church* (Dallas: Presbyterian Heritage Publications, 1989), p. 23.

6   Cf. Alexander Schmemann, *The Eucharist* (Crestwood: St. Vladimir's Seminary Press, 1987), p. 34. Also Chan, *Spiritual Theology*, p. 112.

7   Chan, *Spiritual Theology*, p. 235; cf. Clowney, *The Church*, p. 272.

# 12

## HOW SHALL I RESPOND TO SIN IN THE CHURCH?

### *A Plea to Restore the Third Mark of the Church*

■

Joseph Flatt, Jr.

I read the letter carefully for the second time. Yes, it was clear. If I and the church did not cease and desist we would be sued. At least that is what the menacing letter from the attorney threatened. The situation had been brewing for some time. One of our members was ensnared in blatant sin, and he was being lovingly yet firmly confronted by the church in accordance with our church discipline procedure. As I read the letter for the third time, I experienced an array of emotional responses. My initial incredulity turned to outright anger and then to bitter disappointment. I had played golf with this brother. He had sought my assistance during a difficult personal crisis. He had served in the church. I had observed him grow in his faith. Or so I thought. I had significantly invested in his life. Now it was all up in smoke. Nothing mattered. No amount of reason or appeal to Scripture penetrated his worldly thought patterns. The fleeting pleasure of sin had a death grip on his mind if not also his soul. So I prayed. And I wept. Sin is devastating.

Does this sound familiar? What is a church or pastor to do? Well, the simple answer is: "Follow the directives of the Scripture wherever

All references to discipline situations in this brief essay are actual. They have been changed to disguise identities, however.

they may lead, whatever the cost." Of course, the implementation is a bit more complex. Let's flesh this out a bit.

## SOME BASIC ASSUMPTIONS

Before considering practical suggestions for the practice of church discipline in the local church, it would be helpful to see the bigger picture. In my view there are some basic notions that help focus the sometimes hazy picture of life in the church these days. Though a detailed handling of these particulars is beyond the scope of this brief chapter, a rudimentary grasp of these concepts is essential to the forging of a biblical strategy for confronting sin in the church.

*God expects holiness from His people.*

A bedrock concept in the matter of personal holiness is the fact that the identity of the people of God is linked to His holy character. Consequently, there is no lack of scriptural imperatives regarding holy living in both Testaments:

> *As obedient children, do not conform to the evil desires you had when you lived in ignorance. But just as he who called you is holy, so be holy in all you do; for it is written: "Be holy, because I am holy."*
>
> *—1 Pet. 1:14-16*

> *But you are a chosen people, a royal priesthood, a holy nation, a people belonging to God, that you may declare the praises of him who called you out of darkness into his wonderful light. Once you were not a people, but now you are the people of God; once you had not received mercy, but now you have received mercy.*
>
> *—1 Pet. 2:9-10*

> *For I am the LORD your God; consecrate yourselves and be holy, because I am holy.*
>
> *—Lev. 11:44*

Indeed, though rarely used appropriately, the teaching regarding the separateness of believers is at the crux of the issue of holiness. Paul pointedly admonishes the Corinthians to holiness.

> *Do not be yoked together with unbelievers. For what do righteousness and wickedness have in common? Or what fellowship can light have with darkness? What harmony is there between Christ and Belial? What does a believer have in common with an unbeliever? What agreement is there between the temple of God and idols? For we are the temple of the living God. As God has said: "I will live with them and walk among them, and I will be their God, and they will be my people." "Therefore come out from them and be separate, says the Lord. Touch no unclean thing, and I will receive you." "I will be a Father to you, and you will be my sons and daughters, says the Lord Almighty." Since we have these promises, dear friends, let us purify ourselves from everything that contaminates body and spirit, perfecting holiness out of reverence for God.*
>
> —2 Cor. 6:14—7:1

God's desires for His people are not vague!

### The unholy church is an oxymoron.

The contemporary church is in trouble. Sex, alcohol, and money are doing a brisk business among the faithful. A pollster is not needed (though they are not lacking) to tell us what we know by simple observation: There is virtually no difference between the lifestyles of the typical pagan and the typical Christian. Joe Christian and Paul Pagan both buy tickets to the same indecent movies, tune in to the same trashy television programs, read the same raunchy magazines, use the same colorful vocabulary, stick it to the company, fudge on tax returns, wear the latest provocative apparel, frequent the coolest sports bar . . . well, you can fill in the blanks. And remarkably the church hardly flinches in the face of the pagan practices of its people. In fact, it sometimes endorses them.¹ Little wonder that prison chaplain Samuel Atchison surmises that the church may be its own worst enemy.

It has become common for the entertainment media to portray the Christian church and its clergy as hypocritical, lascivious or out of touch with the world around them. . . . Still, if the purveyors of the new morality are dissatisfied with the traditional concept of holiness, it is in part because the keepers of the biblical flame have left much to be desired. The fact is, many in the Christian church are hypocritical, lascivious and out of touch. Media characterizations of unsavory church folk are unfair in terms of degree and proportion, but not altogether in terms of substance.[2]

*Christ has commissioned the church to confront its own sin.*

Sin should not shock us. We are all sinners. Indeed, if anyone claims to be sinless, he is either woefully out of touch with reality or he is a liar. John makes this plain: "If we claim to be without sin, we deceive ourselves and the truth is not in us" (1 John 1:8). So, as every first-year theology student learns, we should expect sin in the church. Yet the New Testament frequently urges believers to take decisive action in dealing with those in the Christian community who are caught up in aberrant conduct.[3] And on two occasions the role of the church in confronting sin in its midst is directly addressed. The first instance is found in the Lord's tutoring of His disciples.

> *"If your brother sins against you, go and show him his fault, just between the two of you. If he listens to you, you have won your brother over. But if he will not listen, take one or two others along, so that 'every matter may be established by the testimony of two or three witnesses.' If he refuses to listen to them, tell it to the church; and if he refuses to listen even to the church, treat him as you would a pagan or a tax collector."*
> *—Matt. 18:15-17*

Here the Lord establishes the general principle of church discipline. Though this passage should be treated as a statement of principle regarding the handling of sin within the church rather than a detailed regulatory manual, it nonetheless outlines a specific step-by-step process that should guide the church in its discipline practice. In short, the church is granted divine warrant to exercise discipline over its members④ On the other hand, Paul's correspondence with the Corinthian church affords us vivid insight into an actual case of church discipline.

> *It is actually reported that there is immorality among you, and of a kind that does not occur even among pagans: A man has his father's wife. And you are proud! Shouldn't you rather have been filled with grief and have put out of your fellowship the man who did this? Even though I am not physically present, I am with you in spirit. And I have already passed judgment on the one who did this, just as if I were present. When you are assembled in the name of our Lord Jesus and I am with you in spirit, and the power of our Lord Jesus is present, hand this man over to Satan, so that the sinful nature may be destroyed and his spirit saved on the day of the Lord. Your boasting is not good. Don't you know that a little yeast works through the whole batch of dough? Get rid of the old yeast that you may be a new batch without yeast—as you really are. For Christ, our Passover lamb, has been sacrificed. Therefore let us keep the Festival, not with the old yeast, the yeast of malice and wickedness, but with bread without yeast, the bread of sincerity and truth. I have written you in my letter not to associate with sexually immoral people— not at all meaning the people of this world who are immoral, or the greedy and swindlers, or idolaters. In that case you would have to leave this world. But now I am writing you that you must not associate with anyone who calls himself a brother but is sexually immoral or greedy, an idolater or a slanderer, a drunkard or a swindler. With such a man do not even eat. What business is it of mine to judge those outside the church? Are you not to judge those inside? God will judge those outside. "Expel the wicked man from among you."*
>
> —*1 Cor. 5:1-13*

Even a causal reading of these passages leads to the conclusion that the church is not only authorized to exercise discipline over its members but is mandated to do so. It is therefore not surprising that many consider discipline a mark of a true church⑤ Just as surely as

God decisively crushed the outright disobedience of Achan in secretly plundering the banned spoils of victory at Jericho (Josh. 6—7), so the church must deal with sin in its midst. It cannot be ignored. It will not go away.

*God assumes that His people will be part of a local church.*

Commitment to a local church is becoming alarmingly uncommon in the Christian community at large these days. Not only are contemporary believers less likely to place a priority on church attendance than their ancestors, but they are less likely to be a participating member of a local church. Attendance is often a function of convenience, membership a vague matter of personal preference, and recurrent service extraordinary. No wonder, then, that a serious attempt to introduce discipline into the life of a church is often shrugged off like yesterday's stock market correction. "It doesn't really matter" is surely thought, if not verbalized, by many Christians. Perhaps we have forgotten that, by my count, approximately ninety-five of the 114 occurrences of *ekklesia* refer to the local church, that whole epistles are written to local churches, that the New Testament contains long discussions regarding life in the local church, that God goes to the trouble of placing officers in local churches for the care of the saints, and that worldwide evangelism was initiated through the auspices of the local church. At-large Christians clearly are not envisioned in the New Testament!

*Christians are part of a family.*

Privacy reigns supreme in western society. Ernie Executive can communicate by voice mail, E-mail, or fax. His phone calls are screened. His lunch is brought to his office. After work, he can jump in his car parked in the reserved garage, stop by the ATM machine for a cash restock, call his wife on his cell phone on the way home, pull into the drive-thru for some carry-out pasta, and automatically close the garage door behind him when he arrives home. In short he can function nicely day to day without actually having a significant personal encounter with another human being. And he believes this is his inalienable right. No one, including the church or other Christians, has license to invade any part of his life unless he grants it!

This, of course, is in stark contrast to the New Testament picture of the believing community. One of the vivid images of the church in the New Testament is that of a body. One such portrayal is found in Paul's instructions to the Corinthian church. After establishing that every individual part of the body (the eye, the foot, the hand, etc.) is significant to the well-being of the whole body, Paul concludes, "If one part suffers, every part suffers with it; or if one part is honored, every part rejoices with it" (1 Cor. 12:26). Hence, those in Christ's church are uniquely related to one another. What one does affects others. This of course was the underlying dynamic in Achan's sin. As his sin tainted the whole nation (Josh. 6:18; 7:1, 11, 15, 25), so an entire congregation is infected by the sin of one of its constituents.

Because we are so dynamically tied together in the Body of Christ, we are exhorted to intentionally invade each other's space. In fact, I believe this is a logo of a genuine Christian community. The sundry "one another" statements of the New Testament show God's desire for His family. Christians are to be conspicuous because they love each other, they honor each other, they encourage one another, they accept one another, and they even admonish each other. And that is just the beginning! The church is a unique organization indeed.

## THE MECHANICS OF CHURCH DISCIPLINE

As with every other area of church practice, the actual exercise of church discipline must be an operation derived from clear biblical teaching. In short, there must be a demonstrated biblical warrant for this aspect of church life. Because practice proceeds from doctrine, it is essential to establish the theology first. Nonetheless, in the highly volatile area of church discipline it is equally crucial to get the practice right. Though there will always be critics both from within and without no matter how the church engages in church discipline, disaster awaits the church that has the theory down but botches the real-life application! So I would like to offer some suggestions designed to shape the practice of church discipline in such a way as to help keep the church out of the ditch and at the same time reflect the doctrinal underpinnings.

*Adhere as closely as possible to the process outlined in Matthew 18:15-17.*

Obviously the precise procedures followed by the church in Corinth are not given to us. Paul may have exercised an apostolic prerogative in the matter. Nonetheless, he demanded that the church take decisive action. Since New Testament apostles are not present in churches today, it seems wise that the church follow the step-by-step directives of the Lord in disciplinary matters. These steps are: 1) private personal confrontation; 2) private group confrontation; 3) public corporate confrontation; and 4) public corporate action.

*Adopt a corporate discipline procedure statement.*     do this for your church

A written document should be drafted that clearly establishes the course of action the congregation will take in dealing with a matter of discipline. Such a document must clarify where the process is heading and how the congregation gets there as well as lay out the responsibilities of the various persons involved. Yet it should be worded broadly enough so that the congregation can exercise discretion regarding the form and parameters of any disciplinary action. It should also reflect the particular governance of the congregation while preserving the universal biblical principles of church discipline.[6] I strongly recommend that this document be part of an official policy book containing policies, procedures, and guidelines governing various aspects of congregational life. The existence of this book should be well advertised, and it should be readily available to any member of the congregation.

*Incorporate appropriate statements in governing documents.*

The policy statement described above should merely be the logical product of conceptual statements appearing in the basic governing documents of the local congregation. For instance, if the congregation operates under a covenanted concept, then the church covenant should contain a simple statement that all the congregants bound together by covenant agree to submit themselves to the duly constituted discipline of the church. The church constitution should also contain a brief statement describing the congregation's practice of church discipline. If the church's articles of faith are detailed in scope, it would be helpful to include a statement of the church's position on church discipline as well. In short, there should be no doubt to anyone who examines the documents of the church that the congregation is committed to a biblical practice of church discipline.

Almost no detail is insignificant. The wise church will attempt to proactively prepare for as many contingencies as possible. This became immensely lucid to me during one disreputable discipline situation. It had been a long, painful process. God had been honored even though no apparent progress had been made toward repentance. The church and the unrepentant member already had been notified of a meeting at which the unrepentant member was to be dismissed from the congregation. Then the letter arrived. It was from her attorney. It contained her statement of "resignation" from the church along with the attorney's belief that the church no longer had legal authority over his client as well as the blunt suggestion that if the church continued with the church discipline proceedings, it would do so at risk of a lawsuit.

What can a church do in light of the possibility of desperate and calculated "resignations" for the sole purpose of thwarting a church discipline action? The plain answer may be, "Nothing." Informal discussions with legal advisers have led me to the conclusion that some attorneys will argue that anyone who voluntarily joins a loosely knit nonprofit organization such as a church is permitted to voluntarily sever formal relationships with that organization at any time for any reason. Nonetheless, it may be helpful if the official documents of the church contain the specific conditions, circumstances, and procedures regarding entrance into and dismissal from the church. Though that may not prevent a disgruntled member from "resigning" unilaterally, at minimum it will demonstrate that the church has official procedures pertaining to membership issues to which members have agreed. It may provide convincing legal argument and protection as well.

*Secure willingness from each new member to submit to the discipline of the church.*   *i.e., a contract*

*I can't agree to this*

On more than one occasion I have heard it said that it ought to be easy to get into a church but difficult to stay in! Certainly, entrance into a New Testament church should not be an ordeal given a credible profession of faith. However, I contend that the wise church will develop a membership process designed to maintain the integrity of the church and to protect the reputation of Christ. This may be accomplished in several ways. First, a membership information class should be required during which the whole discipline theology and practice is outlined. If the look on the faces of many of those who have attended the classes I have taught is any indication, it is fair to say that many believers have little or no experience with biblical church discipline. Such a class affords a golden opportunity to systematically unwrap this little-spoken-of doctrine.

*accountability*

*trouble & authority*

Second, all those seeking membership should be required to sign a written application in which they are asked to indicate their willingness to voluntarily submit to the discipline of the church as well as to the constituted authority of the congregation.

*there would be no church*

And third, all prospective members should be interviewed by the board of elders or their representatives. This interview, though cordial and informal, ought to be fairly thorough. In addition to exploring the main issues of genuine conversion and Christian testimony, the interviewers should attempt to uncover basic attitudes toward authority.

*person who refuses to repent*

*Discipline only for lack of repentance.*   *repentance / restoration*

*our job*

Though sinful conduct initiates the discipline process, the only sin for which one is disciplined by the church is the failure or refusal to repent. This principle is absolutely essential to successfully exercising biblical discipline. I maintain that fuzziness on this issue is often what topples many well-meaning attempts at discipline. People must never be disciplined for conduct such as rebellion, lying, gossiping, or immorality. Only those who refuse to repent of such sins after being confronted with Christ's demands are proper candidates for the corporate discipline of His church. In exercising discipline, the church thereby recognizes the offender as a functioning nonbeliever because he refuses to respond to the Word.

*Do not allow church discipline to be the exclusive prerogative of one man or a select group.*

I am personally committed to the authority of a godly body of elders in the local congregation in contrast to both the rule of the majority or the dictatorship of the pastor.[7] However, regardless of one's convictions regarding church government, I maintain that the congregation plays a direct and final role in matters of church discipline. To exegetically remove the congregation from the discipline process, in my mind, is to play hermeneutical gymnastics with both Matthew 18 and 1 Corinthians 5. Church discipline must be exercised directly by the corporate whole, not by proxy. No one individual or group should be able to exercise this authority.

*Keep written records detailing the events of each discipline case.*

One of my seminary professors judiciously encouraged his aspiring preachers to keep good written records of significant events. Thus, over the course of my ministry I have done a fairly thorough job of maintaining a written record of matters I deemed momentous or potentially so. And the one occasion I failed to do so came back to haunt me! Church discipline is one of those momentous affairs. It is important that someone (probably one of the elders) manage a case history. This file should include contemporary notes chronicling the who, when, where, and what. It should also contain notations of verbal agreements, correspondence, and meetings, all organized chronologically. Such a record is an invaluable resource in establishing facts and thus guiding decision-making during the discipline process itself. It also can substantiate that the church is attempting to function in an orderly manner and in accord with its own procedures. Furthermore, disciplinary matters occasionally raise their ugly heads years after the fact. A written archive is immensely more reliable than an elder's memory!

*Keep the pastor out of the initial steps of the discipline process if possible.*

Can pray/ make suggestions

Admittedly, involving the pastor in the discipline process only at a later phase may be impossible, especially in a smaller congregation. And doing so may, though it need not, mitigate good shepherding. Yet I would urge that an attempt be made. This simple procedural matter is valuable in that it may prevent, or at least blunt, charges of violation of privacy or confidentiality. Normally such accusations are bogus when proper procedures are followed. However, the mere presence of the pastor in the private stages of discipline may unnecessarily create fertile soil for incriminations by the disgruntled member.

*Strive to produce an atmosphere of compassion.*

Nearly every time our church has been forced to exercise church discipline to the point of exclusion, the cry has gone up from some quarter, "You are a harsh, cold, unloving congregation." Nothing could be further from the truth. We take such action precisely because we *do* care. But this charge always serves as a reminder that we need to constantly cultivate a background of compassion in the church. To this end, great care should be taken to avoid any unguarded private or public statements that would unnecessarily injure the erring party. A helpful question to pose might be, "Will this statement make it more difficult for the erring party to repent and be restored to fellowship?" I have found that details of the erring member's conduct, as a rule, should be kept to the essential minimum. Normally no one is helped by sharing gory details.

The event of public discipline should prompt brutal self-evaluation by every member of the congregation. Paul assumes this in giving his advice for such situations: "Brothers, if someone is caught in a sin, you who are spiritual should restore him gently. But watch yourself, or you also may be tempted" (Gal. 6:1). Spiritual arrogance must be avoided at all cost. An "it could be me" tension should be on the mind of every believer. And that should strike terror into each heart. Hence patience should be graciously extended whenever possible

| *Avoid partiality at all costs.*

Church discipline must be consistently applied regardless of an individual's position in the church or community⑧Having the same last name as one of the church officers, teaching in the Sunday school for half a lifetime, or being a generous donor must have no bearing per se on the application of discipline. At the same time, each situation is unique and must be dealt with individually. Lamentably, there is not a one-size-fits-all discipline garment. Consequently not all cases will be handled with exactly the same procedures or at the same pace. The church may not be able to avoid charges of partiality, but they must never be justified.

*Declare the need for congregational self-judgment.*

Paul expected the Corinthian church to judge its own even though the church itself, as is well known, was far from perfect. "What business is it of mine to judge those outside the church? Are you not to judge those inside?" (1 Cor. 5:12). This tentative judgment by the church does not usurp God's ultimate judgment. The same principle of self-judgment is required in conjunction with the Lord's table (1 Cor. 11) as well as in the matter of potential lawsuits (1 Cor. 6). Hence church discipline cannot validly be construed as "casting the first stone" or some sort of renegade hypocritical action as is often charged.

*Elevate the spiritual well-being of the congregation as a whole.*

The description of the Corinthian disciplinary case alludes to the notion of leaven (1 Cor. 5:6-13). A contrast in size is drawn between a little leaven and its effect on the entire batch. The implication is clear: The stench of immorality of one individual pervaded the whole church. So it became necessary to remove the erring party for his own benefit as well as for the benefit of the church itself. In effect, the church needed to be willing to sacrifice the unrepentant member in favor of the health of the whole body.

*Clarify the concept of exclusion.*

Sadly, the erring party may not repent of his sinful way, even after being lovingly confronted by the church. The New Testament process then requires exclusion.⁹ The force of the phrases "Treat him as you would a pagan or a tax collector" (Matt. 18:17), "Shouldn't you rather have been filled with grief and have put out of your fellowship the man who did this?" (1 Cor. 5:2), "Hand this man over to Satan, so that the sinful nature may be destroyed and his spirit saved on the day of the Lord" (1 Cor. 5:5), and "'Expel the wicked man from among you'" (1 Cor. 5:13) clearly means that the church must withdraw fellowship from the unrepentant member. The church is collectively no longer recognizing him as a fellow believer and is therefore excommunicating him to the realm of Satan so perchance he might be restored as a result of his sensual desires having free but destructive rein in his life. He will no longer enjoy the protective and redemptive umbrella of Christ's church.

*Explain the responsibilities of members after an exclusion.*

I have found it is at the point of exclusion that confusion often pervades a congregation. It is essential that people understand that the discipline process is not over simply because a member has been excluded. The congregation must realize that it bears ongoing responsibilities. We could easily cite the need for prayer, Christian courtesy, compassion, or continued self-confrontation. However, we gain insight into the holy mind of God when we see that 1 Corinthians 5:9-13 focuses on the responsibility to restrict association with the unrepentant individual. What is the Lord saying about how the excluded member is to be treated? I do not believe the passage teaches that individuals in the church are to have nothing to do with the individual in the absolute sense. Yet God wants to send him His message, which is,

"I deplore what you are doing. Change!" And the vehicle for communicating this message is the church. So it is not the act of eating with the unrepentant person that is forbidden per se, but eating as a common social interchange that denotes fellowship and recognition as a Christian. Therefore the Christian can accept a dinner invitation from a nonbelieving neighbor, but not from an unrepentant professing believer! The broader principle must be that any contact with the excluded person must be without acknowledgment of him as a brother in Christ and must be undertaken with a view to his restoration.

*Focus on restoration.*

The *ultimate* goal in any church discipline action, of course, is the glorification of God through obedience to His Word. *Immediately,* however, a congregation ought to exercise discipline for the purpose of overthrowing sin and restoring the sinner (1 Cor. 5:5). The church must always be ready to extend full restoration upon genuine repentance. That churches are sometimes reluctant to grant restoration should not surprise us in light of Paul's need to pointedly admonish the Corinthian church to forgive the sinning brother.

> *Now instead, you ought to forgive and comfort him, so that he will not be overwhelmed by excessive sorrow. I urge you, therefore, to reaffirm your love for him. The reason I wrote you was to see if you would stand the test and be obedient in everything. If you forgive anyone, I also forgive him. And what I have forgiven—if there was anything to forgive—I have forgiven in the sight of Christ for your sake, in order that Satan might not outwit us. For we are not unaware of his schemes.*
>
> —2 Cor. 2:7-11

It is also helpful to demarcate a difference between forgiveness and restoration. Whereas forgiveness is granted immediately, as the conversation between Peter and the Lord implies (Matt. 18:21-22), restoration is conditioned on evidences of genuine repentance. Unfortunately, much repentance is of the showcase variety. In stark

contrast is the Baptist's bombastic demand of those who claimed
repentance: "You brood of vipers! Who warned you to flee from the
coming wrath? Produce fruit in keeping with repentance" (Luke 3:7-
8). Similarly, before Agrippa, Paul implored men everywhere to
"repent and turn to God and prove their repentance by their deeds"
(Acts 26:20). The church must be prepared to discern between real and
pseudo repentance and to demand the former. This obviously requires
divine wisdom and usually necessitates time.

## LEADING A CHURCH TO PRACTICE DISCIPLINE

The rookie pastor had been at the church for a mere two weeks when
fisticuffs nearly broke out in the church basement. And that was only
a harbinger of a sorry set of circumstances. He knew enough to realize
that church discipline was in order. He could not ignore the situation.
However, the details of the practice of church discipline were a little
fuzzy to him. His seminary training was sketchy on the subject, and he
had no recollection of his home church ever practicing church discipline
or teaching it. Furthermore, as far as he could see, his current congregation had no experience with the practice either. How could he lead
the church to the establishment of this vital practice? He was not sure
how to proceed. So he picked up the phone and called a trusted adviser.

There may be no prepackaged answers, but I am convinced there
are certain hallmarks that stand out in a church that successfully practices biblical discipline. In concert with these hallmarks are various
strategies implemented by the leadership of the church. I offer these
thoughts as aids for the commencement or restoration of the practice
of church discipline.

### Above all else, pray!

Frankly, issues surrounding the confrontation of sin have been as
perplexing as any in my ministry. I have often sorely needed wisdom.
So I have resorted to prayer. After all, desperate times call for desperate measures. Thankfully I can testify to the validity of the promise
recorded in James 1:5: "If any of you lacks wisdom, he should ask

God, who gives generously to all without finding fault, and it will be given to him." But the savvy pastor will plead with God for wisdom not just in handling the tough cases but also for wisdom in knowing how to approach the key leaders, the antagonists, and the spiritually anemic in his congregation with the need to return to the Bible in confronting one another about sin. I have learned that all efforts to reform the church in this critical area ultimately are doomed to failure if not bathed in prayer.

*Commit to the long haul.*

Hunker down! Chances are, it has taken decades, maybe even generations, for the church to fall into the ditch on this issue. No matter how persuasive you may be, the likelihood of pulling the church out of the ditch overnight is remote. In many ways patience is to be prized in the arena of church discipline. I may be guilty of overstatement, but if church leaders are not able to exercise reasonable patience in reforming the church in the so-called third mark, I'd rather they not try. The latter state may be worse than the former. This need for operating in the long term is in my estimation one of many reasons for longevity in the ministry. Generally, short pastorates produce temporary fixes at best.

Related to this sometimes difficult need to be patient is the requirement to pick your battles wisely. Not every situation is worth a fatal injury. I am not suggesting compromise or anything remotely close. I am suggesting, however, that because the wise leader is looking down the road, he is willing to lose some battles now in order to win the war then. He has the larger welfare of Christ's church in mind, as well as the reputation of Christ Himself. Because he is well-versed in the big picture, he can think and plan strategically. I first learned this principle from my father, a World War II infantry officer who retired as a brigadier general. He possessed vast information about fighting in war. But he knew more about dealing with God's people.

*Make careful expository preaching and teaching of the Word central.*

I am suggesting a fairly simple line of thought. When people come to believe that the pastor is committed to a journey of teaching the Scripture wherever it takes him, and when people see the pastor actually tackling tough issues head-on rather than skirting them, and when people realize that the pastor teaches in this fashion because he loves God, His Word, and His people, they are more apt to accept painful doctrines such as church discipline. Regardless, it is the Word that the Holy Spirit will use to change hearts anyway, not the pastor's brilliant arguments. Candidly, I have noticed a remarkable corollary between strong teaching in churches and their practicing discipline. So probably the first thing to do (after prayer) is to embark on an extensive study of the key passages dealing with how a church should confront sin.[10] And good, lasting education can't be rushed!

*Emphasize the church's adherence to the authority of Scripture in both faith and practice.*

Somehow the church must embrace afresh a simple notion contained in nearly every doctrinal statement—namely, that it is committed to mining the Scripture for its corporate beliefs and also is committed to following the Scripture in its corporate practice. If this is the underlying explanation for other matters of life in the church, people will more readily sign on to discipline when convinced of its biblical mandate.

*Never bow to the shrine of success.*

I sat in a highly respected pastor's office hoping to receive some helpful guidance regarding how to teach a particular emotionally charged doctrine in a way that avoids as many pitfalls as possible. When I finished my story, I asked him how he had managed to teach this truth throughout his ministry. "I don't," he replied. "People would leave my church." I left his office that day dumbfounded and nearly devastated. I had been expecting some advice in the vein of the apostle's famous confession, "I am innocent of the blood of all men. For I have not hesitated to proclaim to you the whole will of God" (Acts 20:26-27). Unfortunately, teaching and practicing consistent biblical discipline is one of those issues that may require making a choice between filling the pews and offering plates or filling hearts and minds. Make no mistake, the choice is not always that obvious. However, it is also true that "prying into a person's private life" does not sit very well with the average Christian these days.

If a church is not absolutely committed to doing what is right regardless of the potential impact on the corporate vital statistics, the chances are remote that it will practice biblical discipline. Let's admit to what I consider to be a tragic reality: The evangelical church is wildly enamored with a consumer market-driven approach to nearly everything it attempts. "The survey says" is too often right up there with "Thus says the Lord." Have you been turned off by the offering? Fine, leave your money at home. By sacred music? We will deliver the best pop style. By the sermon? Drama will do. Os Guinness, writing of the church's love affair with a modernity-based church growth movement, offers this biting observation: "The preacher, instead of looking out upon the world, looks out upon public opinion, trying to find out what the public would like to hear."[11] As you might guess, church discipline will never play in this kind of environment!

*Speak enthusiastically about the benefits of biblical discipline.*

Never apologize or adopt a defensive posture. Remind people that there are no losers when obedience to God's Word is in operation. And besides, there are great benefits to following the Scripture in this vital area of church life: The name of Christ is protected, the reputation of the church is guarded, gossip is squelched, the way is paved for obedience in other areas of church life, unity is ultimately promoted, others are deterred from sin, the opportunity for self-examination is afforded to all members, the erring person may be rescued from the clutches of sin, real hope for biblical change is encountered, the congregation is strengthened, the pastor and other leaders possess a clear conscience, the church is viewed as a caring body, and Christ's continued presence is assured. These are just a few of the tangible benefits of biblical discipline.[12]

*Ennoble personal holiness.*

Leaders should strive to create an atmosphere in the congregation that is friendly to personal righteousness. This means they must themselves model godliness before the people. It also means the pulpit must resonate the need for, value of, and practical application of sanctification. Godliness must be spoken of in the classrooms as well. Thus when scandal breaks out in the flock, people will easily see the difference and recognize the grotesque nature of such conduct. If there is no holiness, sin loses its absurdity and becomes normal. Churches then become potential recipients of the prophet's pronouncement, "Woe to those who call evil good and good evil, who put darkness for light and light for darkness, who put bitter for sweet and sweet for bitter" (Isa. 5:20).

*Avoid dismissing the Holy Spirit from the church.*

Again, this thought is fairly straightforward. In our well-founded rush to turn loose the Word in the affairs of the church, it is easy to ignore the ministry of the Spirit. We may subconsciously think that if we are persuasive enough, people surely will see the light. We may tend to focus solely on objective truth at the exclusion of legitimate subjective reality. We may exalt the intellect at the expense of the heart. We, just like market-driven ministry, may function as if the Holy Spirit is not needed for success. Only too late will we realize that if the Holy Spirit is dismissed from the church, we cannot deal with sin, sanctification is not possible, and discipline is doomed to fail.

## WHERE FROM HERE?

I hardly had time to reflect on the letter before its author phoned me. Alternating between breathlessness and tears, she spilled out, "Oh, Pastor, how could I have been so blind? Thank you so much for caring for me. I know the church loved me then and loves me now." She spoke of a sad saga of immorality and church discipline that had occurred seven years previously! When she hung up I shouted, "Hallelujah!" Do all cases of church discipline end on such a high note of restoration? Of course not. In fact, most do not. However, there is always cause for hope because we are dealing with the awesome power of the Word mediated by the Holy Spirit. And who knows what God may have in mind!

But the real issue is much more fundamental. Bluntly put, it is whether churches are willing to do what is right regardless of the cost. I cannot help but think that genuine renewal in the church is tied in some way to her willingness to confront sin.

## NOTES

1  It is not uncommon to see churches sponsoring "Christian" nightclubs replete with the whole spectrum of "Christian" music—heavy rock, contemporary, alternative, and praise and worship—in an attempt to duplicate the atmosphere found in the hottest club in town. One Christian organization touted its rally as "A Touch of Class—Raucous Comedy—Live Bands—Hot Dance Moves" (as reported in *Fair Dinkum*, Issue #54, October 1999).

2  Samuel K. Atchison, "Why Violence Invades the Church," Religious News Service, in *The Indianapolis Star*, September 26, 1999.

3  See passages such as Galatians 6:1, Titus 3:10, 2 John 10, Romans 16:17, 2 Thessalonians 3:6, 14, Ephesians 5:11, and 1 Timothy 5:22. These explicit admonitions cause discomfort in the current western church culture, which is driven by a market mentality stamped with pragmatic tolerance.

4  That this passage is a general statement regarding how the church should deal with the sin of fellow members rather than individual reconciliation of fractured relationships is further supported by the omission of the words "against you" (v. 15, NIV) in the majority text. Even Hendriksen, who advocates the inclusion of the words on the basis of internal evidences, agrees: "If the matter is to be decided only on the basis of external textual criticism the phrase must probably be rejected." William Hendriksen, *New Testament Commentary: Exposition of the Gospel According to Matthew* (Grand Rapids, MI: Baker, 1973), p. 697.

5  Typically, the ministry of the Word and the sacraments are cited as essential marks of a true church. A third mark, discipline, is frequently named as well. Calvin implies this in his extensive discussion in *Institutes of the Christian Religion*, Vol. 2 (Grand Rapids, MI: Eerdmans, 1962), pp. 288-296.

6  The following procedure statement, patterned after the document of my own church, is suggested for consideration for adaptation by local congregations:

The following procedures shall be generally followed during a church discipline action in the interest of good order and in an effort to fulfill the directives and implications of Matthew 18:15-17 and 1 Corinthians 5 and in accordance with the Constitution at Article VI, Section IV.

a. The erring member shall be confronted privately in a loving manner with the intent of clarification and, if warranted, repentance of his errant way.

b. Should the member acknowledge his sin and repent, the matter is dropped at this point or similarly at any subsequent point in this procedure.

c. Should the erring member refuse to repent, the confronting member shall meet with the erring member in the presence of one or two witnesses from the congregation in order to further establish the facts and urge repentance. Unless circumstances dictate otherwise, the additional witness should include a church officer.

d. Should the erring member continue in his unrepentant state, the confronting member shall make the matter known to the board of elders. The elders will proceed as they deem appropriate.

e. Should the erring member still refuse to repent, the elders will make the matter known to the congregation in order to urge individual members to appeal to the erring member. At this time the congregation shall use official correspondence to urge the erring member to repent.

f. Should the erring member remain in an unrepentant state, the congregation will vote to exercise appropriate disciplinary action as recommended by the board of elders.

7  I have attempted to argue this point in my unpublished workshop, *The Church, Who Is in Charge?*

8  Paul apparently cites an exception to this principle in 1 Timothy 5:17-20. Special rules are in effect in dealing with erring elders. See John Armstrong's excellent treatment of this subject in *Can Fallen Pastors Be Restored?* (Chicago: Moody Press, 1995).

9  In some quarters lesser sanctions, withholding the Lord's Table being the most popular, are preferred as intermediate steps before exclusion. Though I do not construe such approaches as unbiblical, I am convinced that the only form of corrective discipline that has clear scriptural warrant is exclusion. Other measures may be better used as requirements imposed in order to determine the genuineness of professed repentance.

10  I am thankful for the sage advice of seminary professor W. W. Barndollar, who encouraged all of his young preacher boys to begin their ministries by expositionally working through 1 Corinthians. Of course, nearly every known problem or issue encountered in the church shows up in this letter, including a treatise on church discipline.

11  Os Guinness, *Dining with the Devil* (Grand Rapids, MI: Baker, 1993), p. 59.

12  See Richard Baxter, *The Reformed Pastor* (Carlisle, PA: Banner of Truth Trust, 1974 reprint of 1862 edition), pp. 163-172 for an excellent discussion of the motivations for and value of church discipline.

# 13

---

## PASTORAL SUCCESS IN EVANGELISTIC MINISTRY:

### The Receding Horizon

*Worn Out? — Are Functioning in The Flesh*
*Need To Be Refueled By Jesus*

Mark E. Dever

*Be Refreshed! in your Soul*
*Ask God when is time to be set aside time*

INTRODUCTION *To Him to prepare for His Sheep*

If there is any area of difficulty in the pastor's ministry, it is that of finding success in evangelism. Again and again pastors view their own crowded schedules and neglected families, look in the mirror only to be greeted with a tired face, and then look out at the world around them wondering, "What impact am I making? Am I making any difference at all? What can I do to see more success in evangelism?" It's that aspect of the pastor's work that we want to consider in this chapter.

### SUCCESS

It was said in seventeenth-century France that "to succeed in the world, we do everything to appear successful." It was said in twentieth-century America that "to succeed in the primaries, nothing is needed so much as momentum." Thus we have the image of getting on the bandwagon. It is an age-old proverb that success begets success.

And this, of course, is not only true in politics. Success is desired in whatever we turn our hand to. Which of us reading this in a book on being a pastor does not deeply want to succeed? Which of you reading these words does not have in your mind some hope that you cher-

ish, some dream that drives you on, some level you hope to attain—
something which for *you* would be success?

As important as success is for all people, it may be particularly
idolized among Americans. There seems to be an innate optimism
remaining in Americans that leads us to think that any one of us can
do anything if we just set our minds to it. Classes and castes with pre-
determined boundaries are for others. *We* are all devotees of *The Little
Engine That Could*. And so we each cultivate our own idea of success.
We work for it, strive for it, pay for it, and live for it. And this devotion to success thrives nowhere as much as in my own city of
Washington, D.C. Here party invitations, jobs, and even friends seem
to come and go with success.

For those of you who are younger, let me ask you this question:
What do you imagine success to be? Finish this sentence: "I'll know
I'm successful when _____." Our vision of success is composed
of an individually adjusted amount of health, wealth, status, esteem,
and appearance maintained as fully as possible as long as possible.

All this may seem harmless enough—just the development of the
American dream, right? We're only looking out for ourselves, we
think. Who else will do that? Who else is supposed to do that? But so
deeply rooted is this feeling today that some are even discussing how
much we can allow any of these levels to drop before we decide for
ourselves, or even for others, that that life is no longer qualitatively to
be considered life.

I wonder what you or I—modern Americans—would say to the
following image. Imagine an old man, in failing health, isolated from
family and friends, so poor he can't even afford a winter coat. He
changed careers in midlife, and there was no pension plan or medical
benefits with his own startup organization. Not only that, but his new
enterprise seems to be faltering. Oh, and one more thing—he's incar-
cerated and under capital charges. That means if he's found guilty, he
could lose his life. And it looks like he's going to be found guilty.

Now let me ask you this: Is this man your picture of success? Put
yourself in his place. You probably wouldn't like to do that, would
you? Most of us would probably be more interested in knowing what
ten steps we can take to make sure that we *never* end up in his place.

"Put myself in the place of this old man? Ridiculous!" we may think. But this old man was a Christian, and he wrote to younger Christians about our concern in this chapter. And unless I've misunderstood it badly, I think putting ourselves in his place is pretty much what this old man, Paul, is asking Timothy to do in 2 Timothy 3:10—4:5.

## PAUL'S CALL TO THE PASTOR

*You, however, know all about my teaching, my way of life, my purpose, faith, patience, love, endurance, persecutions, sufferings—what kinds of things happened to me in Antioch, Iconium and Lystra, the persecutions I endured. Yet the Lord rescued me from all of them. In fact, everyone who wants to live a godly life in Christ Jesus will be persecuted, while evil men and impostors will go from bad to worse, deceiving and being deceived. But as for you, continue in what you have learned and have become convinced of, because you know those from whom you learned it, and how from infancy you have known the holy Scriptures, which are able to make you wise for salvation through faith in Christ Jesus. All Scripture is God-breathed and is useful for teaching, rebuking, correcting and training in righteousness, so that the man of God may be thoroughly equipped for every good work. In the presence of God and of Christ Jesus, who will judge the living and the dead, and in view of his appearing and his kingdom, I give you this charge: Preach the Word; be prepared in season and out of season; correct, rebuke and encourage—with great patience and careful instruction. For the time will come when men will not put up with sound doctrine. Instead, to suit their own desires, they will gather around them a great number of teachers to say what their itching ears want to hear. They will turn their ears away from the truth and turn aside to myths. But you, keep your head in all situations, endure hardship, do the work of an evangelist, discharge all the duties of your ministry.*

In this passage Paul calls Timothy to a kind of success that may not always have looked like success—he called Timothy to faithfulness. In considering what faithfulness meant for Timothy, perhaps we'll see more of what success really is for us.

It's interesting to note that here in 2 Timothy 4, in the face of opposition in the Ephesian church, Paul gave Timothy the interesting instruction, "Preach the Word." "In the presence of God and of Christ Jesus, who will judge the living and the dead, and in view of his appearing and his kingdom, I give you this charge: Preach the Word; be prepared in season and out of season; correct, rebuke and encourage—with great patience and careful instruction" (vv. 1-2). This would have been particularly important for Timothy to hear because, just as Paul had said, the persecution he had faced was typical of anyone who tries to lead a godly life in Christ. "For the time will come when men will not put up with sound doctrine. Instead, to suit their own desires, they will gather around them a great number of teachers to say what their itching ears want to hear. They will turn their ears away from the truth and turn aside to myths" (vv. 3-4).

Impatience with the repeating of the truth and a desire for novel teachings—especially those teachings that allow the indulgence of selfish, carnal appetites—would continue, said Paul. Paul had faced these selfish counterfeit Christianities, and Timothy, too, would certainly face them. Therefore Paul charged Timothy in 4:5, "Keep your head in all situations, endure hardship, do the work of an evangelist, discharge all the duties of your ministry."

Back in 2 Timothy 1:11 Paul had said that he had been appointed a preacher, a herald. Now here he solemnly charges Timothy, not for the first time, but probably for the last, "Preach the word. Herald it. Give the message you were sent to proclaim."

In olden days the town crier didn't sound his trumpet, let the people gather around him, and then start making up some things that he himself wanted. Today the mail carriers don't stand outside your door, scrawl a few little notes, and shove them through your door or put them in your mailbox. No! They've had messages committed to them, and *they must deliver them.*

In the same way Paul stressed that Timothy had a ministry of preserving the truth (it was the Word that he was to preach; with the Word he was to be prepared to correct and rebuke). But Timothy was to preserve and present the truth kindly. He was to "encourage—with great patience and careful instruction." Timothy was to be constantly prepared to proclaim the Word, so that he could correct, rebuke, and encourage as needed. In view of all the opposition he would face, much of his preaching would have a negative character—denying false, unbiblical teaching and rebuking the sinful behavior that comes from it.

But though Timothy's preaching often had to be in one sense negative, it all also had to be colored by, flavored by, his gracious message. So the preaching must be patient. And this patient preaching must be the preaching of the Word. It must center on instruction in the faith, not simply secular problem-solving techniques or motivational psychology, personnel management, or conflict resolution. Intellectual doubts must be addressed, immoral sin must be rebuked, lurking fears must be dispersed—but all by the patient preaching of the Word. Timothy was not to be deceived by the false teachers but was to follow Paul's example of continuing to be faithful even in the face of opposition.

And he could best do this by doing the work of an evangelist as he continued to hold out the Gospel that he had heard from Paul. Paul appropriately summed up this charge with the comprehensive call to Timothy to "discharge all the duties of your ministry" (4:5). The call that Timothy had been given placed him in a special debt to those around him, even as Paul's call had done, and so Timothy was to discharge this debt not by a gift of money, but by the complete gift of himself.

When I first went off to college, I was shocked by the blatant disregard for all moral conventions. Freedom was the apparent essence of the behavior code. Unlike what many of my friends who went to other universities experienced, I was told there were no rules about who was to be where or when. Consenting sexual activity was a matter of complete indifference to the university authorities. I even found that the campus police requested that you not let them know about any activities that involved drugs. Alcohol was unregulated, as were bedtimes, bank accounts, and (happily for me anyway) book purchases.

One thing, and one thing only, seemed to cause the very soul of the academic community to rise up in indignation and to promise expulsion from their midst—plagiarism. Plagiarism is, of course, taking and using another person's thoughts as one's own.

Now while I, as a Christian pastor and evangelist, stand foursquare against any kind of deception, which plagiarism entails, I must say that as a Christian pastor and evangelist I do appreciate the derivative nature of plagiarism. Plagiarists eschew original thought. They refuse to produce their own work and instead attempt to wholly own the work of others. In this second sense, you could say that's what is behind our teaching ministry when we present the Gospel of God to others.

We're committed to plagiarism in our churches and conversations, in our expositional preaching and in our evangelism, *not* by trying to take credit for what is not ours, but in the sense that we attempt to present ideas that are not originally our own but belong to God and are from His Book. We understand that this is the essence of godliness—God's own revelation of Himself. If you would find mercy and forgiveness and peace with God, if you would serve Him, please Him, come to know Him, absolutely nothing will be as fruitful for you as familiarity with and faith in the message of His Book.

In his disputes with Erasmus in the early sixteenth century, Martin Luther wrote: "It is not the mark of a Christian mind to take no delight in assertions; on the contrary, a man must delight in assertions or he will be no Christian. And by assertion . . . I mean a constant adhering, affirming, confessing, maintaining, and an invincible persevering."[1] Luther was right. Asserting God's truth in the context of spiritual darkness is, of course, the great evangelistic work of the church. And the reason for this is quite simple—because we believe that we are in a spiritual fog, even darkness, as Jesus called it, and we need the clear light of God's revelation of Himself to dispel our darkness.

This is not simply a theological point for pastors like myself to know. All who are Christians, committed to the ministry of the church, need to know that however difficult or unpopular it may be, they must encourage their ministers in the activity of preaching the Word, of doing the work of an evangelist, of heralding God's life-giving truth. Though it is often difficult—witness how many deserted Paul and his message, seen later in 2 Timothy 4—such faithfulness is always worthwhile.

Opposition to the Gospel was not, however, to cause Timothy to despair. Remember how Paul had charged Timothy in 4:1, "In the presence of God and of Christ Jesus, who will judge the living and the dead, and in view of his appearing and his kingdom . . ." This One is the final Judge—not those many who look for flattering teachers or those teachers who prostitute themselves to their desires. Not even Nero with his sword would be the final judge.

Paul, you see, was concerned about more than Timothy's simply following his example. Paul knew that Timothy had a specific calling, and so Paul knew that Timothy must be faithful not only in following the apostle's example, but particularly by being faithful in heeding Paul's charge here.

Again that charge was, in short, that Timothy should "preach the Word" (4:2; cf. 1 Tim. 6:20; 2 Timothy 1:14). The word used here for "preach" is the word for *proclaim*. Timothy, you see, was not only to hear the Word, to believe it, obey it, guard it, suffer for it, and continue in it. He was certainly to do all those things, but he was also to *preach* it, to *herald* it, like the imperial herald going into a city or the medieval town crier going into the marketplace, as we thought of above; or today like the press spokesman or the anchorperson broadcasting on TV. Timothy was to herald, to proclaim, to broadcast.

And he was to broadcast *what*? The Word, the message, the "deposit" from chapter 1, the body of doctrine that Paul had taught Timothy. The "sound doctrine" of 4:3, "the truth" of 4:4, "the faith" of 4:7.

Once more, notice that we have no license or liberty to preach anything but the message of Christ. I don't think I was called merely to preach; I was called to preach *the Word*. It is not the activity itself, regardless of content; it is the compulsion that comes along with bearing this message.

What would Timothy's heralding this message involve? In verse 2 Paul mentions four aspects of it: "Be prepared in season and out of season; correct, rebuke and encourage." First, *"be prepared in season and out of season."* Timothy was to do this whether it was convenient or not—and even more to the point, given the difficult situation in Ephesus, whether or not the hearers wanted to hear it. Timothy was to continue to be faithful to his charge to proclaim this Word because *it was (and is) an urgent proclamation.*

The Puritan pastor Richard Baxter said, "You cannot break men's hearts by jesting with them, or telling them a smooth tale, or patching up a gaudy oration. Men will not cast away their dearest pleasures upon a drowsy request of one that seemeth not to mean as he speaks."[2] Baxter encouraged people to ask serious questions of themselves, and he as their pastor took it as his job to press issues home to the hearers from the pulpit and in private conversation. Baxter had a sense of the seriousness of the charge he had been given.

George Whitefield, the great evangelist of the eighteenth century, once remarked to Mr. Betterton, a famous actor, "Why is it that the clergy, who speak of *real* things, affect people so little, and the players, who speak of imaginary things, affect them so much?" Betterton responded, "My lord, I can assign but one reason—we players speak of things imaginary as though they were real, and too many of the clergy speak of things real as though they were imaginary."

It's true, isn't it, that too many of us like actors who are compellingly realistic and ministers who are reasonable and coolly controlled, almost dispassionate? But because we have an urgent message, we must "be prepared in season and out of season."

What this means, Paul now breaks down for us even more. We must "correct" some—that is, convince those in error. Being faithful will involve us in arguments with those who are wrong in their doctrine. It will also mean that we must sometimes "rebuke," reproach, or warn those in sin. And, too, it will mean that we must "encourage" or, perhaps better, exhort or urge or appeal to those haunted by fears or immobilized by insecurity. This is some of what preaching the Word will involve.

And do notice *how* this is to be done, seen in the last phrase of 4:2: "with great patience and careful instruction." It is interesting that, even as urgent as the message is, Timothy is to preach it "with great patience" (cf. 2:24-25). And he is to do it essentially through "careful instruction."

We may not think of our calling, even as evangelists, as a teaching ministry, but that seems to be how Paul presented it here. This will often require the very unusual art of standing or speaking contrary to someone's misplaced fears or misplaced self-confidence, and of doing so with appropriate authority and urgency, and yet "with great patience and careful instruction." All of us who are Christians must pray that God will give us wisdom to do our evangelism in such a way.

This is *what* Paul's charge to Timothy is and something of *how* he should fulfill it, but *why* should Timothy be faithful in heeding Paul's charge to preach the Word and to do the work of an evangelist? Paul said he should do so because of the imminent coming of Christ and because of the dire current situation. Let's look at both of these in turn briefly.

First, Timothy should be faithful in preaching the Word *because of the future coming of Christ* (4:1). Did you notice the very impressive, even awesome, fourfold basis of Paul's charge to Timothy in that verse? Paul charges Timothy "in the presence of God." And he goes on to charge Timothy in the presence "of Christ Jesus, who will judge the living and the dead." Paul is exhorting Timothy here to live with the end in view. Then he goes on to exhort him to do this in view of Christ's "appearing" and in view of Christ's "kingdom."

Of course, many of us today live as if we're on earth forever, though the truth is that we're not. People think it idiotic to deny themselves or expend themselves today because of some promised event tomorrow. But it's no more foolish to live today in view of the accounting we must give to God tomorrow than it is for us to study for a test or pack for a trip or prepare for the birth of a baby. If we're to live responsibly, we *must* live with the future in view. So Paul exhorted Timothy here to preach the Word—to hold out the Gospel—because of what the future holds.

But Paul also particularly exhorted Timothy to preach the word *because of what this present life holds*, which in Ephesus seemed to be rising opposition to the truth. "For the time will come when men will not put up with sound doctrine. Instead, to suit their own desires, they will gather around them a great number of teachers to say what their itching ears want to hear. They will turn their ears away from the truth and turn aside to myths. But you, keep your head in all situations, endure hardship, do the work of an evangelist, discharge all the duties of your ministry" (vv. 3-5).

So Timothy should not only preach the Word because of the coming judgment but also because of the growing darkness. The time will come, Paul says, when some will desert true teaching (v. 3a). The picture is clear and sad. These people will turn to teaching that fits their own inclinations. They will "suit their own desires." They will gather "a great number of teachers" who will say "what their itching ears want to hear." He summarizes the problem by saying, "They will turn their ears away from the truth and turn aside to myths"(v. 4). If you remember, this desertion of the Gospel, this turning away from the faith to false doctrines and myths, was exactly what occasioned Paul's previous letter to Timothy (see 1 Tim. 1:3-7). Now here he is warning again of people being swindled, apparently willingly, into bartering life-giving truth for lies, legends, fables, and myths, which instead of changing hearts and minds and giving new life simply tickle ears. This is a tragic exchange.

Also take note that Paul concentrates here not on the false teachers, but on those who actually create them by listening to them. During the 1630s and 1640s in England, Archbishop William Laud would refer to the Puritan lecturers by the dismissive and unfair title of "the peoples' creatures," meaning that these preachers often held lectureships that were not connected with the pastorate of a church but were simply paid for by lay subscribers or sponsors. In this sense these false teachers in Timothy's days were creatures of the people, and the people who paid for them shared in the responsibility for their errant teaching. Our congregations are responsible for the falsehoods they endure from their pulpits, and the more serious the errors, the more responsibility is borne.

So Timothy was to remain faithful in the face of opposition to the truth, and in 2 Timothy 4:5 Paul spells out something of what this faithfulness will look like. First, Timothy should "keep [his] head in all situations." He must exert some self-control. He must not fall into the trap so many of the Ephesians apparently had. He must not be led around by his own desires. He must not be shifting and unstable; rather, he must be sober, well-balanced, calm, and sane. And Timothy had to be willing to endure hardship and suffering.

Listeners as selfish as these will, of course, find the message of the cross offensive. And so they might well ignore or even act to silence Timothy.

Again, looking at verse 5, we see that Timothy was to do the work of an evangelist (cf. Eph. 4:11; cf. Acts 21:8). He should continue preaching the Word, the message of Jesus Christ, *especially* since this was what was in danger of being lost. And so in the midst of this opposition Timothy was to discharge all the duties of his ministry. He should perform his whole duty as a servant of God. Regardless of the response of his hearers, he was to persevere until his whole God-given task was completed.

Calvin said, "The more determined men become to despise the teaching of Christ, the more zealous should godly ministers assert it and the more strenuous their efforts to preserve it entire." Some people have used the image of a kite for a faithful Christian facing opposition. The stronger the winds against it, the higher it flies. Whatever image we want to use, the truth is this: The human heart loves sin and is offended by any message that will divorce us from our sin. You and I must know this if we are to be faithful with the Gospel. We can anticipate opposition, and rather than discouraging us, this opposition should only show us the need all the more clearly.

Timothy was to be faithful to follow Paul's example, and Timothy was to be faithful to heed Paul's charge to preach the Word.

## WHAT WE'VE SEEN HAPPEN AT OUR CHURCH

Several years ago I pledged myself to be an elder and the pastor in our congregation in Washington. At that time I formally took vows before the congregation and received a charge. The charge was given by Don Carson, and at one point during it Don charged me, saying:

> You are an ambassador. You will faithfully declare the whole counsel of God. You will proclaim the holy birth, the perfect life, the atoning death, the bodily resurrection, the glorious ascension, the present session and the personal return in judgment of the Lord Jesus. How great is this responsibility as set forth by Saint Paul: "We are ambassadors for Christ, as though God did beseech you by us: we pray you in Christ's stead, be ye reconciled to God."

You are a steward. You are entrusted with the mysteries of God, and it will be your obligation faithfully to proclaim the Word of God, to follow the ordinances instituted by Christ, and so to uphold the work and worship of the church that He who is the great Head of the Church may be glorified.

I charge you therefore before God and the Lord Jesus Christ, who shall judge the living and the dead at His appearing and His kingdom: preach the Word; be instant in season, out of season; reprove, rebuke, exhort, with all long-suffering. Endure hardship; do the work of an evangelist; fulfill your ministry.

By God's grace, this is the work that I have undertaken at our church. In the years that have passed since then, we have had many encouragements in our evangelism. Some of them have come from others who have visited the church. One intern at our church (Bert Daniel) recently wrote that though the church has a heavy emphasis on community,

> one should not [therefore] assume that the church lacks evangelistic zeal or missionary vision. I do not believe I have ever witnessed a church have a greater fervor for evangelism that does not have an official evangelistic program. Evangelism seems to be the emphasis in all the church does and for many has become a natural part of their lives and conversations. In conjunction with the members actively seeking to evangelize at school and in the workplace, Mark's preaching encourages members to invite unbelievers to attend on Sunday morning. The sermons always contain questions that aim to provoke the thinking of the unconverted or a presentation of gospel truth that would probe their hearts.

A church planter friend from another evangelistic and Reformed denomination was with us for a year. One Sunday night before he left, he shared with the congregation that the thing he and his wife had been most struck by during their time with us was the concern that God had worked in our hearts for evangelism. They said that though they had been involved with a couple of evangelistically intense church plants, they had never before been in a church where the concern for evangelism so permeated the congregation. They observed that evangelism was simply the lifestyle of the church and that it was always in our conversation and our prayers.

Because visiting pastors often comment on this, I am sometimes asked what we have done to bring about such an evangelistic congregation. As the pastor, I am keenly aware that all that is good has its source in God. Too, I am aware of our shortcomings, coldness, and missed opportunities. Having said all that, it is probably appropriate for me to try to summarize some of what we have seen and done in evangelism in our local church's life.

Let me first take just a few sentences to describe this church. If there was ever a normal church, this is it. Solidly evangelical, a little over 100 years old when I came, it had known numerical decline for the previous forty-five years, since the mid-twentieth century. Once a prominent city church, it had become a much smaller and more elderly congregation, with most of the congregation living outside the city and driving in. In the last five years we have seen a number of changes. The average age has probably dropped from seventy to twenty-five. The majority of the members now come from inside the city. The congregation is more racially diverse. The total number of members is half of what it was, but the number of attenders has tripled. The budget has gone from the red to the black, and from about $300,000 to more than twice that. Our missions support is increasing as a percentage of the budget, and there is a life and vibrancy in the congregation that is simply a pleasure. The services are traditional Baptist—Sunday morning, Sunday evening, and Wednesday evening midweek. The sermons are long (some of them over seventy minutes!) and the music blended, with an emphasis given to congregational singing over performed music.

What have I as a pastor done specifically to be faithful to fulfill my calling to do the work of an evangelist? In many ways, of course, doing the work of an evangelist simply means being a faithful pastor. In terms of a practical theology of evangelism, it begins with an understanding that Scripture is the primary tool God's Spirit uses in evangelism. With that in mind, here is some of what I as the pastor, along with other members, have done at Capitol Hill Baptist Church in terms of evangelism.

These days, we're more well-known for being Reformed in our theology or having expositional preaching or elders or meaningful membership (including practicing church discipline) or the Center for Church Reform (www.churchreform.org) or for having a remarkable community than we are for our evangelism.

But amidst all the other concern for reform in the life of the church, God has also been doing a great evangelistic work among us. Not, however, in the ways that people usually think of when they hear that. We have no regular door-to-door visitation program. We don't do many mass mailings or telephone surveys. The members are not encouraged to pray "the prayer" with people immediately upon sharing the Gospel with them and to then assure them they are now Christians. We have no altar calls at the end of our services. In the scores of people I've baptized here in recent years, the youngest one has been sixteen, and only a handful have been under twenty. We do exhort children to trust in Christ, though we do not baptize them, lest we create a culture of sincere but merely nominal Christians. There is no emphasis on numbers per se. I do not want the congregation to begin focusing on short-term attendance or nose-counting as an index of success in evangelism.

So if that's all the stuff we're *not* doing, what *are* we doing? I have concentrated on praying, modeling, teaching, and working to create in the church a culture of faithfulness and prayerfulness in relationships, and friendliness and spiritual conversation among members of the church.

We pastors know that sometimes it is easier to get our members talking about Saturday's football game than about their own spiritual lives. I have deliberately encouraged copies of the membership list to be taken by all members, to use them as prayer lists, encouraging people in how to pray even for people whom they don't know well or at all. I have encouraged them to speak about the sermon or other spiritual matters after the services and to do so in honest and realistic ways.

Though we do not have *programs* for evangelism, I have encouraged providing church members with *tools* for evangelism. So, for example, we have had a lot of evangelism training in Sunday school. We've used various courses—for example, *Living Proof 1 & 2*, *Speaking of Jesus*, *Tell the Truth*, *Two Ways to Live*, and *Christianity Explained* (an evangelistic Bible study on Mark's Gospel). We have taught various brief courses on apologetics. Throughout all of this I have wanted to clearly present evangelism in the context of a biblical understanding of conversion, and conversion in the light of a biblical understanding of the Gospel. I have worked in my public teaching of Scripture to give such biblical understandings.

I plan our services and deliberately work to make sure that we do not artificially hype emotion. Don't misunderstand me. The Gospel certainly engages our whole person, including our emotions. But I am aware that there are things Christians sometimes do in the name of evangelism that are not helpful. Momentary emotional engagements can be dangerously deceptive. We must treat people's souls with care. We at Capitol Hill have no great pageants with national flags—either for missions or for patriotic days. We have no music for entertainment's sake; almost all of our music is congregational in nature. Our services are deliberately simple, direct, reflective, and plain.

I think one of the most powerful evangelistic tools that is often ignored is the discipline of corporate silence, which shuts us up to our own consciences and to the echoes of God's Word in our own souls. So in our services at Capitol Hill, we have built in silent reflection, particularly after the sermon. The absence of this in many evangelical services is a serious deficit and a wrongly lightening agent. One of the ways that I think the altar call most seriously damages our evangelism is by turning the work of the Word into a spectacle. When the Word has been preached, it should be allowed to sink into the heart of every person present. Even a few moments of silence at the end of the sermon and the service can help tremendously.

I have assumed throughout my ministry here that the most important evangelistic tool I have is expository preaching. God has always used His Word to bring life. Therefore my sermons are based on specific biblical texts. As I mention them in the sermon, I deliberately explain to people how to find the book and the references in it.

These sermons are long because I think that meat is helpful to

*preach to the heart of the people*

growing Christians, young Christians, and non-Christians. I remember one sermon in Lamentations some time ago in which I preached passionately on the judgment of God on sin. One member came up to me afterwards and said it was a great sermon, except for the fact that I didn't tell people the Gospel. My friend was right.

Since then I have tried to be clear with the Gospel in each sermon. In every sermon I appeal to people to come to Christ. In the sermon I may well invite people to talk to the Christian friend they've come with or to me after the service. I try to make the sermons clearly relevant to non-Christians, particularly in the introductions.

I design the sermon titles to pique the interest of Christians and non-Christians alike, and I publish them months ahead of time in a church card. I have encouraged members to use the church card, to circle a sermon title that may have to do with a conversation the member has had with a non-Christian friend, and to invite them to church for that date, with lunch and conversation afterwards.

One of the things I do in sermons and services is deliberately to refer explicitly to Christians and non-Christians in church services. Non-Christians have told me that they appreciate their presence being acknowledged and that it makes them feel like it is appropriate for them to be present.

One thing that I have tried to do to heighten our awareness of the Gospel is to teach people that questioning one's salvation is not wrong, but that it is better and more wise to examine oneself to make sure one is in fact saved. Such discussions draw attention to what it means to be a Christian and how one becomes a Christian. Indeed, such discussions draw attention to the Gospel.

Part of this must include an honesty about the cost and the difficulties of the Christian life. We are not trying to sell anyone a bill of goods. We have nothing to fear from honesty. And, indeed, we have a good pattern for this in the One who invited his disciples to "Take up your cross and follow Me." At the same time, we should not be shy about bringing out the hope that we do have in Christ. I am not ashamed to preach about heaven. We should not be slow to tell people of the great gift God has given us in Christ.

Of course, there are many things beyond the sermon that I have encouraged to help our church be obedient in evangelism. We regularly have baptismal testimonies in the morning service. We celebrate the joy of the conversions that God gives us, and we assume that these testimonies to new life in Christ will present the Christian life with the winsomeness and attractiveness that it has. We encourage members to stand around after the services in order to talk to people. We encourage people to have deliberately spiritual conversations. We have even changed the building to accommodate this time; we have refurbished our West Hall in order to provide space for coffee and cookies and to have a bookstall with interesting and helpful literature.

The community itself is to be one of the chief evangelistic tools. The family life of the church is built up in such conversations and in the Sunday evening services. We assume that as we are built up as the Body of Christ, the Spirit of Christ in us will be attractive to those made in God's image. Knowing Jesus' words in John 13:35 that Christians' love for one another will be a powerful evangelistic testimony, we build community not just for ourselves but for those outside of us, in the darkness of the world.

Having a church body that is composed of people who genuinely are growing in Christ is therefore an important aspect of evangelism, because it holds out hope to non-Christians as they see other people struggling, yet changing for the good. If you can get a reputation in the community as a church in which people's lives are actually changed, you will begin to see some amazing things. I have had members of the community (not of my church) ask for Bible studies, to have meals together in order to explain what's going on, and even to stop by for a "spiritual checkup."

As the pastor, I deliberately cultivate a seriousness about church membership for a number of reasons, one of which is to encourage evangelism. Being serious about membership to me means that I begin laying the foundation for a Richard Baxter-like spiritual visitation at the point of someone applying for membership. The person who desires to join the church must meet with me (usually with another church member, often an elder, present). At that meeting I ask to hear the person's testimony of their Christian experience. I also ask them for a one-minute explanation of the sum of the Gospel. Many times

one or both of these questions have led to good evangelistic opportunities with people who have not yet come to know Christ. For the
Christians, this is a good time of evangelistic training as I help them
reflect on their own testimony and what God used to bring them to
Christ and pray that God will use that to sensitize them to the evangelistic opportunities He has given them. The gospel summary, too,
gives me a chance to sharpen the Christian's presentation of the
Gospel. With almost everyone I remind them of Jesus' simple summary
of the response that he calls for—"repent and believe."

In our Sunday evening service we share openly about non-
Christian friends, evangelistic ideas, or ministries and pray for all of
the above. I have worked to lead the church to pray for other people's
physical needs (e.g., a cousin's hospitalization), then their own needs,
even if physical, then for the spiritual needs of themselves and others,
then the spiritual needs of the church corporate, including the building up of the church through conversions. All of these things are
appropriate topics of prayer, but I am attempting to cultivate a bias
toward the latter ones. One of the effects of this should be better
awareness of evangelistic responsibilities and opportunities and good
prayer to God for those around us.

Our Wednesday night Bible study is a close and careful discussion
study through the New Testament epistles. So far we have spent about
two and a half years in James and three years to date going through
Galatians. Such careful studies help people understand election, faith
and works, justification by faith alone, the nature of Christian assurance and therefore true Christian conversion and appropriate evangelism. This is where the engine of the church gets fine-tuned by
corporate consideration of God's Word.

Continuing to go through various meetings of the church, with an
eye to their implications for evangelism, there is also a Thursday morning theology breakfast. By means of this smaller meeting in my study,
and my practice of handing out good books to read on Sunday
evening and Wednesday evening, I attempt to help people understand
Christianity more thoroughly. If the members have a better grasp of
the Gospel, and indeed of all of Scripture, addressing questions they
naturally have, they will find evangelistic opportunities in their lives

more easily and naturally. All of life points back to our Creator and Judge. Every way I help them to see and understand that truth is a way I help to equip them and remind them of the occasions they have to share the Good News.

A whole network of small groups has grown up, and those groups have been encouraged to take responsibility for, among other things, encouraging each other in evangelism. Each day through the week some groups are probably meeting somewhere to hold each other accountable, to study Scripture, to read a book together, to pray, or even specifically to plan for evangelism.

There are some things that we as a church do specifically and primarily for evangelism. We have established a series of public lectures called Henry Forums at which we have brought in speakers such as Carl F. H. Henry (a member of our church and the "Henry" of the Forum's name), J. I. Packer, Timothy George, Philip Johnson, R. Albert Mohler, Jr., Iain Murray, and D. A. Carson, among others, to address contemporary issues from a biblical viewpoint. These issues may range from postmodernism to evolution to evidence for the resurrection of Jesus Christ. Most of the addresses will not interest everyone, but we encourage those who can to bring along friends who would be interested in the topic and then to talk with them afterward.

Doing the work of an evangelist is not necessarily lonely work. Part of my work is to encourage others to come up with their own evangelistic initiatives. So here at Capitol Hill, members actually initiate evangelistic ministries that they have a passion for. There have been many of these, sometimes happening only once, other times continuing on for years. I encourage them to try different things and to realize that something like this doesn't have to continue in order to be a success. The evangelistic ministries that have been begun have taken on many forms. Members who work with children and young people have been some of the most inventive. One member has worked to give out sermon tapes at a nearby child day-care center. Others have helped to organize an Angel Tree party through Prison Fellowship. A Mothers and Others group has been started on Thursday mornings just to give area stay-at-home mothers "and others" a chance to get together for coffee, talk, and fun. We recently had a traditional

Vacation Bible School in the summer. For adults, an evangelistic book-stall at Eastern Market, a nearby public market, has recently begun. Another member, a fairly recent convert himself, has begun a "book forum" in which Christians read pieces by important authors (Christians and non-Christians) with their non-Christian friends and get together once a month to discuss them.

All of this can take place, in part, because we deliberately do not clog the members' lives with trying to fulfill our programs. We give them tools—Wednesday night Bible study, my deliberately preaching through all kinds of Scripture, *Christianity Explained*, *Two Ways to Live*, my question to them about the Gospel in one minute or less, the Henry Forums, classes on apologetics—but not programs.

One very simple thing that I have done is to encourage people to talk about evangelism. I have tried to model the fact that talking about evangelistic situations with other people is a normal thing for Christians to discuss and talk about, and that it should be done regularly.

The basic evangelistic tool that I use myself and that I have trained other members in using is a six-part study through Mark's Gospel called *Christianity Explained*. Using this, I have led evangelistic Bible studies through Mark's Gospel, sometimes with an individual and other times with small groups of people. I have also deliberately worked at training and encouraging others to do the same.

We talk here not about having seeker-sensitive sermons or services, but about having seeker-sensitive lives. Being aware of the Gospel and being prayerful is the basis of such a seeker-sensitive life. Living in the neighborhood and encouraging church members to get to know their neighbors, whether from other churches or non-Christians, is a basic building block for an evangelistic church. Our own church is in the process of what I would call re-indigenizing, reintegrating in the community. As part of this, our members have naturally participated in activities like Neighborhood Watch, the Garden Club, and various social ministries in the area—including crisis pregnancy centers, after-school tutoring, and meals for the homeless.

I myself chose to move my family to a house near the church in order to encourage this re-indigenizing. Now a growing percentage of our membership lives within five or ten minutes from the church.

Geography is an advantage to be used, both in sanctification—by sharing our lives together—and also in evangelism.

We want to encourage the membership to think and pray about evangelism as a normal part of their Christian lives. We teach them they can do this from either of two ends. The first end is what we've already talked about—coming up with creative ministries that they have a vision for, like the Book Forum, Mothers and Others, or the Eastern Market Bookstall. The other end they can begin praying through, however, is not a certain ministry but a certain person or people that need to be reached. We would like members of the congregation to think creatively about what they can do with their friends at work, their neighbors, their families, or other natural relational networks that they have.

There is so much else I could say about the work of an evangelist that God has called me to as the pastor of Capitol Hill Baptist Church. Our church, of course, also supports traditional means of evangelism. I have publicly stated my desire to increase annually the percentage of our budget going to support missions work overseas. We support area campus staff workers with Inter-Varsity and Campus Crusade. I do evangelistic speaking at area campuses when invited by the college Christian fellowships there. The church has begun having the Sunday morning sermons reproduced for radio and the Internet. We have a website (www.capitolhillbaptist.org) at which visitors can download sermons in audio form. We have purchased time on a local radio station to broadcast the sermons, and other stations around the country have also picked them up for no additional charge.

When I first came to visit, the pulpit committee asked me what my plans for the church would be. I said that I had no programs to bring and that in one sense I was quite content for everything but the preaching to fail, though I trusted it wouldn't. I would simply come and preach the Word, pray, build personal relationships, and try to patiently persevere and see what God would do.

And that is what I've done here so far. Certainly we've had some disappointments. Some of those I thought I saw come to Christ have not ended up persevering. We've had discipline cases that have broken my heart. But a remarkable group of people have found new life in Christ.

One fellow who was the legal adviser for a member of Congress was just jogging by and felt he should come to church though he hadn't been in years. After a few months of hearing the Gospel, God graciously converted him. Another neighbor I met at a dinner and talked with about the Gospel ended up studying all of Mark's Gospel and becoming a Christian. In one remarkable story we've seen the conversion of a mother and her two grown sons. She was a Unitarian who simply started coming to church and was converted through her own study, our preaching, and going through Mark's Gospel. Her sons started coming with her to church as a way of having family time. They were both undergraduates at Georgetown at the time and were not particularly disposed toward Christianity or even religion. One became a Christian a couple of years after his mother did, and his brother did the same a few months later. And there have been many more.

Of course, we are always a work in progress. In the Reformation, Rome's motto of *semper eadem*—always the same—beckoned to questioning Europeans as an apparent bulwark of certainty. The motto of the Reformed churches, on the other hand, was *Ecclesia Reformata, semper reformanda secundum verbum dei.* That is, "the church reformed, always to be reformed according to the Word of God." May such be our testimony in the great work of evangelism that God has called us to perform and to encourage in our churches.

## CONCLUSION

So what about success? At the point Paul wrote to Timothy, Paul had been laboring for about thirty years as an itinerant evangelist. In 2 Timothy 5 he says that he had taught, lived, purposed, believed, had patience, loved, endured, been persecuted, suffered, been rescued. He had "fought the good fight . . . finished the race . . . kept the faith." He had been deserted and opposed, strengthened and delivered. And now he was being poured out and was ready to depart. And he was certain that the Lord would bring him safely to heaven. This is, of course, the last letter we have that was written by Paul.

According to tradition, within a few months, perhaps weeks or even days, of writing these words Nero gave his verdict on Paul, and Paul was led out to one of the main roads leading into Rome, the Ostian Way, and beheaded.

Nero passed his verdict on Paul, but Christ had another. So was Paul successful? Another question: Did Paul's letters to Timothy fail? It seems as if the church in Ephesus continued to struggle after he had written the first one, so he had to write this second one. What happened to that church? We have information about the church from earlier days in Acts and in Paul's letter to the Ephesians. But we also have information in the New Testament about the Ephesian church from about thirty years later.

*To the angel of the church in Ephesus write: These are the words of him who holds the seven stars in his right hand and walks among the seven golden lampstands: I know your deeds, your hard work and your perseverance. I know that you cannot tolerate wicked men, that you have tested those who claim to be apostles but are not, and have found them false. You have persevered and have endured hardships for my name, and have not grown weary. Yet I hold this against you: You have forsaken your first love. Remember the height from which you have fallen! Repent and do the things you did at first. If you do not repent, I will come to you and remove your lampstand from its place. But you have this in your favor: You hate the practices of the Nicolaitans, which I also hate. He who has an ear, let him hear what the Spirit says to the churches. To him who overcomes, I will give the right to eat from the tree of life, which is in the paradise of God.*

*—Rev. 2:1-7*

Was the Ephesian church successful? And what about Timothy, the pastor? In 2 Timothy 4 Timothy was exhorted to continue, to preach, to be prepared, to correct, rebuke, and encourage, to keep his head, endure, do the work of an evangelist and discharge all the duties of his ministry, to do his best to come to Paul, bring Mark and Paul's cloak and parchments, to be on his guard against Alexander, and to greet some folks. We don't know if Timothy made it to Paul before Paul was executed, but tradition has it that Timothy was in Ephesus for many years as the pastor of the church there. So he might very well have been the "lampstand" of the Ephesian church referred to in the letter in Revelation.

Apparently one time late in the first century, during the reign of the emperor Nerva (that dates it to 97 A.D.), a public celebration—really, an orgy—was going on in Ephesus in celebration of the god Dionysius. Timothy openly opposed this public frenzy. And when he did, the mob was enraged. So they picked up stones and clubs and beat him until he died.

Was Timothy successful? Maybe I should put the question this way: In all this activity, do you think *God* was successful? As one old poem says, "God buries his workmen, but carries on His work."

Now let's bring this home. Is *your* church successful? Are things going well? Are you, in your ministry, successfully doing the work of an evangelist? What if your body is aging and your health failing, if you are separated from family and friends, if your employment is ended and your bank account is empty, if you're cold and perhaps even in prison, in danger, very real danger, of losing your life? Then, friend, are you successful? Are you doing the work of an evangelist?

NOTES

1  Martin Luther, *Bondage of the Will* (Philadelphia: Westminster Press, 1969), p. 105.

2  Richard Baxter, *The Reformed Pastor*, John T. Wilkensin, ed. (London: Epworth Press, 1939), p. 145.

you reap what you sow
Let God give you wisdom

*Don't complain - pray*

# 14

## THE PASTOR AND CHURCH GROWTH:

### How to Deal with the Modern Problem of Pragmatism

■

### Phil A. Newton

*Jesus started c 12; only need 2; #'s aren't important*

*Be faithful, where you are*
*└ in house*

Instead of me fitting religion, I found a religion to fit me," explained one person in a *Newsweek* article. The feature addressed the growing trend of churches adapting to their "market." As the writer aptly stated, "They don't convert—they choose." He added, "The market-place is now the most widely used system of evaluation by younger churchgoers," and "by this standard, the most successful churches are those that most resemble a suburban shopping mall."[1]

On a recent Sunday morning I visited such a church. I drove into the spacious parking lot, directed by volunteers to an empty spot amid hundreds of other automobiles. The casually dressed attendees received smiles from well-placed greeters. On the way to the worship center, I walked past kiosks offering coffee, gifts, and information on the church's ministries. My sport coat and tie pegged me as a "visitor."

The worship service began with a lively band led by a former rock musician. A large screen projected choruses and hymns offering music with theological content supplemented by pieces that offered no sub-stance at all. When his band turned up the volume, the mixture of cou-ples, singles, and teenagers appeared laid-back in their response. The congregation seemingly viewed this as a time of wholesome enter-tainment rather than passionate worship.

As attendees made their way back and forth from the worship cen-ter to the coffee kiosk, I felt as though I was attending a concert or athletic competition. Perhaps a motivational seminar would best describe the scene. This hit home as the senior minister began his sermon. He was preaching on leadership, occasionally referring to Nehemiah, though lacking any stimulating exegesis. It seemed to be more like a Peter Drucker seminar than biblical exposition. Throughout the sermon the pastor alluded to their church and himself as models for leadership. He referred to his entrepreneurial spirit and the success they had attained through following the leadership principles he espoused.

In the midst of the sermon he stated that for leaders to bring others into a working relationship, they must look for integrity and godliness, though no explanation was given of what he meant by godliness. He carefully gauged his language to avoid biblical terms he thought might be offensive.

I waited to hear some morsel of the Gospel, but none was offered. While the worship leader did make a couple of pointed statements about the cross of Christ, the pastor never hinted at the sufficiency of the cross, the work of Christ, or even the meaning of salvation. Jesus was only "used" as a means to achieve a certain level of leadership. I looked around the building at the hundreds attending, realizing they would leave without being pointed to the sufficiency of Jesus Christ.

The service described is not unusual across the North American evangelical landscape. Hundreds of churches have adopted a pragmatic, seeker-friendly approach to "doing church." Does it work? If you mean, does it produce numbers? Absolutely! With the right techniques, a church placed in a suitable location can almost be guaranteed an increase in attendance and finances. If one approach fails to produce results, the pragmatic leader switches to a different approach. The validation for this is found in the definition given for *pragmatism* by church growth leaders: "The principle that demands results from biblically sound strategies; *when no results are recorded*, the strategy is changed to another one that is equally sound theologically."[2]

In such churches the Bible is subjected to strained interpretations in order to fit into the latest marketing schemes foisted upon the church. Biblical soundness yields to pragmatic results. Once a new method produces results, church growth strategists declare it to be a *church growth principle*. The late Donald McGavran, father of the church growth movement, explained that he first discovered church growth principles by observing churches of various denominations while serving as a missionary in India. He explained that he visited "Mennonite, Methodist, Presbyterian, and Anglican fields, observing what procedures God was blessing to the growth of his churches and what he was not." His conclusions were *not* the result of careful biblical exegesis but rather observation of what worked. He continued, "Thus I formed and tested any principles of church growth. During those long, hard years God granted me considerable insight into how churches grow. *The basic theory and theology of the church growth movement was being hammered out on the anvil of the disciplined observance and analysis of the Church's experience among many peoples of India.*"[3]

Experience, not biblical truth, led the way into church growth as a movement. With such an approach, the Bible is secondary, being utilized only to "prove" a principle. McGavran stated, "Discovering Church Growth principles is not difficult." What is required? "One observes where the church is growing, where God is blessing the efforts of his servants with factual, actual church growth, where the number of members is increasing and new congregations are being born, and where men and women are introduced to Jesus, commit their lives to him, and become responsible members of his church."[4] When one witnesses such a situation, he need only analyze it and hammer it out into a new church growth principle.

Where has this movement taken the evangelical church? No one can deny that many churches are growing to mammoth proportions, with attendances topping 5,000 to 10,000 each weekend. Nor can anyone deny that most of the growth has been the result of draining smaller, less programmatic churches. Even small and midsize churches have climbed aboard the church growth train, adopting as many "principles" as possible to enlarge their numbers and budgets. But is there evidence of new, regenerate life? Is there a significant change in the character and morals of those professing faith in Christ among the growing churches? Is there a new wave of selfless sacrifice for the work of missions? Is there a new passion for the truth of God's Word? Is there a new love for holiness?

Bill Hull offers a stinging indictment of the condition in most churches: "The test of a congregation, apart from personal holiness, is how effectively members penetrate the world. American churches are filled with pew-filling, sermon-tasting, spiritual schizophrenics, whose belief and behavior are not congruent." He further observes, "Christians' use of money, priorities of time, attitudes about work and leisure, divorce and remarriage, increasingly reflect culture rather than Scripture. Therefore, the church is weak in skills and weak in character."[5] If we fill church buildings with multitudes who have no intent to live out the demands of the Gospel, what have we accomplished? We may have built huge monuments to the marketing skills of church leaders, but we have done little to further the work of God's kingdom and transform a sin-darkened society.

Contrast this with the growth that occurred during periods of spiritual awakenings. Pubs in towns and villages along the eastern seaboard shut down for lack of business in the wake of God-breathed revival. Tens of thousands would stand in scorching heat to hear two-hour-long doctrinal sermons by George Whitefield. In the Welsh revival, pit ponies in the coal mines were confused about their work. Their masters had experienced such radical transformation of character and life that their language was different. The ponies, accustomed to the profanity of coal miners, now had to reckon with the gracious conversation of the redeemed!

## WHAT IS THE ISSUE?

I maintain that church growth is *not* the issue for evangelicals. Does this mean that I join the ranks of those who loathe the idea of growing churches? Certainly not. As long as the growth of the church is due to God-ordained means and Holy Spirit-born work, then I long to see it. With Isaac Watts, I can sing:

> We long to see Thy churches full,
> That all the chosen race
> May, with one voice and heart and soul,
> Sing Thy redeeming grace.[6]

Rather than spending so much time and money on developing new marketing strategies for growing numbers, congregations would benefit from their leadership immersing themselves in the Word of God. *What has the Lord of the Church commanded for His people? What are the principles and commands set forth to direct the church of Jesus Christ through the centuries?*

Few evangelicals have had an impact on the present generation like that of Pastor Rick Warren of Saddleback Valley Community Church in Mission Viejo, California. After intensively studying growing churches while a seminary student, in 1980 he planted his life in Southern California. The seminal work describing Warren's philosophy of ministry is his book *The Purpose Driven Church.*[7] His church currently averages nearly 15,000 in attendance. Warren's genuineness shows in his writing and speaking. Certainly he must be admired for the diligence he has shown in accomplishing his goals. Because of his success, hundreds of Saddleback clones have sprung up in every imaginable setting. Pastors seek to imitate Warren's sermons, as well as attempting to style their worship services after his own seeker-sensitive approach.

What does Rick Warren teach about attracting such large crowds? He maintains that Jesus attracted large crowds by loving unbelievers, meeting their needs, and teaching them "in interesting and practical ways."[8] I do not doubt that crowds will be attracted to any church following this formula. However, in an effort to affirm his own philosophy of ministry, Warren fails to examine the *response* of the crowds to Jesus' ministry.

While many passages refer to the multitudes that crowded around Jesus to receive something from Him, John's Gospel gives an extended analysis of one such multitude. In the sixth chapter of his Gospel, John records the story of Jesus feeding 5,000 men and their families. Growling stomachs provided a need, or to use Warren's term, "a felt need" of the multitude.[9] Jesus accommodated them by multiplying five loaves and two fish into an incomparable feast for these poor Galileans.

Then Jesus withdrew from this crowd that had their felt needs met. Why would He leave when things were just getting started? "Jesus, knowing that they intended to come and make him king by force, withdrew again to a mountain by himself" (6:15).⑩ Was the multitude satisfied with the teaching of Christ? No. Their desire was to shape Jesus into an earthly king rather than being shaped through Jesus' spiritual reign over their lives. *The crowd was more interested in Jesus adapting to them than in submitting to Him as Lord.* So Jesus left the multitude and sent His disciples across the Sea of Galilee by boat while he withdrew to the mountain.

After walking on water and rescuing His disciples from a blustery sea, Jesus came to the other side of the Galilee. Meanwhile, the crowd, still eager to have their "felt needs" met, journeyed all night by foot and in small boats to meet up with Christ again. Does Jesus commend their eager search for Him? No; He rebukes them for impure motives and sensual desires. "I tell you the truth, you are looking for me, not because you saw miraculous signs [i.e., Messianic signs], but because you ate the loaves and had your fill" (6:26). In other words, "You were not interested in what I had to say that addressed your spiritual lives. You simply wanted another 'felt need' met." He went on, "Do not work for food that spoils, but for food that endures to eternal life, which the Son of Man will give you. On him God the Father has placed his seal of approval" (6:27). When they questioned Him further about His "food that endures to eternal life," Jesus explained that it could not be gained through their works but only by believing in Him (6:29). *Jesus always discerned the crowds*

The multitude asked for more signs in order to believe. Imagine that. Though they had been miraculously fed in the wilderness and understood that Jesus crossed the Sea of Galilee by supernatural means, they wanted more signs. They sought to fill their vain desires with whatever spectacle Jesus might show them. Their minds craved entertainment. But the Lord refused to accommodate what the crowd considered their "felt needs." Instead He taught them the difference between temporal satisfaction with bread and eternal satisfaction with "the Bread of Life." Then Jesus Christ made the most radical demand upon the crowd they had ever heard: "I tell you the truth, unless you eat the flesh of the Son of Man and drink his blood, you have no life in you. Whoever eats my flesh and drinks my blood has eternal life, and I will raise him up at the last day. For my flesh is real food and my blood is real drink" (6:53-55).

No one could doubt that Jesus Christ spoke and ministered to these people in the most loving way, that He had met their "felt need" of food, and that He spoke in a most "interesting and practical way" in explaining eternal life. But what was the result? Did the crowd commit to keep following Jesus Christ? Once they understood the intent of the divine message with its narrow, austere conclusion, would they "decide for Christ"? John's analysis of the crowd who claimed to be disciples was that due to the demand of the Gospel, "many of his disciples turned back and no longer followed him" (6:66). The multitude hung around as long as the message of the Gospel did not get too close. They looked for the miracles and baskets of bread, but they had no love for the truth of the Gospel proclaimed.

Here is precisely the issue: It is only by the foolishness of the Gospel preached that unbelieving people can be saved (1 Cor. 1:18—2:5). Yes, Jesus spoke in interesting and understandable ways; and so should we who proclaim the Gospel. But He never sought to "dress up" the Gospel to make it more palatable for unbelieving ears. The "Gospel" does not even sound like the "Gospel" in many churches that claim to love the message of Christ. They have become so conscious of attracting crowds that they have demeaned the Gospel to accommodate the tastes of the multitude. Bill Hull squarely explains the nature of the gospel message:

> The gospel is confrontational in its very nature. Any presentation of the gospel that does not present a challenge to the unbeliever to radically change his or her thinking and attitudes toward God and his saving work in Christ is not the same gospel preached in the pages of the New Testament! Today, people can be happy, healthy members of evangelical churches without ever having to face a God who is anything more than a "buddy," a Savior who is anything more than an example, and a Holy Spirit who is anything more than a power source. And that can happen without faith, without repentance, indeed, without conversion.[11]

## How Far Does It Go?

The concepts of the church growth movement, particularly the issues of pragmatism, are promoted as "transferable." These principles are no longer confined to conservative, evangelical churches. Liberal churches, pseudo-evangelicals, and even cults have benefited from the strategies of the church growth movement. Indeed, a diverse group drinks from the wells of church growth in order to increase their numbers.

My community's local newspaper featured the story of a notably liberal congregation that had adopted a "seeker-friendly" approach to worship. The article told of a pop singer who entertained on Saturday night and the wee hours of Sunday morning on Beale Street (Memphis's nightclub street), grabbed a few hours sleep, then made his way to the platform of this church where he led its first contemporary worship service. The pastor made a frank assertion: "This is legitimate worship." He explained, "This is not alternative worship. Some people may not like me saying this, but it's a part of *entertainment worship*."[12] Unfortunately, he learned about entertainment worship from evangelical Christians who claim to believe in the sufficiency of Scripture.

The effects of entertainment worship or seeker-formats upon churches are devastating. The appetite of Christians for the richness of biblical exposition has been dulled. Man-centered techniques for evangelism have multiplied so that the bottom line with churches is adding numbers, not true disciples. Church growth has become the goal of churches rather than the glory of Christ. Peter Wagner went so far as to claim, "Not only did Jesus die on the cross for church growth and command church growth, but he also set an example for church growth through his ministry."[13] Where does God's Word tell us that Jesus died on the cross for church growth? How does that statement fit into the doctrines of justification, propitiation, and atonement?

A friend from the Midwest wrote me to express his burden for his own evangelical congregation that is moving into pragmatism. After watching a skit and then hearing a sermon devoid of biblical content, he commented, "I don't know which was worse: the fact that feel-good psychological self help has replaced the clear preaching and teaching of the Word, or the fact that I heard several people say afterward that it was a good message. I guess if the church has been dumbed down, and only felt needs are addressed, that is the result."

## Is God in Need of Our Help?

The movement away from the sufficiency of Scripture and the power of the Gospel of grace subtly suggests that God is in need of our help. Times have changed. What "worked" in previous generations cannot work today. Why depend upon the regenerating power of the Holy Spirit when we have the methodology to pick the locks on men's hearts?

This presumption fomented by the church growth movement can be seen in the way that the prerogatives of God have been shifted to the best marketing techniques. Although Paul writes that unbelieving men are dead in their trespasses and sins and must be made alive by God (Eph. 2:1-7), Warren can declare, "It is my deep conviction that anybody can be won to Christ if you discover the key to his or her heart. That key to each person's heart is unique so it is sometimes difficult to discover. It may take some time to identify it. But the most likely place to start is with the person's felt needs."[14] What is wrong with the Gospel being the "power of God for the salvation of everyone who believes" (Rom. 1:16) rather than dependent on finding the right felt need?

When Paul encountered the pagan-minded Athenians, he did not try to locate the key to their hearts by appealing to felt needs (Acts 17:16-34). He understood that they lacked a proper view of God and consequently had an elevated view of themselves. So he expounded the doctrine of God to them. This was front-line missionary work by a seasoned veteran. Paul resorted to teaching the theology of God to his audience before even broaching the subject of Jesus Christ. Until they understood something of the nature and character of God, the Gospel would not make sense to them.

In doing evangelistic preaching, we may assume that our audiences understand the nature of God. This is not always the case, especially in our postmodern society. Rather than trying to locate a key to people's hearts, we could begin by expounding the nature of God. Joseph Tracy records the description of the kind of preaching that prevailed during the Great Awakening:

> We cannot but also observe that the principal means of the late revival were, the more than ordinary preaching of such Scripture and most important doctrines as these, namely: The all seeing eye, purity, justice, truth, power, majesty and sovereignty of God; the spirituality, holiness, extent and strictness of his law; our original sin, guilt, depravity and corruption by the fall; including a miserable ignorance of God and enmity against him, our predominant and constant bent to sin; our impotence and aversion to return to him; . . . the necessity that his law should be fulfilled, his justice satisfied, the honor of his holiness, authority and truth maintained in his conduct toward us; . . . the difference between his saving graces and merely moral virtues without sanctification, whereby multitudes are deceived to their eternal ruin; in special, the nature and necessity of receiving Christ, so as to be actually united to him and having entire and everlasting interest in him, to be forthwith justified by his imputed righteousness, adopted into the number of the children of God, entitled to all their privileges assured in the covenant of grace, having Christ as our mediatorial and vital Head of all good, with his constant dwelling and acting by his Spirit in us[15]

We cannot doubt the "success" of this preaching in producing lasting effects. What would happen if we returned to doctrinal preaching rather than bending to marketing techniques? Instead of allowing the whims of the crowd to dictate the content of a sermon, which is precisely what happens in seeker-friendly preaching, the preacher would boldly expound the Word of God. Christ would be magnified in His churches rather than attention being given to skilled preachers, big buildings, and clever techniques (2 Cor. 4:1-6; Gal. 6:14). The glory of God would be evident against the backdrop of human inability (Rom. 11:33-36; 1 Cor. 1:26-31). The righteousness of the law would be raised as the holy standard that holds men accountable before God (Rom. 3:19-20; Gal. 3:19-22). The sufficiency of Jesus Christ would be elevated as the only means for saving sinners (Gal. 2:15-21; Col. 1:15-20). The adequacy of the Holy Spirit would be depended upon to bring revelation, conviction, and regeneration to unbelievers (John 16:7-11; 1 Cor. 2:6-16; Titus 3:5). The church would be known as the Body of Christ (1 Cor. 12:12-31; Eph. 4:7-16), a dwelling of the Holy Spirit (1 Cor. 3:16-17; Eph. 2:19-22), a proclaimer of the excellencies of the One who called unbelievers out of darkness into His light (1 Pet. 2:9), and the pillar and support of the truth (1 Tim. 3:14-16).

## HOW ARE WE TO LABOR?

If we are not to go the way of pragmatism and seeker-friendly orientation, then how are we to labor in Christian ministry? We cannot simply be *against everything* but *for nothing*. I believe we must begin with a thoroughly biblical passion for the work of ministry. The leadership of a church must be convinced that what God has spoken in His Word cannot be improved upon, even with all our ingenuity and technology.

*We must begin with a conviction of the sufficiency of Scripture for both our faith and our practice.* The past two decades have witnessed a rallying toward biblical inerrancy. Churches and ministers have battled for "the faith that was once for all entrusted to the saints" (Jude 3). Though there is much talk of the Scripture's sufficiency for our *belief*, there is less evidence that we find it sufficient for our *practice*. The dependence upon marketing techniques implies that God's Word is just not adequate, that biblical doctrine lacks the practical edge to carry the torch of Christianity.

The renowned liberal Harry Emerson Fosdick promoted this idea, asserting, "Nobody who talks to the public so assumes that the vital interests of the people are located in the meaning of words spoken two thousand years ago."[16] Conservative, Bible-believing preachers following Fosdick's assumption have made biblical exposition nearly extinct. Preachers scour for clever stories and illustrations, tying them together with a verse or two and then trying to make a seeker-appealing application. He then uses clever means to bring his audience to a point of decision.

Why not go back to the Word of God? After all, the so-called

Rom 1: 16-17

"seeker" will not believe the Gospel unless the truth of the Good News has affected his *thinking*. It cannot affect his thinking unless it is clearly *proclaimed*. Russ Bush and Tom Nettles clarify what being convinced of the Scripture's sufficiency means:

> The New Testament doctrine of justification by faith implies the necessity of a positive personal response to the truth of the Good News. *Positive response implies some degree of perception.* Therefore, each man *must understand the central message of Scripture for himself in order to make his personal response to God.* The affirmation of the sufficiency of Scripture implies an affirmation of the clarity of the essential message of the Bible.(17)

*To move away from pragmatic preaching, the preacher must be convinced of the Gospel as the power of God for salvation for all who believe* (Rom. 1:16-17). The early church scattered throughout the regions surrounding Judea and then into the Gentile world, preaching the Gospel of Jesus Christ (Acts 8:4; 11:19-21). Paul identified the contents of the Gospel preached:

> *For what I received I passed on to you as of first importance: that Christ died for our sins according to the Scriptures, that he was buried, that he was raised on the third day according to the Scriptures, and that he appeared to Peter, and then to the Twelve. After that, he appeared to more than five hundred of the brothers at the same time, most of whom are still living, though some have fallen asleep. Then he appeared to James, then to all the apostles, and last of all he appeared to me also, as to one abnormally born.*
>
> —*1 Cor. 15:3-8*

The death, burial, and resurrection of Jesus Christ must ever be at the heart of Christian proclamation. It must be woven through the fabric of our sermons, lest those sermons lack a biblical ring. Consequently, without such content and the doctrines that attend it, the preacher has failed to proclaim the Gospel.

Phil 1:6                                        mt 16: 18

*Ministers of the Gospel must also be convinced of their roles as messengers or heralds of the Gospel, not confusing their role with that of the Holy Spirit.* The New Testament term for preacher (*kerux*) means one who is a "herald." Such a person's duty was to clearly bear the message of his superior to a given audience. In the case of a gospel preacher, that preacher has no room to take liberties with the Gospel. He must be diligent to set forth the good news of Christ's redemptive work as revealed in the Word of God. The Gospel *will* do its work! It is innately powerful and applied by the Holy Spirit to the minds and hearts of the unbelieving. The preacher cannot improve upon the purity of the Gospel, nor should he attempt to coerce responses to the Gospel as though the Holy Spirit lacked power through the Gospel to bring about conversion. "Moreover, to be ashamed of the Gospel is a fault of cowardice in pastors," rang out Martin Luther. "But to contradict it and not to listen to it is a fault of stupidity in church members."[18]

The preacher must never let the audience's desires dictate the message. The common, seeker-friendly approach is to survey a community to discover what they want in a church, then shape the church and message to fit its desires. Yet Paul warned Timothy, "For the time will come when men will not put up with sound doctrine. Instead, to suit their own desires, they will gather around them a great number of teachers to say what their itching ears want to hear. They will turn their ears away from the truth and turn aside to myths" (2 Tim. 4:3-4). Did Paul then instruct Timothy that in light of the cultural context, he should by all means adapt his message to fit his hearers' "desires"? In those enduring words he rather instructed Timothy, "Preach the Word" (v. 2). A pragmatic minister might insist that such preaching would drive people away, that the goal is to get people into church. I do not deny that the pragmatic approach will bring in numbers. But since it contradicts the clear biblical mandate for Christian ministry, I am concerned that what it produces will be less than Christian. The late James Montgomery Boice has poignantly stated this truth:

Churches that allow people to choose from things they might want rather than proclaiming what they actually need will grow, just like churches that major in religious entertainment. Vaudeville, talk shows, pop concerts, free therapy, and aerobic dancing, whether secular or religious, may bring in crowds. But these things do not satisfy genuine spiritual hunger. Therefore, although they attract large crowds, they also detract people from finding what is truly worthwhile, just as the secular entertainment industry does by its diversions.[19]

*The minister of the Gospel must be convinced that the Lord can and will save the lost as well as sanctify the saints.* We have the divine assurance that Jesus Christ has purchased with His blood "men for God from every tribe and language and people and nation" (Rev. 5:9). He is the one who begins the saving work and completes it (Phil. 1:6). Therefore, the Lord is the One who has taken responsibility for growing His church. As He declared to the disciples, "I will build my church; and the gates of Hades will not overcome it" (Matt. 16:18). This is never an excuse for laziness or irresponsibility on the part of the minister. Rather, he is to faithfully serve as unto the Lord, diligently utilizing every means of spiritual labor, knowing that the Lord alone can grow His church.

## Utilizing God-given Means for Growth

So much attention is given to creating growth in our churches that we may very well be forcing what should be a more natural process by the grace of God. Paul spoke of the local church functioning rightly, with the pastors and teachers equipping the flock, the members doing the works of Christian service, the whole body growing together in doctrinal unity, and each member making his or her own contribution to the body's needs. Out of this process, growth naturally occurs. It is not forced or programmed. It is not a plan to carefully follow. Rather, it is the Body of Christ living like the Body of Christ (Eph. 4:11-16).

I would propose four areas that demand attention for churches to develop healthy growth.

*First, priority must be given to biblical proclamation.* By this, I refer to an emphasis on expository preaching rather than a diet of topical preaching. The central message must be proclaiming Jesus Christ in all of His fullness and sufficiency (Col. 1:28). Pastors must major on feeding the flock "the whole will of God" (Acts 20:27). They have the responsibility, every time the Body of Christ assembles, to open the Word and expound its truth. The pattern set for us in the book of Acts is that of biblical preaching. We must keep in mind that the Greek world was quite accustomed to drama and skits in their culture; yet we find no evidence of New Testament preachers substituting or even supplementing their preaching with clever skits.

*Second, the church must unashamedly function as a church.* The church is not a business or a for-profit corporation. It is a dynamic body, with each member gifted to help the whole body function as a corporate servant of Christ. Though the technology of our century differs from the first century, the saturation of pure paganism in the culture certainly was no less in the first-century world. The distinctiveness of a worshiping community, living in unity with one another, loving each other, ministering to people in need, walking in humility, and glorying in Jesus Christ, stirred the amazement of the first century just as it does in our own day. When we muddle the beauty of the church with entertainment that resembles the world or an emphasis on the recreation that is so much part of the world, we have lost our distinctiveness. We find ourselves in competition with the theater, recreational outlets, and entertainment centers.

When as a church we neglect to function as a church, we put ourselves on a different plane. Therefore we are forced to produce bigger splashes than our worldly competition for time and attention. All the while we have forgotten the simplicity of being the Body of Christ *in* the world but not *of* the world (John 17:9-19). As the people of God, we must be unapologetic about God-centered worship. Our goal in worship is not to attract or entertain the world but to give glory to our great God.

The natural function of the Body of Christ is faithfully witnessing about our Redeemer. Our lives are testimonies of being transferred from the kingdom of darkness into the kingdom of Christ (Col. 1:13). Our lips give testimony as we have immersed ourselves in the truth of God's Word, being ready to give an answer for the hope that keeps us joyfully going through this world (1 Pet. 3:15). I have found that the most effective training for personal witnessing is constantly teaching the Gospel to my people. The more familiar they are with the whole Gospel, the more ready they are to witness in any setting.

*Third, we must learn to discern what is and is not legitimate as New Testament believers in our community outreach.* It is important to use our creativity and imagination in reaching the lost without compromising the purity of the Gospel or the integrity of Christianity. Members of the congregation, as well as staff ministers, can be involved in beginning community or neighborhood Bible studies for outreach, businessmen's luncheons, or evangelistic studies in the office place. The use of retreats or special conferences can also open the door for effective outreach. Literature can be one of the finest tools in our hands to point others to Christ or to help struggling believers in the community begin to grow. One young man I met in the Washington, D.C. area started a monthly literary discussion in his apartment in which he analyzes a popular book and then makes pointed biblical application to his primarily unbelieving guests. They keep coming back because he is able to answer their questions with a sense of authority.

*Fourth, maintain continuity in all the ministries of the church.* Every facet of the church needs to be aimed in the same direction, having the same focus. There are to be no contradictions between what is emphasized in the sermon or the worship service or the Sunday school or the youth ministry. This is what is expressed so clearly in Colossians 1:28: "We proclaim him, admonishing and teaching everyone with all wisdom, so that we may present everyone perfect in Christ." This text has become a mooring point for all our ministries: Does this ministry proclaim Jesus Christ clearly and in His fullness? Does it serve to admonish and instruct so that the hearers will be more on their way to spiritual maturity? When you have a common focus throughout the church, you never have to be embarrassed to bring guests, knowing they will be pointed to Jesus Christ. There is nothing to hide, no ministry to camouflage.

Rather than searching the landscape of Christendom for "what works," the serious-minded believer is exhorted to go to the Word of God. See how the early church functioned in its own historical context and then apply that to your setting. Be creative within the biblical framework. There are no rigid patterns to follow, but plenty of fresh ideas that can be found throughout the Scriptures. Learn from others, but do not accept any idea without discernment.

Evaluate all that you do in light of God's Word and the glory of Christ. Does it draw attention to Jesus Christ or to the cleverness of men (1 Cor. 2:1-5)? Does it set forth the whole Gospel or is it manipulative? Does it leave men thirsting for Christ or desiring more of men? Does it move believers into spiritual maturity or leave them waiting for the next spiritual fix to keep them going? May the Lord grant you fruit that remains.

## NOTES

1 Quoted by James Montgomery Boice, "On My Mind: Salad Bar Sanctuaries," *Modern Reformation*, September/October 1999, p. 52.

2 C. Peter Wagner, Win Arn, and Elmer Towns, eds., *Church Growth State of the Art* (Wheaton, IL: Tyndale House, 1988), p. 297 (italics added).

3 Donald McGavran and George Hunter III, *Church Growth Strategies That Work* (Nashville: Abingdon, 1984), p. 17 (italics added).

4 Donald McGavran and Win Arn, *Ten Steps for Church Growth* (San Francisco: Harper & Row, 1977), pp. 15-16.

5 Bill Hull, *The Disciple Making Pastor* (Old Tappan, NJ: Revell, 1988), pp. 20-22.

6 Isaac Watts, "How Sweet and Awful Is the Place," 1707.

7 Rick Warren, *The Purpose Driven Church: Growth Without Compromising Your Message & Mission* (Grand Rapids, MI: Zondervan, 1995).

8 Ibid., p. 208.

9 Ibid., p. 219.

10 Scripture taken from *The New American Standard Bible®*, copyright © 1960, 1962, 1963, 1968, 1971, 1973, 1975, 1977, 1995 by The Lockman Foundation. Used by permission.

11 Bill Hull, "Is the Church Growth Movement Really Working?" in Michael Scott Horton, ed., *Power Religion: The Selling Out of the Evangelical Church* (Chicago: Moody Press, 1992), p. 144.

12 "Lights! Camera! Action! It's Worship on a Whole New Set," *The Commercial Appeal*, September 13, 1999, Sec. B, p. 1, italics added.

13 C. Peter Wagner, *Your Church Can Grow* (Ventura, CA: Regal Books, 1984), p. 199.

14 Warren, *Purpose Driven Church*, p. 219.

15 Joseph Tracy, *The Great Awakening: A History of the Revival of Religion in the Time of Edwards & Whitefield* (Edinburgh: The Banner of Truth Trust, 1997, first published in 1842), pp. 400-401.

16  Quoted by John MacArthur, *Our Sufficiency in Christ* (Dallas: Word, 1991; reprint Wheaton, IL: Crossway Books, 1998), p. 147.

17  L. Russ Bush and Tom J. Nettles, *Baptists and the Bible* (revised and expanded) (Nashville: Broadman & Holman, 1999), p. 48 (italics added).

18  Martin Luther, *Luther's Works: Lectures on Romans*, Vol. 25 (St. Louis: Concordia, 1955), p. 150.

19  Boice, "Salad Bar Sanctuaries," p. 52.

# REFORMATION & REVIVAL
# MINISTRIES

■

Reformation & Revival Ministries, in a partnership with Christian Focus Publications, began an imprint line of books in the year 2000 for the purpose of providing resources for the reformation of the Christian church through the life and work of Christian leaders. Our goal is to publish and distribute new works of pastoral and theological substance aimed at reforming the leadership, life and vision of the church around the world.

Reformation & Revival Ministries was incorporated in 1991, through the labors of John H. Armstrong, who had been a pastor for the previous twenty-one years, for the purpose of serving the church as an educational and evangelistic resource. The desire from the beginning has been to encourage doctrinal and ethical reformation joined with informed prayer for spiritual awakening. The foundational convictions of the ministry can be summarized in the great truths of the sixteenth-century Protestant Reformation and the evangelical revivals of the eighteenth and nineteenth centuries.

To accomplish this vision the ministry publishes a quarterly journal (since 1992), *Reformation & Revival Journal,* designed for pastors and serious readers of theology and church renewal. A more popular magazine, *Viewpoint,* is published six times per year. The ministry also has an extensive array of books and tapes.

Dr. Armstrong speaks in conferences, local churches and various ministerial groups across the United States and abroad. The ministry has a no-debt policy and is financed only by the gifts of interested people. The policy from the beginning has been to never ask for funds through solicitation, believing that God provides as He will, where He will, and when He will. An office and support staff operate the ministry in suburban Chicago.

Further information on the ministry and the above resources can be found in the following ways:

**Reformation & Revival Ministries**
P.O. Box 88216
Carol Stream, Illinois 60188
630-980-1810
630-980-1820, fax

E-mail: RRMinistry@aol.com
Web: www.randr.org

# INDEX

■

*walk a life of holiness*